Welcome to

THE
EVERYTHING
DOG BREED GUIDES ®

A S THE OWNER of a particular type of dog—or someone who is thinking about adopting one—you probably have some questions about that dog breed that can't be answered anywhere else. In particular, you want to know what breed-specific health issues and behavioral traits might arise as you plan for the future with your beloved canine family member.

THE EVERYTHING® DOG BREED GUIDES give you clear-cut answers to all your pressing questions. These authoritative books give you all you need to know about identifying common characteristics; choosing the right puppy or adult dog; coping with personality quirks; instilling obedience; and raising your pet in a healthy, positive environment.

THE EVERYTHING® DOG BREED GUIDES are an extension of the bestselling EVERYTHING® series in the pets category, which include *The Everything® Dog Book* and *The Everything® Dog Training and Tricks Book*. These authoritative, family-friendly books are specially designed to be one-stop guides for anyone looking to explore a specific breed in depth.

Visit the entire Everything® series at www.everything.com

THE EVERYTHING

Pug Book

Dear Reader:

I have always loved pugs. Their fine qualities—a wicked sense of humor, intelligence, and charm—and even their long and interesting breed history all combine to make them a companion much to be desired. Not everyone is suited to life with a pug, however. Pugs have some quirks that are interesting, to say the least. If you're planning to get a pug, knowing about these quirks in advance will help you adjust more smoothly to your new pal's antics. If you already have a pug, this book may help answer some of those questions you've had about his behavior or physical needs.

As a lifelong dog-lover and writer who specializes in the subject of dogs, it's my goal to help people get along with the dogs that share their lives. This book will help you by providing pug-specific tips on choosing a puppy, training, health, exercise, and more. Good luck!

Kim Campbell Thornton

THE
EVERYTHING®
PUG
BOOK

A complete guide to raising, training,
and caring for your pug

Kim Campbell Thornton

Adams Media
Avon, Massachusetts

Dedication:
To Dr. John and Susan Hamil and
Xena the Warrior Pug and Dr G. and Otis

Publishing Director: Gary M. Krebs
Managing Editor: Kate McBride
Copy Chief: Laura M. Daly
Acquisitions Editor: Kate Burgo
Development Editor: Bridget Brace
Production Editors: Jamie Wielgus,
          Bridget Brace

Production Director: Susan Beale
Production Manager: Michelle Roy Kelly
Series Design: Daria Perreault and John Paulhus
Cover Design: Paul Beatrice, Frank Rivera
Layout and Graphics: Colleen Cunningham
          Rachael Eiben, John Paulhus,
          Daria Perreault, Erin Ring

An Everything® Series Book.
Everything® and everything.com® are registered trademarks of F+W Publications, Inc.

Published by Adams Media, an F+W Publications Company
57 Littlefield Street, Avon, MA 02322 U.S.A.
www.adamsmedia.com

ISBN: 1-59337-314-7
Printed in the United States of America.

J I H G F E D C B A

Library of Congress Cataloging-in-Publication Data
Thornton, Kim Campbell.
The everything pug book / Kim Campbell Thornton.
    p.   cm. — (An everything series book)
ISBN 1-59337-314-7
1. Pug. I. Title. II. Series: Everything series.

SF429.P9T5 2005
636.76—dc22
2004026802

This publication is designed to provide accurate and authoritative information with regard to
the subject matter covered. It is sold with the understanding that the publisher is not engaged
in rendering legal, accounting, or other professional advice. If legal advice or other expert
assistance is required, the services of a competent professional person should be sought.
    —From a *Declaration of Principles* jointly adopted by a Committee of the American Bar
                Association and a Committee of Publishers and Associations

Many of the designations used by manufacturers and sellers to distinguish their products are
claimed as trademarks. Where those designations appear in this book and Adams Media was
aware of a trademark claim, the designations have been printed with initial capital letters.

Cover photo ©Kaelson, Carol J. / Animals Animals / Earth Scenes
Interior Photography: Karen Hocker Photography

This book is available at quantity discounts for bulk purchases.
For information, call 1-800-872-5627.

BREED SPECIFICATIONS

According to the American Kennel Club, the pug breed specifications include:

- **General appearance:** Pugs are generally one of three colors—silver, apricot-fawn, or black. In silver and apricot-fawn pugs, the colors should contrast between the black mask of the face and the rest of the pug. The trace, or black line extending along the back of the body, should be black.
- **Temperament:** Even-tempered, playful, charming, dignified, extroverted and loving
- **Size:** Compact, square-shaped, with a wide chest; a "cobby" body with hard, developed muscles. The ideal weight for a male or female pug is 14 to 18 pounds.
- **Head:** Large and round, not apple-shaped.
- **Eyes:** Very large, round, and dark. The pug is known for its prominent round eyes.
- **Ears:** Velvety and thin; should be small. There are two kinds of ears, the "rose" and the "button" (preferred).
- **Muzzle:** Should have deep wrinkles. Short, square muzzle with a slightly undershot bite.
- **Coat:** Soft, short, and glossy, with fine fur

Acknowledgments

The author wishes to thank the following pug maniacs for sharing their knowledge of and love for their dogs: Gershon K. Alaluf, D.V.M.; Andrew Bubeck; Laurie Buckley; Libby Crookham; Dee Dee Drake; Robin Downing, D.V.M.; Christine Dresser, D.V.M.; Ros Grimshaw; John Hamil, D.V.M.; Susan Hamil; Marcy Heathman; Andy Linton; Monika Potemra; Alan Radcliffe; Kristina Reid; Luana Rivera-Palacio; Alice Staples; Jamie Swanson; Phyllis Thompson; Kimberly Wilkinson; and Katie Williams.

. . .

Contents

Chapter 13: Basic Grooming 163

Chapter 14: Common Illnesses, Injuries, and Emergencies 179

Introduction

DOGS AND HUMANS paired off 15,000 or so years ago, and they've been best friends ever since. While the relationship between dogs and humans began as a working partnership, people soon realized the dog's potential simply as a companion. The pug is one of the many breeds developed solely to keep people company and provide entertainment. The pug excels in both these capacities.

Pugs are independent, headstrong, and spunky. They love to play, making them ideal for families with children. Small but sturdy, with a muscular build, they even appeal to people who otherwise wouldn't consider keeping a small dog.

In general, pugs are crazy about people. Most are extremely outgoing, happy to meet strangers, and always ready to play with kids. Some slug pugs live to lie in a lap and eat bonbons, while others are more active, willing to go anywhere and do anything as long as it means being with their people.

The beginning of a perfect day for a pug is sleeping late—under the covers, of course, with his head on the pillow, right next to you. He'll move fast, though, when he hears breakfast being prepared. He eats, plays, naps, plays, goes for a walk, naps some more, and eats again. Eating and spending time with his people are the favorite parts of a pug's day. At night, he goes to bed with you, ready to do it all over again the next day.

This book offers advice on acquiring a pug, as well as tips on housetraining, manners, socialization, nutrition, health, and just about anything else you might need to know to live happily with a pug. A pug is a guaranteed best friend for life. He wants to be with you every minute of every day. If that's what you want in a dog, you can't do better than a pug.

Meet the Pug

BRED FOR CENTURIES AS A COMPANION, the pug is a dual-personality dog. Content to share a sofa with his people, he is also active and playful. The pug is capable of great charm and dignity, and he wins friends and influences people with his outgoing, loving disposition. And his small size makes him suited to any home, from city *pied-a-terre* to country estate. With all of those advantages, it's not surprising that the pug is one of the most popular breeds in the United States.

Pug Popularity: A Pleasing Personality

Pugs are completely focused on their people. They'd rather be with you than anyone else in the world. A pug will follow you from room to room, sticking closer than your shadow. It's this strong desire to be with people, combined with a stable, even temperament, that makes the pug so desirable as a companion to adults and mature children alike.

Another characteristic that distinguishes pugs is their sense of humor. They are often described as the clowns of the canine world. If they can make you laugh, they will. That even includes a willingness to wear funny costumes while marching in parades or participating in just-for-fun dog events.

While pugs are generally friendly and outgoing, you will find a range of temperaments in the breed. Some pugs can be shy, introverted, or aggressive, although these characteristics are rare. When you see pugs with these traits, you can almost bet that they weren't well socialized as puppies.

Fortunately, it's rare to nonexistent to find a pug that's snappish. It's not unknown for a pug to bite in self-defense or in the face of severe provocation—being repeatedly hit or teased by a child, for instance. It's more typical of the breed to forgive such a behavior with a smiling face and a wag of the tail. (That doesn't mean, of course, that a pug should have to tolerate such behavior.)

▲ Pugs are popular and friendly. These happy dogs make great companions that will follow you anywhere.

Whether he's bossy, calm, submissive, or mischievous, expect a pug to always want to be with you, especially in your lap. Pugs have been known to accompany their people to work, to shopping malls, and even to restaurants and movie theaters. And the pug's alert nature, small size, and love of people have allowed him to take on the important jobs of therapy dog and hearing dog.

Not surprisingly, the American Kennel Club registered 21,340 pugs in 2003. That places the pug at number twelve in the AKC breed hit-parade, up from number sixteen in 1999 and number fourteen in 2002. Pugs have held steady in the AKC's top twenty breeds for many years.

Pug Needs

With their flat faces, prominent eyes, chunky bodies, curly tails, and playful, loving dispositions, pugs endear themselves to people almost instantly. In return for their affectionate and entertaining companionship, they have certain needs that must be met for their comfort and happiness.

 Essential

Pugs are easy to groom, but they do have a few special requirements. Their facial wrinkles and ears must be kept clean to help prevent infections.

Besides regular meals and a sturdy roof over their heads, pugs need consistent training, regular exercise, a comfortable environment, and lots of interaction with their people. The pug that's provided these things can't help but become your best friend.

Training

As with any breed, intelligence and trainability vary from dog to dog, but for the most part pugs are smart and have good memories. If they're properly motivated—usually with food—and kept entertained, they are quick to learn. On the other hand, reliability (to the extent that pugs can become reliable) comes only with frequent repetition over a long period of time.

Expect your pug to learn undesirable behaviors more quickly than good ones. You can counter that tendency by giving your pug plenty of opportunities to do things the right way and few opportunities to get into trouble. Just because your pug is smart doesn't mean he's always going to be well behaved.

Exercise

One of the great things about pugs is their adaptability. They are content to spend much of their time asleep on the sofa while you're at work, but they enjoy outings whenever they're offered. Unlike some breeds, they don't need a brisk daily workout to burn excess energy. A nice stroll through the neighborhood will suit a pug just fine and is important to help prevent obesity, which is common in the breed. Occasionally missing a walk because of bad weather or lack of time isn't a problem. Your pug will be just as satisfied with indoor play.

Pugs are sturdy dogs, capable of going on long walks as long as it's not too hot outdoors. Pugs in good shape have been known to walk distances of up to five miles, but a walk of a mile is a good distance for a pug. In any case, be sensitive to temperature. Pugs don't do well in the heat.

Shelter

One of the attractive qualities of the pug is his small size. If you're one of those people who would like to have a big dog but lack the room, then the pug is definitely a breed to consider. He's the epitome of "a big dog in a small body." A pug is the ideal breed for apartment and condo dwellers, especially in urban environments. Pugs need and enjoy regular walks, but they don't need a yard. In fact, pugs aren't good "outside dogs" at all. Because of their squashy faces, they're especially sensitive to heat and require a temperature-controlled environment. A pug doesn't need a lot of space, but he does need to be comfortable.

Companionship

Most important, your pug needs lots of love and attention. He's a people-pleasing, people-loving dog, and his greatest joy in life is spending time with you. After all, he's been bred for centuries to do a dog's most important work: serve as a companion. By training your pug and providing him with daily play and exercise, you're not only creating a dog with nice house manners, you're also spending quality time with him. In return, he'll bring you a lot of laughter and happiness.

A Pug by Any Other Name

Theories abound as to the derivation of the pug's name. Because of his studly body, wrinkled head, and association with the Netherlands, the early pug was sometimes called the Dutch mastiff or the Dutch pug. He also went by the name dwarf mastiff, a reference to his small size. Some pug historians suggest that the breed took its name from the marmoset monkeys that were popular pets in the seventeenth and eighteenth centuries. The wrinkled marmosets were often referred to as pugs, and people may have taken to calling the wrinkle-faced dog a pug as well. A nineteenth-century dog writer named J. H. Walsh theorized that the breed name came from the Latin word *pugnus*, meaning "fist"—the shadow of a clenched fist was said to resemble the pug's profile. In the Netherlands and Germany, the pug's frowning expression gave rise to the nickname "mops" or *mopshond,* from the Dutch word meaning "to grumble." That's not to say that the pug is pugnacious, however. He's a lover, not a fighter. In English-speaking countries today, the pug is affectionately nicknamed Puggy, Pugsley, Puggly, Puglet, and any number of similar derivations.

A Brief History of the Pug

Pugs have been companions to people for centuries. Pug fanciers believe the breed has been known for more than 2,400 years, but such claims are difficult to substantiate. It wasn't until the nineteenth century that detailed breeding records became common, and from pictures we know that the breed has changed a great deal just in the past 200 years. What is known is that the breed originated some-where in Asia. Early pug-type dogs existed in Tibetan monasteries and in the imperial courts of China and Japan.

Pug-type dogs in China were referred to as Lo-Sze, or sometimes as Foo dogs. The Lo-Sze was similar in build to the Pekingese but was distinguished by a short coat and smooth tail.

On the Trade Route

When enterprising European traders made their way to the Far East, these intriguing little dogs captivated them. Dutch and Portuguese merchants are generally credited with bringing the pug to the Western world. Easy to transport and care for, pugs would have made fine cargo to bring back to the royal courts of Europe, where toy breeds led pampered lives as lap dogs, foot warmers, and flea catchers. The unusual pug was sure to find favor.

Find favor he did, not only for his striking looks but also for his loyalty. The pug became the official dog of Holland's House of Orange in 1572 after Pompey, a pug belonging to William the Silent, Prince of Orange, aroused his master from a sound sleep as Spanish soldiers crept through William's camp at Hermigny. Pompey's timely alarm allowed William to escape capture, and the prince vowed never to be without one of the little dogs. A carving of Pompey on William's tomb in Delft Cathedral memorializes the brave pug.

 **Fact**

Queen Victoria kept pugs. She was a noted dog lover, and pugs were among the many breeds that she kept in the royal kennels.

A little more than a century later, pugs were still popular with the House of Orange. In 1688, pugs accompanied William III and his English wife, Mary II, when they sailed from Holland to ascend the English throne after the overthrow of Mary's father, James II. William and Mary's pugs, in turn, overthrew the toy spaniels that had been the favorites of England's Stuart kings.

Soon, everyone wanted a pug, and the breed's popularity continued through the eighteenth century. Among the breed's fans was Josephine Beauharnais, the future empress of Napoleon Bonaparte.

Her devoted pug, named Fortune, kept her company while she was imprisoned during the French Revolution, and he served as a messenger, carrying concealed messages to Napoleon.

The Rise of the Modern Pug

After the British sacked the Imperial Palace in Beijing in 1860, several pugs found there were brought to England. Among them were black pugs, a novelty at the time. The pugs from China helped bring about a change in the breed's looks, having shorter legs and flatter faces than the pugs that had been in Europe for the past three centuries. When Britain's Kennel Club was formed in 1873, its first studbook listed sixty-six pugs. The British Pug Dog Club was formed in 1882, and black pugs were first exhibited in an English dog show in 1886.

The first known pugs in the United States arrived after the Civil War. Records show that twenty-four of them made their dog show debut in New York in 1879. The AKC accepted the breed for registration in 1885, making the pug one of the earliest AKC-recognized breeds.

The pug was still prized as a companion in the late nineteenth century, but by the beginning of the twentieth century the fickle public preferred other dogs. In 1926, only fifteen pugs were registered with the AKC. Nonetheless, a few breeders persevered and kept the breed alive in the United States. A group of East Coast pug fanciers formed the Pug Dog Club of America in 1931, and by 1944, 155 dogs were registered. In the 1950s and 1960s, the pug's popularity grew substantially, and the breed has remained a favorite ever since.

Art Affair

As a favorite of royalty and commoner alike, it's not surprising that the pug has been immortalized in various forms of media through the centuries. He has appeared in numerous works of art, from paintings to modern photography. In addition, the pug has played starring and supporting roles on the silver screen and romped through the pages of literature.

Before the advent of photography, people had portraits painted of their loved ones or their prized possessions, including dogs. A painting of a dog could indicate much more than that, however. During the turbulent late seventeenth century, when Protestants and Catholics battled over who would control the British throne, a pug in a portrait served as subtle social commentary, symbolizing that the person portrayed was a supporter of William III over the deposed Catholic monarch James II.

 Fact

Many well-known personalities have loved pugs, including Winston Churchill; fashion designer Valentino; and entertainment stars Paula Abdul, Jenna Elfman, Billy Joel, Charlie Sheen, and Denise Richards. The Duke and Duchess of Windsor pandered to their pugs in a way that most pugs can only dream of. Their dogs traveled the world with them and had their own entourage, including a chef and a poop scooper.

Some dogs, of course, appeared in paintings because of their proximity to artist or subject. The British artist William Hogarth was a noted pug lover. Among his works is a self-portrait—*The Painter and His Pug*—that included his pug, Trump. Forty years later, Spanish court painter Francisco de Goya immortalized the Marquesa de Pontejos and her pug. Through such works of art, we can see not only the pug's role as a companion but also the evolution of the modern pug. Hogarth's dog looks more like a white bulldog than the pug we know today, while the Marquesa's dog looks more like a modern pug.

Early nineteenth-century pug portraits include an engraving from Philip Reinagle's *The Sportsman's Cabinet*, dated 1803, and an oil portrait entitled *Pug in a Landscape*, artist unknown, dated 1808. The pugs in these works appear larger than modern pugs and have a distinct muzzle. A later work, *Pug*, by B. A. Howe, circa 1850, shows a pug with tightly cropped ears, a style that didn't go out of fashion until 1895, when ear-cropping was outlawed in Britain as inhumane.

Paintings also tell us of the pug's stature in society. *Pug and Terrier*, by John Sargent Noble, shows a clearly well-kept pug wearing an almost-human expression of disdain as he looks down at a lesser dog wearing a begging cup around his neck.

The pug's fun-loving personality shines out in *Rover and Puggy*. Painted by Charles Burton Barber in 1878, it shows a pug and collie standing amid discarded tennis rackets and balls. Both dogs look as if they're just waiting for someone to start a game.

Most of the pugs portrayed in Victorian and earlier works of art are fawn-colored, but one picture from 1895 portrays a black pug from Queen Victoria's kennel. The dog has a white blaze on the chest, a common characteristic of black pugs at that time. A more modern portrait of a black pug is that of Nero, dated 1986. The artist, Neil Winokur, prepared a triptych of three cibachrome photographs with Nero in the center. He's flanked by his favorite rubber chew toys—a lamb chop and a lady's foot.

Film Works

Besides being companions to entertainers, pugs are entertainment stars in their own right. One of the best-loved films featuring a pug is the 1986 movie *The Adventures of Milo and Otis* (Otis was the pug). Japanese filmmaker Masanori Hata made this family film about two friends—a pug and a cat—that go on an unanticipated adventure when one falls into a river and is swept downstream and the other follows.

In the 1997 movie *Men in Black*, an alien named Frank, in the form of a pug (played by seven-year-old Mushu), stole the show from stars Tommy Lee Jones and Will Smith. He made a repeat appearance in the 2002 sequel, *Men in Black II*, in which Frank becomes an agent partnered with Smith. If you look closely, you'll also find pugs in the movies *Pocahontas*, *Runaway Bride*, *The Great Race*, and *Dune*.

Pugs Through the Pages

A number of books feature pugs and for good reason: they're funny and photogenic. One of the most laugh-out-loud portrayals of pugs is *Clara, The Early Years,* by the late Margo Kaufman. Clara was the pug that ruled Kaufman's life, and the book is her uproarious account of life with the imperious pug. In one episode from the book, the author writes: "Five minutes after her arrival, she inspected our junior suite like Leona Helmsley checking to see if the chocolate mints on the pillows were lined up at the right angles."

In *PugSpotting: A True History of How Pugs Saved Civilization,* author Susanne McCaffery-Saville explores the historical relationship between pugs and people and discusses how pugs have influenced art, literature, and music.

Pugs in Public, by photographer George Bennett, is a tribute to the pugs that inspire slavish devotion in their people and amusement in all who encounter them. Some of the pugs you'll meet in its pages are Tuck, who spends his days in his owner's art gallery, with a three o'clock break for biscuits at the Four Seasons hotel; Buddy, the quality-control specialist at a bicycle shop; and Pee Wee, who runs things at a chic café.

Another photographer, Jim Dratfield, captures pugs in all their many moods: philosophical, dignified, puzzled, content, and cool. The sepia-toned and full-color photographs include pugs getting married in a Las Vegas chapel, studying the architecture of a Gothic cathedral, and trying on a new toupee.

Pug Alert

If you've read this far, you've probably already been captivated by the pug's comical charm. And who wouldn't be? Pugs are incredibly cute. They're the original party dogs, always ready for a good time and a laugh or two. They love people and will do anything to entertain them. But beware! The pug is addictive. Once you've had a pug, you'll never want to be without one. You may even move into the realm of multiple pugs. To learn more about the pug's physical attributes and personality, read on!

The Pug Defined

FROM THE FIRST domesticated canine 15,000 years ago, dogs have evolved into an incredible variety of shapes, sizes, and temperaments (witness the pug!). Over the millennia, people molded those dogs into companions and workers. The pug, for one, has always been a companion. Today, each breed has written guidelines, known as standards, that describe how each type of dog should look and act. Here, you'll learn about the pug's appearance and temperament.

The AKC Pug Breed Standard

The dictionary describes the pug as a small, sturdy, compact dog; a breed of Asian origin with a close coat, tightly curled tail, and broad, wrinkled face. That's certainly the breed in a nutshell, but there's a lot more to know about what a pug should look like, how it should be built, and how it should move and act. That's where the breed standard comes in.

What's a breed standard? It's a picture in words that describes what the perfect dog in each breed should be like, detailing the physical and mental qualities that make up a particular breed. Of course, there is no such thing as a perfect dog, but the standard gives breeders something to strive for. It also ensures that a pug looks like a pug and not like a Brussels griffon, a bulldog, or a French bulldog.

Whether you want your pug to be a companion, show dog, or

both, the breed standard will help you understand which characteristics are most important for each job. For instance, if your pug will be primarily a family companion, it doesn't matter if his eyes aren't dark enough or his mask isn't well defined. In the show ring, however, those flaws would count against him. By knowing what's behind each requirement in the standard, you can decide which characteristics are most important to you in choosing your pug.

▲ Pugs bred by reputable breeders will conform to the breed standard.

The Overall Picture

The breed standard calls for the pug to be *multum in parvo,* a Latin phrase meaning "much encompassed in little," or, to put it another way, "a lot of dog in a small body." That's an apt description for this breed, which is known for being small but mighty. The pug is a decidedly square dog, with a compact, muscular body supported by strong, straight legs of moderate length. The hindquarters are in balance with the forequarters. The pug should look neither lean and leggy nor short-legged and long-bodied. The breed's ideal weight is fourteen to eighteen pounds, but larger pugs are common. Pugs belong to the AKC's Toy Group, a collection of breeds that, in general, stand no more than fifteen inches high and weigh no more than twenty pounds.

 **Fact**

The only pug to win Best in Show at the Westminster Kennel Club show was Ch. Dhandy's Favorite Woodchuck, in 1981. He was also a two-time winner of the Pug Dog Club of America (PDCA) national specialty, taking Best of Breed in 1980 and 1981.

Round Head

The pug's head is large, massive, and round, but the breed shouldn't be apple-headed—that is, it shouldn't have a domed-top skull that is rounded in all directions. Nor should there be any indentation of the skull. The jaw is wide enough to balance the top of the head; a narrow lower jaw is a flaw.

Bold, dark eyes give this breed a soft expression, but when a pug is excited, his round, lustrous eyes are full of fire. The breed standard describes the eyes as dark, very large, bold and prominent, and globular in shape, with a solicitous expression. Solicitous is a good word to use with the pug. This is a dog that's always soliciting you for attention or food! Large, deep wrinkles crease the pug's face, and the short muzzle is blunt and square. The muzzle shouldn't be upfaced (a term meaning that the lower jaw is positioned upward). A pug's bite—the relative position of the upper and lower teeth when the jaws are closed—should be just slightly undershot, meaning the front teeth of the lower jaw overlap the front teeth of the upper jaw.

At the sound of his name, a pug twitches his small, thin ears, which are described as being soft as velvet. The pug's ear comes in one of two shapes: button, which is preferred, or rose. A button ear is defined as one in which the ear flap folds forward, with the tip lying close to the skull so as to cover the opening. A rose ear folds over and back, revealing the burr, or inside of the ear. Either type of ear should be small and neatly folded so it doesn't detract from the head's overall round appearance.

Square Body

The height of the pug from floor to withers should equal the dog's length from forechest to tail. The pug has a slightly arched neck that's strong and thick, long enough to carry the head proudly. The cobby body is wide in the chest. The shoulders are moderately laid back. The back is short, level from the withers to the high tail set. Speaking of the tail, it's curled as tightly as possible over the hip. A tail with a double curl is perfection.

 Alert!

"Cobby" means short-bodied and compact. "Layback" is the angle of the shoulder blade when viewed from the side. The withers are the dog's shoulders. "Tail set" refers to how the base of the tail sets on the rump. In the case of the pug, the tail is set high.

The pug's body is supported by strong, straight, and moderately long legs. The elbows (where the forelegs bend) should be directly beneath the withers when the dog is viewed from the side. The pasterns (the area of the foreleg between the wrist and toes) are strong, neither steep nor down. This means that the pasterns aren't set at an incorrect angle, one that's too high or too low.

The rear legs have a moderate bend of stifle (the knee) and short hocks (the heels) that are perpendicular to the ground. When a pug is viewed from behind, the rear legs are parallel. The thighs and rear end are full and muscular. Pug feet have well split-up toes with black nails. In shape, they're neither long nor round, but somewhere in between. Usually the dewclaws are removed when a puppy is still very young. This helps prevent injury to the eyes.

Movement

The pug moves with a gait that's free, self-assured, and jaunty. It's a rhythmic two-beat, diagonal gait in which the feet at opposite ends of the body strike the ground together. There's a slight roll of the hips from side to side. Viewed from the front, the forelegs should be carried well forward, with the paws landing squarely and the central toes straight ahead. The hind legs should follow in line with the front. You shouldn't see any turning in or out at the joints.

Coat and Color

Covering the body is a coat that's fine, smooth, soft, short, and shiny. The pug's coat should never be hard or woolly.

The breed comes in three colors: silver, apricot-fawn, and black. Silver and apricot-fawn pugs sport a black mask and ears, the more well defined the better. Some pugs bear a black thumb- or diamond-shaped mark on the forehead. You may occasionally see a trace along the back, a black line extending from the occiput (the back part of the skull) to the tail. The mask and markings should be as black as possible.

Silver pugs are rarely seen. The silver color has been described as cold stone with silver hairs. A silver pug has no black hairs on the body (with the exception of the mask and ears). Fawn or apricot-fawn pugs have a warm, clear coat color with no black hairs on the body except for the mask, ears, and the trace along the spine. A black pug can appear blue-black or rusty black. The blue-black coat is preferred.

Temperament

A pug's temperament is just as important and just as distinctive to the breed as all the other elements combined. The ideal pug is even-tempered, stable, and playful. He exhibits great charm, dignity, and a loving, outgoing disposition.

Black pugs can have very different personalities from their silver and apricot-fawn siblings. Some pug lovers describe them as almost a breed apart. They are creative, to put it mildly, in deciding how they will respond to commands, but in competition they have the ability to deliver an exemplary performance—should they so choose. A black pug can be assertive and challenging to live with, but lovable nonetheless.

Faults and Disqualifications

Faults are weaknesses that can cost a pug points in the show ring. A structural fault involves the way the dog is put together or the way it moves. A cosmetic fault is aesthetic in nature, affecting only the dog's appearance.

Faults range from the superficial to the serious, although they may not affect a pug's ability to be a good companion, except as they relate to your personal preference. The following list includes examples of faults that might be seen in the pug:

- Lean and leggy body
- Long body with short legs
- Apple-shaped head
- Wry mouth (one in which the teeth or tongue are showing)
- Overbite
- Long nose, one that sticks out from under the nose wrinkle
- Small white spot (or spots) on the chest or toes
- Hard or woolly coat
- Straight legs that don't turn in or out at the joints
- Tail that doesn't curl

A disqualification is a serious flaw that makes a pug ineligible for the show ring. A pug with disqualifications should not be bred. The following conditions or faults are disqualifications for pugs:

- Unilateral or bilateral cryptorchid (one or both testicles are undescended)
- Viciousness or extreme shyness
- Albinism
- Brindle coloring

The Versatile Pug

One of the many virtues of the pug is its adaptability. The pug can be a family friend, show dog, obedience or agility competitor, or therapy dog. All of these aspects can be found in a single pug, or you may have a dog that excels in only one or two of them. Whatever the case, the following information will help you find the pug that's just right for you.

What you want in a dog will determine the type of pug you look for. The qualities of a companion dog vary, depending on your lifestyle and whether you have children. A show dog, of course, must have a certain appearance and personality. A pug that excels in the obedience ring may have a very different personality and physical abilities than one that excels in agility or as a therapy dog. Decide what you want in a pug before you start looking at puppies.

The Family Pug

Your family dog is a big investment, and you should want to get the most for your money. A pug that's going to be a family companion should have a calm, stable temperament. He should come from parents that have this same temperament and that have health certifications indicating healthy eyes. Ideally, a puppy's parents have proven themselves to be good examples of the breed by earning a championship in the show ring.

Even the best-quality pugs don't produce all show-quality pups, however. Don't be concerned if the puppy you're interested in is labeled "pet-quality." That term doesn't mean substandard. It simply means that the dog doesn't have what it takes to compete successfully in the show ring. He can, however, be a winner in your home.

The Show Pug

Show pugs, besides having the potential for excellent conformation—it's impossible to know for sure at eight weeks of age, no matter what a breeder may tell you—have a charisma that's obvious even in puppyhood. Dog-show judges often say that the dogs they choose are "asking for the win," and it's this level of appeal that can help ensure a show dog's winning career. If you want to show your pug, choose a pup with no obvious disqualifications and only minor faults. Naturally, the parents should have the same health certifications you would expect if you were buying a family dog. They should have proven themselves in the show ring by earning a championship.

Conformation is the form and structure of a dog as defined by the breed standard. A conformation show is a competitive event where dogs compete in several classes at various levels to determine the one that most closely resembles the breed standard. Dogs that earn the required number of points earn the title of champion.

Performance Pug

Pugs aren't the most athletic of dogs, but they are certainly capable of competing in various canine sports, including obedience trials, agility trials, freestyle, and tracking (yes, tracking!) tests. Any pug, family companion or show dog, can participate in these types of events if it has positive training, a patient owner, and a love of performing in public. The only possible bars to a pug's performance in canine sports are structural or movement faults that might affect, say, its ability to jump or run well.

Therapy Pug

It's well known that simply petting a dog can lower blood pressure. A visit from a dog to patients at nursing homes and hospitals can raise spirits and soothe agitation. Therapy dogs, or facility dogs as they're sometimes called, receive training from organizations such as Therapy Dog International, the Delta Society Pet Partners, and Love on a Leash. Therapy dogs don't need formal obedience training, but they are expected to have certain skills. These include being able to meet strangers in a friendly manner, sit politely for petting, walk nicely on leash, walk through crowds, be comfortable around walkers and crutches, and get along well with other dogs.

Not surprisingly, the good-natured and comical pug is a natural at therapy work. Pugs enjoy meeting people and love being petted. Their ability to learn tricks and willingness to play dress-up can earn them smiles, laughter, and applause as they make their rounds, all of which are strokes to the pug's healthy ego.

Besides being personable, pugs have other advantages that make them good therapy dogs. Their short coats are easy to groom, so they're good to go on short notice. They're small enough to be portable, yet still sturdy enough to withstand all the handling they'll receive. All of these traits and attributes combine to make the pug a desirable and successful therapy dog. Therapy work is a great way to spread the pug love around.

Understanding the Pug Character

Pugs love everyone. That's a given. Individual pugs, however, display a range of personalities, from laidback and cuddly to wild and crazy. So before you begin your search for a pug, decide what type of personality best suits you and your family. A mismatch can mean unhappiness for you and the dog.

Think long and hard about what you want in a dog. If you prefer a mild-mannered dog, be sure to tell the breeder so, because an ebullient pug will lead you a merry and exhausting dance. Be aware that an active, assertive pug puppy is likely to retain those characteristics into adulthood. And know that the shy pug that sits in the corner won't magically turn into a confident, outgoing dog once you take him home.

In general, however, you'll find that pugs are comical, mischievous, sweet, and loving. They retain their toddler-like enjoyment of life long into maturity. Even old pugs still get a thrill out of playing with a stuffed animal or acting goofy.

Pug Mania

Expect your pug to greet people by jumping up and down frantically until he's noticed. A pug won't stand for being ignored. He will bug people relentlessly until properly acknowledged. Some pugs are so excited to see visitors that they'll twirl around and snort to express their pleasure for a good ten minutes before choosing a lap to grace with their presence.

On the surface, a pug might seem like a laidback kind of dog, but that's before you've seen him in action. When the mood strikes them, pugs tuck their butts down and streak through the house or around the yard, tail out, ears flying, and a big grin on their face. This common pug antic is referred to as low-riding, the pug scuttle, or in some households, the Pugtona 500.

Victorian novelist George Eliot gives perhaps the best description of life with a pug. Writing to a friend about the pug he had bought for her, she says, "I wish you could see him in his best pose—when I have arrested him in a violent career of carpet-scratching—and he looks at me with forelegs very wide apart, trying to penetrate the deep mystery of this arbitrary, not to say capricious, prohibition. He is snoring by my side at this moment, with a serene promise of remaining quiet for any length of time: he couldn't behave better if he had been expressly educated for me."

Pugs and Children

Pugs love kids. A pug's rowdy, mischievous nature makes him a good partner in crime for the right child, and unlike most dogs, pugs love playing dress-up. Pugs are small, which is appealing to children, but they're sturdy enough to make good playmates for mature children. A pug will greet roughhousing with a grin, but that doesn't mean he should have to tolerate children who pull his ears and tail or poke him in the eye.

Before you get a pug, consider whether your child is old enough to interact with a dog. This breed is best suited to playing with children who are at least six years old. If you have younger children in your household, teach them how to pet the dog nicely, and always supervise all interaction between young children and pugs to prevent them from hurting one another.

Pugs and Other Pets

When it comes to company, other pugs are best (at least in the mind of a pug). If there aren't any available, pugs are just as happy with other dogs or cats. With its tendency to be bossy, the pug may even become the leader of the pet pack, in spite of the size or age of other animals. Pugs have been known to chase cats, sometimes obsessively, but most cats are well able to put a single pug in its place very quickly (so keep Kitty's nails trimmed to prevent pug eye injuries). In general, however, you'll find that pugs are accepting and loving toward most other animals. If you have a larger dog, you'll need to supervise play so your pug doesn't get hurt accidentally.

What to Expect

Expect a pug's personality and activity level to develop as the dog matures. Almost all puppies are active, outgoing, and even hyper. Those little flat noses are into everything. When they're not exploring, pugs want to be with people—right beside them, in their lap, or directly beneath or on their feet.

As pugs mature, a stage that can last from two to four years, they tend to mellow. It's not as important to run off the energy, to bark at every imaginary burglar, or to express an opinion on every little thing that goes on inside or outside the home. Until then, however, expect them to run around the house, bounce off the furniture, jump on people and other pets, and in general behave like the wacky, fun-loving dogs they are.

Finally, be prepared for a pug's idiosyncrasies. For instance, most people know that pugs snore, but they don't realize just how loud they can be. If you're already used to someone snoring in bed with you, a pug probably won't be a problem, but if you like quiet when you sleep, it's definitely something to consider.

Pugs are also flatulent. There's a reason some people nickname their pugs "Fartdog." They will emit smelly gas, and there's not really much you can do about it. If you have a sensitive nose, be sure you're willing to live with the pug's emissions.

To Your Pug's Good Health

I S THERE ANYTHING ELSE you should consider before getting a pug? Absolutely! Like all breeds, pugs are prone to certain genetic health problems, diseases that are passed from parents to pups. A careful breeder works hard to eliminate these problems from her line, but there's no such thing as a perfect dog. No matter how much testing is done or how careful the breeding, sometimes these diseases just pop up and must be dealt with.

Hereditary Problems

Pugs are generally healthy as a breed, but that doesn't mean they're free from hereditary diseases. Hereditary problems seen in pugs include eye problems; orthopedic (musculoskeletal) problems; pug-dog encephalitis; epilepsy; and respiratory problems. Find out more about the pug's propensity for these conditions so you know exactly what you're getting into and—when possible—how to avoid them. By knowing how to recognize and care for the various problems that can affect your pug, you'll be better prepared than most dog owners to give him a safe and healthy life.

Eye Disease

Because pugs are prone to eye disease, the best breeders have their breeding stock annually certified clear of eye problems by the

Canine Eye Registry Foundation (CERF). Eye diseases that are commonly seen in pugs are keratoconjunctivitis sicca, pigmentary keratitis, cataracts, entropion, progressive retinal atrophy, and trichiasis. Keratoconjunctivitis sicca and pigmentary keratitis are the main health concerns of PDCA members.

▲ Pugs can suffer from overheating; keeping them cool is a must.

Keratoconjunctivitis Sicca

More commonly known as dry eye, this condition is common in pugs, especially older dogs. Because the dog isn't producing enough tears, the eyes become dry and irritated and may produce a thick, sticky discharge. Left untreated, dry eye can cause permanent damage, but effective medications are available to help keep it under control. These may include cyclosporin eye drops, antibiotics, steroids to control infection and inflammation, or the use of artificial tears to lubricate the eyes. Avoid using saline solution, which can make the condition worse.

Pigmentary Keratitis

This inflammation of the cornea, known as PK, is characterized by the spread of dark pigmentation (color) across the surface of the eye. The cause of pigmentary keratitis is unknown, although it's often associated with dry eye, entropion, or environmental irritants such as dust or wind. It usually develops in young to middle-aged dogs. PK is a serious condition that progresses to blindness unless it's diagnosed and treated early. It begins as a red patch, supplied with blood vessels, and sometimes mixed with darker pigment. The pigment can spread across the cornea until the dog is no longer able to see.

Fortunately, medications such as cyclosporin, an immunosuppressant drug that seems to stimulate tear production, and surgery to remove the pigmented layers of the eye, have made PK more treatable. With surgery and cyclosporin, a pug can regain almost 100 percent of his eyesight, although the success of treatment varies from pug to pug. Check your pug's eyes regularly for cloudy or dark spots that may indicate a problem. The earlier PK is caught, the more successful treatment will be.

Cataracts

A cataract is an opaque spot on the lens of the eye that can be a result of the aging process or inherited. Pugs are one of the breeds in which congenital, or juvenile, cataracts have been documented. Hereditary cataracts are found most often in dogs that are five years of age or younger, and they may occur in both eyes (bilateral cataracts). Cataracts can often be removed surgically with excellent results, but if this isn't possible, your pug can still lead a near-normal life. Many dogs with cataracts retain enough vision to get around without a problem, and most are fully capable of compensating for decreased vision with their sense of smell.

Entropion

Entropion is the most common congenital defect of the eyelids in dogs. The eyelid rolls inward, causing the eyelid hairs to rub against the eyeball. The result is irritation or injury, indicated by tearing and squinting. This condition can be corrected surgically. Pugs that have had entropion surgically corrected cannot be shown in conformation. It's unethical to show a dog that has had any kind of corrective surgery, because the dog is not a good breeding prospect.

Progressive Retinal Atrophy

Progressive retinal atrophy (PRA) is an inherited retinal degeneration. Dogs with PRA have trouble seeing in dim light and eventually lose their vision altogether. Early signs of PRA are reluctance to move around in dimly lit areas or to go down stairs, or staying unusually close to the owner. PRA can't be treated, although genetic research offers promise, but again, blind dogs learn to get around quite well by relying on their sense of smell. The best way to prevent PRA is to breed only pugs that are certified free of the disease.

 Essential

Catch eye problems early by having your pug puppy examined by a veterinary ophthalmologist for irritants such as entropion, ingrown lashes, and inadequate tear production. These conditions will almost certainly result in keratitis (dry eye) and corneal ulcers if they go untreated. Have your vet tear-test your pug's eyes annually.

Trichiasis

The pug's prominent nasal folds are the culprit in trichiasis, a condition that arises when facial hair or eyelashes make contact with the cornea, causing excessive tearing, squinting, and corneal inflammation. Trichiasis is painful and may result in a corneal ulcer if left untreated.

Corneal Ulcers

Corneal ulcers result from a defect or hole in the surface of the cornea and can be caused by irritation or injury or through bacterial, viral, or fungal infection. Depending on whether they are superficial or deep, ulcers may produce little or no scarring or large scars and impaired eyesight. Treatment usually involves the application of topical antibiotics, but in severe cases, surgery is the only remedy.

Conjunctivitis

Conjunctivitis, also known as pink eye, occurs when the eye's normal population of bacteria and fungi gets out of control. The viruses that cause distemper and canine hepatitis can also cause conjunctivitis. Some forms of conjunctivitis are highly contagious among dogs. Keratitis, or inflammation of the cornea, results from injury or infection.

Orthopedic Problems

Dogs walk on their toes and carry 75 percent of their weight on their shoulders and front legs. It's easy to see, then, how easily they can suffer from orthopedic diseases. Musculoskeletal, or orthopedic, problems affect the bones, joints, and muscles. Hereditary orthopedic problems are common in dogs, and pugs are no exception. They can develop patellar luxation, hip dysplasia, and Legg-Calve-Perthes disease. Pugs with inherited orthopedic conditions should not be bred.

Patellar Luxation

Patellar luxation is a fancy way of saying dislocated kneecap. You may also hear the condition referred to as luxating patella or slipped stifle. When the patella (the knee) luxates, it slips out of the socket. Dogs that are prone to patellar luxation usually have weak ligaments, misaligned tendons, or grooves that are too shallow or narrow to hold the knee in place.

What a Luxating Patella Looks Like

The type of patellar luxation seen most often in pugs is called medial luxation. When the knee pops out, usually toward the body, your pug may hop like a bunny or have a difficult time straightening the knee. The knee can do the hokey-pokey, slipping in and out of place, or it can slip out and stay out. Diagnosis is made with a physical exam and radiographs (x-rays).

Grading Luxations

The severity of patellar luxation is graded from one to four, with one being the least severe and four being the worst. The knee slips out of place only slightly in grade one luxations. The knee locks up momentarily in grade two luxations, causing the dog to skip or hop until it slips back into place. Dogs with grade one or two luxations usually experience no pain. In grade three luxations, the patella won't stay in place. The angulation of the bones can change, and the dog may show signs of lameness. Pugs with grade four luxations show serious skeletal changes and are clearly lame.

Treatment

If your pug has grade one or two patellar luxation, you should be able to control the condition by keeping his weight at a normal level and strengthening the muscles around the knee with mild uphill exercise. Your veterinarian may recommend nutraceuticals such as chondroitin or glucosamine to help rebuild cartilage.

 Essential

A nutraceutical is a food or ingredient that's believed to have health benefits with few or no side effects. They aren't a quick fix, though—it can take up to two months to see results. Glucosamine and chondroitin are extracted from animal tissues such as the shells of crab or shrimp (glucosamine) or cartilage (chondroitin).

Surgery is an option for dogs with grade three or four luxations. After surgery, encourage use of the joint with slow exercise on a leash and on level ground. Keep the pace at a walk so your pug doesn't "cheat" by skipping on his bum knee. Patellar luxation can be diagnosed in pugs as early as five to eight weeks of age, especially in severe cases. Other pugs may have the deformities that cause luxation but never show signs. Keeping your pug at a healthy weight can help prevent the problem from developing.

Hip Dysplasia

This condition is primarily thought of as affecting large breeds, but it can occur in smaller dogs as well and is quite common in pugs. Hip dysplasia, or HD, occurs when the head of the femur (thigh bone) doesn't fit properly in the cup (acetabulum) of the hip joint. When the cup is too shallow, the joint is lax, meaning that the bone slips around inside it instead of fitting securely. Despite the frequency of hip dysplasia in pugs, many breeders don't test their dogs for it because few pugs that develop HD suffer serious lameness or pain from it. That said, pugs with HD shouldn't be bred, and pugs that produce puppies with HD should be removed from a breeding program.

Diagnosis

Hip dysplasia is diagnosed through x-rays. It can range from mild to severe, with some dogs never showing signs and others developing lameness at an early age. The good news is that it usually doesn't affect a pug's mobility as severely as it does in larger breeds. Take your pug to the veterinarian if you see him limping after exercise, walking with a waddling gait, having trouble getting up or lying down, or showing reluctance to move.

Treatment

Mild cases of hip dysplasia can be treated with anti-inflammatory drugs and nutraceuticals, plus moderate exercise to encourage muscle mass and tone. In severe cases, however, surgery—ranging from making minor changes in the shape of the femur to total hip replacement—is the only way to relieve the dog's pain.

The development of hip dysplasia depends on multiple factors, both genetic and environmental. If both parents are free of hip dysplasia, there's a much greater chance that their offspring won't have hip problems. Keeping your pug on a proper diet and minimizing weight gain can help reduce the risk of hip problems as well. Rapid growth hastens the development of orthopedic problems. It can also make problems more severe than they might have been otherwise, so don't let your pug puppy get fat. To prevent injury, provide nonskid footing such as area rugs if you have slick wood or tile flooring.

 Alert!

Nonsteroidal anti-inflammatory drugs (NSAIDs) made for humans—Tylenol, ibuprofen, acetaminophen, for instance—can be fatal to dogs. Never give these pain relievers to your dog. Your veterinarian can prescribe an NSAID formulated for dogs.

Legg-Calve-Perthes Disease

This disease occurs when the blood supply to the ball of the hip is impaired, gradually destroying the hip joint. The condition is most common in young toy breeds such as pugs, usually occurring between four and ten months of age. The condition can be hereditary or the result of trauma to the hip. Pugs with this disease suffer severe lameness and may be unable to bear weight on the affected leg. The surrounding muscles waste away, and the result is loss of motion at the joint and even shortening of the leg. Anti-inflammatory medications can help relieve pain, but the best results may require surgical removal of the head of the femur. Some cases have been known to improve without surgery, however.

Hemivertebrae

This spinal malformation isn't seen often in pugs, but it's most common in dogs with curved backs and short, twisty, or curly tails, so it's something to be aware of. The condition is present at birth and usually becomes apparent at six to twelve months of age, when the misshapen vertebrae begin interfering with the nerves controlling the hindquarters, causing the puppy to trip frequently or even to become paralyzed. Some dogs respond well to acupuncture, but others are permanently paralyzed. Although hemivertebrae is uncommon in pugs, it's a good idea to ask the breeder if she's experienced it in her lines.

Pug-Dog Encephalitis

Sadly, not much is known about this disease, a fatal condition for which there is no treatment. Encephalitis is an inflammation of the brain and brain membranes. This particular variety, known as PDE, usually affects young pugs, under the age of two years, with females appearing to be at slightly higher risk than males.

The signs of PDE include seizures, circling, head pressing, lethargy, a staggering gait, and blindness. There's no way to test for predisposition to the disease, and no treatment has yet been found to work. Death usually comes fairly quickly, and it's not until then that a definite diagnosis can be made through examination of the brain tissue by a veterinary neuropathologist.

Veterinary researchers are working to discover how the disease is passed on. Once that mystery is solved, it will be easier to identify carriers, analyze pedigrees to select breeding stock, and develop a test for the disease. Researchers also hope to identify a viral agent for the disorder, which would allow them to develop a vaccine against PDE.

Epilepsy

Epilepsy is a brain disorder that causes recurrent seizures—convulsions that are set off by abnormal bursts of electrical activity in the brain. Epilepsy is one of the most common neurological diseases in dogs, and some forms are heritable. Inherited epilepsy is referred to as idiopathic, meaning the cause is unknown. Pugs are one of the breeds prone to idiopathic epilepsy.

The length of epileptic seizures can range from a few seconds to a few minutes. In rare cases, they can continue for an hour or more. Mild forms of epilepsy can be treated with medication to control the seizures, but the disease has no cure. There's no screening test for epilepsy, and it often doesn't appear until a dog is older. The incidence of epilepsy can be reduced through selective breeding, however. The breeder should be able to tell you the frequency of epilepsy in his dogs.

 **Essential**

The AKC Canine Health Foundation funds research into understanding epilepsy. This information could help scientists develop tests to identify carrier, clear, and affected dogs, allowing breeders to make more informed choices in their breeding programs. Owners of pugs with epilepsy can contribute to this research by providing blood samples to the Canine Epilepsy Research Consortium. (See Appendix A for contact information).

Respiratory Diseases

Short-faced dogs such as pugs often have difficulty breathing, especially in hot, humid conditions or after exertion. Breathing difficulty can be worsened if the dog has deformities that affect breathing, such as pinched nostrils or an elongated soft palate. Pugs commonly have problems with stenotic nares and elongated soft palates. Fortunately, both conditions can be corrected surgically to help the pug breathe easier. These problems grow worse with age, so it's best to deal with them early on in your pug's life. The cost of surgery for brachycephalic syndrome (a term that encompasses both conditions) varies regionally, but in general you can expect to pay $800 to $1,000, which includes anesthesia and laser surgery. Pug owners say the results are well worth the expense.

Stenotic Nares

The nares are the two halves of the nasal passage, and the word "stenotic" refers to a narrowed or constricted passage. Thus, stenotic nares are tiny or narrowed nostrils, and they're most common in brachycephalic, or short-nosed, dogs such as pugs. When the nostrils are too small or the nasal cartilage is too soft, the dog has difficulty breathing. Dogs with this condition often breathe through their mouths and must work extra hard to get enough air. These dogs are noisy breathers, especially after even the mildest exertion or excitement. The nostrils may even collapse when the dog inhales, or you may see a foamy nasal discharge. Mild cases can be treated medically by preventing the dog from gaining too much weight, avoiding exertion during hot weather, and using a harness instead of a neck collar. Surgery can be performed on dogs with more serious respiratory difficulty.

Stenotic nares can become obvious at an early age, but sometimes they don't become a problem until the dog is several years old. In the case of a puppy, the nasal cartilage may firm up by six months of age, relieving the breathing difficulty. Your veterinarian may recommend waiting until that age before deciding on surgery, which can open up the dog's nostrils and ease his breathing. The surgery involves removing a wedge of nasal skin and cartilage, and when it's performed before the problem becomes serious, it has good results. Pugs that are surgically treated later in the course of the disease may not respond as well. If left untreated, the results can be an enlarged heart and eventual heart failure.

Elongated Soft Palate

Elongated soft palate is closely related to stenotic nares. A long soft palate can block part of the airway into the lungs, causing difficulty breathing. Pugs with an elongated soft palate snort, snore, gurgle, and gag. Like stenotic nares, this condition is most common in short-nosed dogs. To determine whether the palate is too long, the dog must be anesthetized and examined by your veterinarian. If that's the problem, it can be corrected surgically right then and there with great success, especially if the dog is less than a year old. A long soft palate and stenotic nares are often corrected at the same time. For both conditions, surgery is easiest and most successful if performed before serious clinical signs develop, such as fainting or cyanosis (blue gums and tongue caused by lack of oxygen in the bloodstream). If left uncorrected, an elongated soft palate puts a strain on the heart and lungs, and the dog's breathing ability worsens with age.

Pug Health Research

Pug owners are fortunate to have a national breed club (the Pug Dog Club of America, or PDCA) that's dedicated to supporting research into the breed's health problems. Assisting the PDCA in this goal are the AKC Canine Health Foundation and the Morris Animal Foundation.

Along with the AKC Canine Health Foundation, the PDCA is cosponsoring a study to type the DNA of normal pugs. By piecing together the genetic sequence of a normal pug, researchers hope to develop genetic tests to determine which pugs are carriers of, affected with, or free from certain genetic diseases. The PDCA is also sponsoring two research projects on pug-dog encephalitis (PDE).

The AKC Canine Health Foundation, founded in 1995, helps bring together grants from individuals, breed clubs, and corporate sponsors to fund research projects. One of the pug-related research projects funded by AKC Canine Health Foundation will study new molecular procedures to identify a viral basis for PDE. Another hopes to discover the cause of PDE, focusing on the possibilities of genetic transmission of the disease, viral, or autoimmune causes.

The mission of the Morris Animal Foundation is to improve the health and well-being of companion animals and wildlife by funding humane health studies and disseminating information about the results of those studies. An MAF study is currently evaluating a new anti-epilepsy drug that researchers hope will offer advantages over current medications—potential good news for owners of pugs with epilepsy.

Acquiring a Pug

YOU'VE EVALUATED YOUR LIFESTYLE and personality, concluding that you have the time, patience, and sense of humor required to live happily with a pug. You've studied the breed standard and have a good idea of what you want in a pug. Your children are at least six years old, mature enough to know how to handle a small but sturdy dog, and old enough to take on simple dog-care tasks under supervision. Now you need to decide where to get the pug of your dreams.

Looking for Pugs in All the Right Places

Pugs are a popular breed, so they tend to be widely available without a long wait. When you're ready to get your pug, you have a number of choices to make in deciding where to acquire your new dog. You can purchase a pug from a breeder or adopt one from an animal shelter or pug rescue group. Each source has advantages and disadvantages. Take a look at the possibilities so you can make the decision that's right for you.

The Reputable Breeder

Anyone can breed two pugs and sell the puppies. Breeders aren't required to have a license or even to know anything about dogs. Ideally, however, you'll purchase your pug from a hobby breeder (also referred to as a reputable or responsible breeder), someone who has been breeding and showing pugs in conformation classes for several years. Finding a good breeder is paramount. You want to deal with someone whose primary concern is the best interest of the breed, not a person who's simply capitalizing on the pug's popularity to make a quick buck.

 Alert!

A reputable breeder's priority is that his puppies go to a good home where they'll be loved all their lives. Be wary of a breeder who seems anxious to get rid of puppies or who pressures you to take one of his puppies.

Reputable breeders show their dogs in conformation classes so their quality can be seen and evaluated by other pug experts. They're knowledgeable about the breed's history and health, genetics, and breed type. They don't breed their dogs until they're physically mature—at least two years old—and they usually skip at least one cycle between breedings to give the female a rest from the hard work of pregnancy, labor, and raising a litter.

Reputable breeders also test their breeding stock to ensure that they're free of hereditary diseases before breeding and submit results of those tests to health registries, such as the Orthopedic Foundation of America (OFA). They monitor their dogs' health through eye exams, hip and knee evaluations, and other outwardly observable expressions of genetic conditions. When genetic tests for specific diseases are available, reputable breeders make them an integral part of their breeding program. They also test breeding stock for brucellosis, a sexually transmitted disease, and hypothyroidism.

This perfect pug breeder belongs to the Pug Dog Club of America as well as to local all-breed or specialty dog clubs. Club membership indicates a desire to keep up with what's happening in the breed, especially in the area of health. Reputable breeders study pedigrees carefully, looking to find the best matches for their dogs' strengths and weaknesses.

Some health conditions can't be tested for or don't show up until later in life, but the breeder should be using dogs that are currently free of disease and that have a family history that's relatively free of these diseases (no dog or breed is entirely disease-free). A pug breeder whose dogs have eye clearances from the Canine Eye Registry Foundation (CERF), who x-rays the hips and patellas (knees) of breeding stock, and who has the radiographs evaluated by the Orthopedic Foundation of America or PennHIP is to be highly commended.

The Advantages of a Reputable Breeder

When you buy from a hobby breeder, you can meet your pug's mother in the flesh and sometimes the father if he's in the same locale. (Females are often shipped long distances to be bred with the right male.) Even if the father isn't in the area, the breeder may have photos or videos of him. You may also be able to meet other relatives of the puppy you're considering. This is a plus because it gives you a good idea of what your pug will be like as an adult.

When he breeds a litter, the reputable breeder handles the pups frequently and accustoms them to the sights and sounds they'll encounter in a typical home. This helps them adjust quickly when they go to live with their new families.

Breeders can also become mentors. They're there to answer questions as your pug goes through adolescence—which can be a trying time—and if you want to show your pug, they can guide you through the process. If you live in the same area as the breeder, she may board your dog while you're traveling, allowing him to stay in a familiar place and giving you peace of mind that he's being well cared for. And if there's ever a reason you can't keep your pug—because of divorce, or a death in the family, say—a truly reputable breeder will take the dog back and keep it or place it in a new home.

Sometimes reputable breeders can be difficult to find. It takes patience and persistence to find the one who's right for you. But if you want to get your money's worth, a hobby breeder is the way to go. You will know that your new pup is the offspring of healthy, high-quality dogs and has been raised in a home by a knowledgeable breeder who provides her pups with good nutrition, veterinary care, and early socialization to the world around them.

▲ Buying through a well-known breeder
is a good way to find a strong, healthy pug.

Finding a Breeder

Word of mouth is a good way to start your search for a breeder. Ask a satisfied pug-owning friend for a recommendation. Your veterinarian may have a reputable pug breeder as a client. The veterinarian can advise you on the health of that person's dogs and confirm whether he had proper preliminary health certifications performed.

Visit a dog show, and talk to the pug breeders there. They won't have puppies for sale at the show, but it's a good place to get to know a breeder informally. Be sure to wait until after breeders have come out of the ring before you try to talk to them. Before they go in, they'll be too busy getting their dogs ready to be able to spend much time with you.

If you meet some breeders you like, ask to set up an appointment to visit their homes and meet their other dogs and puppies. Talk to several breeders and look at lots of puppies so you can get a good overview of the breed.

 **Fact**

Dog shows are often advertised in your local newspaper. You can also buy a copy of the *AKC Gazette* at most newsstands and check its calendar listings to see if there are any upcoming shows in your area.

The AKC's Web site provides a link to the PDCA Web site (*www. pugs.org*), where you can find a directory of breeders organized by state, along with an extensive list of breeder selection tips. If you don't have Internet access, the PDCA's address is listed in Appendix A. The club's secretary or breed information representative can refer you to reputable breeders in your area. If you write to the club or to a breeder, be sure to send a self-addressed, stamped envelope for a reply.

Interviewing a Breeder

Once you've found some breeders you're interested in, you can start the interview process. Here are some questions to get you started:

- How long have you worked with pugs?
- What breed clubs do you belong to?
- Do you show your dogs?
- What are the show records of the sire and dam?
- What's the goal of your breeding program?
- What health problems do you have in your lines?
- What steps do you take to reduce the risk of health problems?
- Can I see the health certifications for the puppy's parents and grandparents?
- How often do you produce litters?

- How old are the puppy's parents?
- Do you guarantee the health of your puppies?

The answers will give you an idea of how committed the breeder is to pugs and their well-being. Breeders who exhibit their dogs are proud of what they've produced and are willing for their dogs to be judged by other pug experts. A breeder who admits to problems in the breed, or even in his own line, is simply being honest. No breed is free of hereditary problems, and anyone who makes that claim is not someone from whom you want to buy a pug.

 Essential

Ask the breeder to go over the pedigree with you and tell you about the medical history of her pups' ancestors. Problems such as epilepsy and hypothyroidism usually don't show up until a dog is middle-aged or older, after it has already passed on its genes.

Besides telling you a pug's good points, a breeder should also emphasize the breed's negatives. These include health problems, year-round shedding, frequent flatulence, and loud snoring. Beware of a breeder who tells you only the good stuff.

Your interview with the breeder should give you a good idea of how committed she is to pugs and how long she has been in the breed. Don't be afraid that the breeder will think your questions are odd, rude, or intrusive. If she's a reputable breeder, she's more likely to be impressed that you've done your homework. Be wary of someone who ignores your questions or is offended by them.

The Breeder's Concerns

An interview with a breeder is a two-way street. Expect to be thoroughly grilled by a caring breeder. He wants to make sure each puppy goes to a loving home where it will be loved and appreciated. Rather than taking the questions personally or being insulted if the breeder has concerns about some aspect of your lifestyle, such as your children's ages, remember that he is only concerned for the welfare of his pups. You'd ask lots of questions, too, if your children were going to a new home. Your brain should send up a red flag if the breeder doesn't have any interest in finding out about you and what kind of home you'd offer. Good breeders will require that the pug be returned to them if there's ever any reason you can't keep it—no matter how many years later it is.

 Alert!

Don't be suckered by a breeder's professional-looking Web site. A good Web designer and writer can make the worst puppy mill or backyard breeder seem legitimate. Look beyond the pretty pictures, and ask the tough questions that will help you distinguish good breeders from bad.

Questions to expect include whether someone will be home during the day, who will be responsible for the dog's care, whether everyone in the family wants a pug, whether you have a fenced yard, where you expect the pug to sleep, whether you plan to spay or neuter your pet, what your plans are for training the dog, whether anyone in the family has allergies, and what happened to previous pets—for instance, whether they died of old age or were hit by cars after only a couple of years.

Pug Rescue Organizations

What if you want a pug but you like the idea of giving a home to a dog in need? A pug rescue group can give you the best of both worlds. A pug may be placed with a rescue group because it's elderly and has health problems its owners can't afford to treat. Many pugs in rescue groups are those whose sight is compromised in some way. Others are given up because of housetraining problems or because the owners have a new baby and don't have time for the dog. The Pug Dog Club of America supports rescue efforts by maintaining a list of rescue groups nationwide that help place lost or abandoned pugs.

A rescue group is not the place to go if you are simply hoping to find an inexpensive puppy. Rescue pugs are almost always six months or older. Most rescue dogs are adults, and some have even entered their golden years. Don't expect to find a one-year-old female that doesn't shed, is already housetrained, and doesn't have any health problems.

The important thing to remember is that pugs stay young for a long time. Pugs can live to be fifteen years old, and a three-, four-, or five-year-old pug can be as agile and active a dog as you could hope for—and is likely to stay that way for several years to come. Whatever their circumstances, pugs adopted from breed rescue groups usually go on to become wonderful family companions.

Breed Rescue Advantages

Generally, people involved in pug rescue are committed to the welfare of the dogs they work with. They try hard to match people with the right dog. They follow up with new owners after the adoption and offer advice and counseling as needed.

You also know exactly what you're getting. You know what size the dog will be, whether he's already housetrained or knows other commands, what his personality and activity level are like, whether he gets along with kids and other animals, and whether he has any health problems.

Breed Rescue Disadvantages

Puppies are rarely available, and the heritage of a puppy or dog adopted through a pug rescue group is rarely known. If it is known, it may not be of very high quality. Generally speaking, the people who surrender a pug to a rescue program are not the people who have carefully selected a breeder. Furthermore, you don't have the advantage of being able to see the health clearances on the parents. Eye disease or other hereditary problems often don't appear until later in life.

Adopting from a breed rescue group isn't as simple as going in, picking the dog you want, and writing a check for it. Like reputable breeders, breed rescue volunteers want to place each dog in the best possible home. This requires a period of evaluation that takes time. The length of the wait is influenced by the number of dogs available and the number of other equally or sometimes more suitable applicants.

Keep in mind that pugs placed with rescue groups often have health or behavioral problems that must be dealt with. You'll need to give a rescue pug extra patience, care, and understanding for the adoption to be successful.

Adopting a Pug from a Rescue Group

First, you'll need to find a pug rescue group in your area. Start by contacting the Pug Dog Club of America (see Appendix A for address). Or you can go to your favorite search engine, such as Google or Yahoo!, and type in "pug breed rescue [your city or state]."

When you find a pug rescue group, ask for literature on the program, such as a brochure or newsletter. Take a look at the adoption contract. It should state that the program will accept the return of the dog for any reason, should you be unable to keep it.

 Essential

Expect to be treated respectfully during the adoption process. In return, truthfully provide all the information requested about yourself, your family, and your home environment. Be willing to permit the home visit, and don't be offended by what may seem to be personal questions. Just as you want a nice pug, the rescue group wants nice homes for its dogs so they don't end up being returned.

If you decide you're interested, you'll be asked to fill out an application. Most groups require and check references, usually from a veterinarian or dog trainer. Many groups also schedule home visits so they can evaluate the environment where the pug will be living, as well as your readiness for a pug.

Rescue groups may have specific adoption requirements, or they may consider each application on a case-by-case basis. Reasons an application may be rejected include unrealistic expectations, such as wanting the dog to live outdoors, or because the applicant's previous dogs were all hit by cars before the age of two. Requirements for adopting a pug may include having a fenced yard and letting the dog live indoors. Expect to be required to spay or neuter the dog (with occasional exceptions for age or medical conditions).

Adoption fees usually range from $100 to $150. The thought of paying that much for a homeless dog might seem outrageous to you, but the fees are important because they help support adoption efforts and pay for the veterinary expenses that many of these dogs incur before they're ready for adoption. An adoption fee may also include spaying or neutering, vaccinations, and a health check. That's a pretty good deal, when you think about it. Sometimes adoption fees are assessed on a case-by-case basis. Some groups waive the fee for elderly dogs or those that are facing expensive veterinary treatment.

If your budget allows, throw in a little extra on top of the adoption fee to help other homeless pugs.

Animal Shelters and Humane Societies

Believe it or not, you can find a pug in an animal shelter or humane society. Sometimes puppies are turned in to shelters when the family that bred them hasn't been able to sell them. Other times, adolescent or older pugs are given up because their people decided they didn't have time for them. If you are considering acquiring an older pug or you like the idea of giving a home to a dog that really needs one, but there's not a pug rescue group in your area, the shelter can be a great place to look.

Shelter Advantages

The greatest advantage of adopting a pug from a shelter is that warm, fuzzy feeling you get from giving a needy dog a good home. Another advantage is the variety of services provided by some shelters. You may go home with a pug that has been health-checked, spayed or neutered, and vaccinated. He may even be housetrained or know basic obedience skills. Some shelters offer training classes and behavioral counseling so the two of you can get off to a good start.

 **Fact**

If your local shelter doesn't have any pugs available and there's no pug rescue group in your area, consider looking online. An organization called Petfinder has a Web site (*www.petfinder.com*) where rescue groups and animal shelters can post descriptions and photos of animals that need homes. You can search the site by breed, area, and other parameters.

Shelter Disadvantages

The disadvantages of adopting from a shelter are similar to the those than come with adopting from a pug rescue group. The main disadvantage—if you can call it that—is that most shelters don't provide instant gratification. Like breeders and pug rescue groups, many shelters nowadays have a rigorous screening process. They want to make sure that the dogs they place go to forever homes, not temporary housing. While it might seem onerous, think of it as a benefit to the dog rather than as a hoop you must jump through.

Before Any Adoption

Evaluate a pug from a breed rescue or animal shelter to make sure the dog will suit your family and lifestyle. If you're considering an adolescent or mature dog, ask ahead of time if you can take the dog for a walk through the neighborhood or at a nearby park. Note the dog's reaction to the approach of bicycles, cars, or strollers, and to sudden sounds or movements. Ideally, he will be confident and relaxed, recovering quickly from a startling or unusual situation.

As you approach people, pay attention to the dog's response. Be wary of taking home a pug that shrinks away from people or tries frantically to climb up into your arms. This dog will require lots of socialization. Acceptable reactions range from indifference to cautiousness to friendliness to curiosity.

Ask what type of situation the dog came from. If he was given up because he didn't get along with a family's children or other pets, you don't want to take him home to your children or other pets. Some pugs simply want to be the center of attention, and they do best with childless or older couples, that is, people who can give them the time they need. On the other hand, if the dog was given up for behavior problems caused by lack of attention, that's something you can remedy with training and time. Ask yourself the following questions before adopting a pug:

- What is the dog's activity level?
- How much exercise does he need? (Some pugs are more active than others.)
- Does he have any severe health problems, and do I have the time, money, and desire to deal with them?
- Does he get along with children and other animals?
- Does someone need to be home with him during the day?

Adoption is by no means the route to a free dog, but the return on investment can be tremendous. Having a pug means you have a guaranteed best friend for life, a dog that wants to be with you every minute of the day. If that's what you want, that's what you get.

Looking for Pugs in All the Wrong Places

Because pugs are so popular, many people breed them just to make a fast buck. It's easy to find a pug from these people, but the thing to remember is that you get what you pay for. These breeders usually don't start out with high-quality pugs, and they don't do the pedigree searches and health screenings that characterize hobby breeders.

With this in mind, here are some places to avoid when looking for that perfect pug puppy.

The Pug Next Door

Not every breeder is a hobby breeder who's knowledgeable about and committed to the pug breed. So-called backyard breeders are usually pet owners looking to get a little money back on the purchase price of their dog or who are under the mistaken impression that their little Petunia needs to have a litter before she's spayed. They're often unfamiliar with the breed's health problems, and they don't do any health checks before mating her with another pug that may or may not have health or temperament problems.

How can you recognize backyard breeders? They usually advertise their pups in the newspaper, unlike hobby breeders, who often have a waiting list before they ever breed a litter. Other tip-offs that someone is a backyard breeder include use of the word "thoroughbred" to describe the pups (instead of "purebred"), a failure to screen buyers carefully, or willingness to let the pups go before eight weeks of age.

Run of the Mill

Commercial breeders, often referred to as puppy mills, produce puppies on a large scale and wholesale them to pet stores. Their pups are not raised in the home but in kennels, which may or may not be well kept. Because the numbers of pups they produce are so great, they're not able to give the dogs much human attention during their early formative weeks, when they should be learning to love people.

Commercial breeders don't usually sell to the public, although there are some exceptions. These people may have three or more breeds, and they always have litters available. Hobby breeders, on the other hand, breed once a year or sometimes only once every two years. Their goal is to improve the breed, not to make money. If a breeder can't show proof of involvement with the breed—Pug Dog Club of America membership, conformation championships on their breeding stock, health screening for the breed's genetic problems—walk away. Puppy millers and backyard breeders don't do these things.

How Much Is That Puppy in the Window?

Without a doubt, a pet store is the most convenient place to find a pug puppy, but it's definitely not the best place. At a pet store, you can't meet the parents or other relatives. Nor do you have any way of knowing the conditions in which the pup was raised or whether the parents were screened for health problems.

The puppies at pet stores come from puppy mills, not reputable breeders. Even if the pet store says its pugs come from local breeders rather than being trucked in from the Midwest (where most puppy mills are located), that's still no guarantee of quality. No reputable breeder sells puppies to a pet store. Hobby breeders want to screen buyers directly to ensure that their pups are going to good homes.

Another consideration is that a pet store purchase is often an impulse buy. You see an adorable pug puppy in the window, and you just have to have it immediately. There's no time to research the breed's temperament and health problems—and all breeds have them. A few weeks or months later, that cute puppy turns into a regretted purchase and often ends up at the animal shelter or passed on to another family.

Is it always bad to get a pug from a pet store? Not necessarily. Some pet supply stores don't sell pups themselves but instead team up with a local animal shelter or breed rescue group to offer pets for adoption. This is a win-win situation. Pups get the visibility from being on display, and the adoption group can still screen adopters before letting the pup go.

Pug Price Tag

Whether you buy from a hobby breeder, a backyard breeder, or a pet store, you can expect to pay anywhere from $450 to $1,500, depending on the quality of the puppy and where the breeder is located. A reputable breeder who performs the proper testing on breeding stock—CERF eye clearances and OFA patella and/or hip clearances—usually sells puppies for $450 in the South and Midwest, a price that can rise to $900 or more on the East and West coasts.

A pug puppy with show potential can sell for as much as $1,500, again depending on where the breeder is located. Price can also vary by gender. Females generally cost more than males.

Some breeders charge less for pet-quality puppies than for puppies with potential as show dogs. Reasons a puppy might be sold as pet quality include being too big or having such aesthetic flaws as light eyes or an incorrect coat. Some breeders don't like to keep dogs with white toenails in their breeding programs. If the dog is healthy, however, none of these flaws will detract from his ability to be a great companion. On the other hand, some breeders charge the same amount for pet- or show-quality puppies because all of the pups have had the same good health care, nutrition, and socialization. Neither philosophy is right or wrong.

Expect to find prices in pet stores as high or higher than those from reputable breeders. You get the most for your money, though, when you buy from a reputable hobby breeder who has put thought, time, expertise, and expense into the breeding of his litter. The money you invest in a healthy puppy will give you a return of many years of pug love.

CHAPTER 5

Choosing a Pug

BECAUSE PUGS ARE SO CUTE and charming, it's difficult to resist going home with the first one you see. First you need to decide your preferences regarding a puppy or an adult dog, whether you want a male or female, whether to get one or two dogs, and whether you plan to show the dog. You need to be aware of all the details involved in getting a puppy, from choosing the one with the right personality to understanding the papers that come with a pup.

Puppy Versus Adult

Everyone wants a puppy, don't they? Not always. Puppies aren't without charm, but adult dogs have advantages you might not have considered. Before you make a decision, discuss the pros and cons with your family, and don't forget to consider whether your lifestyle is suited to bringing up a puppy.

Puppies: Sugar, Spice, Naughty, Nice

Puppies are cute. There's no denying that. Puppies are maddening. There's no denying that, either. Raising a puppy is a full-time job, comparable to having a curious and active toddler in the home. If you have children, you may take a new puppy in stride, or he may push you over the edge.

Puppies require constant supervision to ensure that they don't pee or poop on your new carpet, chew the drywall, and gnaw on the cords beneath your desk. They need to go out for potty breaks every two to four hours, if not more often, and they eat more frequently than an adult dog. Their energy is boundless.

On the upside, a puppy gives you the opportunity to mold your pug into the dog of your dreams. If you want to have the greatest amount of influence over your pug's development into adulthood, it's best to get an eight- to ten-week-old pup from a reputable breeder. You have even more control over your pug's behavioral development if you start training and socialization at an early age. It's much easier to teach a puppy than it is an adolescent.

Adults: What You See Is What You Get

It might not have occurred to you to acquire an adult pug, but the idea has merits you might not have considered. First, there are no surprises with an adult pug. You know exactly what you're getting as far as size, conformation, and personality.

 Fact

An adult pug requires fewer initial veterinary visits and vaccinations than a puppy. Usually, by the time a dog reaches maturity, any health problems it may have are evident. Adopting an older pug allows you to choose one that you know is healthy or at least to be aware of any health problems instead of being surprised by them down the road.

An adult pug may already be familiar with family life and household routines. He may be already be housetrained and have some familiarity with obedience commands. This is a plus if you're not home during the day to take a puppy out and give him the supervision he needs. Adult pugs are less active than puppies and more content to sleep the day away while you're at work, as long as they receive plenty of attention and a walk when you get home.

Consider an adult pug if you have children. Adult pugs usually have a laid-back attitude about children's antics. They know that kids move suddenly and sometimes pull tails, and they're calm enough to take it all in stride. Puppies, on the other hand, are still learning about living with people, especially the pint-size versions.

Don't be worried that an older pug won't bond with you and your family. A steady supply of treats and a welcoming lap are all you need to win a pug's heart. If you can pass up the pleasures of puppyhood for the joy of building a relationship with a pug that has retired from the show ring or whose first home didn't work out, an adult dog is a good choice for you.

The Art of Compromise

Your kids want a puppy but you think an older dog sounds like less work. Consider compromising by selecting an adolescent pug that's six or seven months old. A dog this age is still full of puppy vim and vigor, but his bladder capacity is greater, and he needs meals only twice a day instead of three or four times a day. He's young enough to be adaptable, and his attention span is greater than that of a puppy. On the other hand, a dog this age is just entering adolescence, which can be a trying time, but you'd have to face it at some point if you got a younger puppy.

Where do you find this adolescent dog? Often, breeders keep several pups to "run on," in the hope that they'll develop into good show prospects. Those that don't make it are sold to families as companion dogs.

Male or Female?

When it comes to gender, most people want female dogs. They have a reputation for being easier to handle and "cleaner" as far as not marking in the house. Pugs can have differences between the sexes, however, so don't automatically rule out one over the other. Males tend to be cuddlier, while females can be aloof and tend to make better watchdogs. Males also have a tendency to be calmer, although there are always exceptions. A pug of either sex is cheerful, amusing, mischievous, and sensitive.

Naturally, there are physical differences as well. Unless a female is spayed, she'll go into season (heat, or estrus) for about three weeks, twice a year. This usually occurs every five to seven months. A bitch (female) in season has swollen genitals, which she licks frequently, and a bloody discharge that can be light or heavy. During this hormone-driven period, your pug may enthusiastically hump anything or anyone she can find. Without careful supervision, she'll become an escape artist in search of any male—pug or not—to satisfy her urges.

 **Fact**

Males and females have different elimination habits. Males will lift their legs on almost anything, from your freshly painted fence to a wall or sofa. Females generally squat neatly, although it's not unheard of for a dominant female to lift her leg.

In both sexes, spaying or neutering can reduce or eliminate these unpleasant behaviors. Spay/neuter surgery also has health advantages. Spaying prevents uterine infections. If a bitch is spayed before her first heat, her risk of developing breast cancer later in life is reduced significantly. Spayed females are also spared the hormonal disruption of a false pregnancy, in which the uterus swells and the nipples engorge with milk. This can be disturbing to the dog both emotionally and physically.

Neutered males are protected from testicular cancer, prostate disease, and perianal adenomas, growths around the anus that are testosterone-dependent. Neutered males are also less likely to lick their genitals, lift their legs, or hump guests. Nor do they have any reason to roam in search of a willing and able female. Because neutered animals of both sexes have no desire to reproduce, they can focus all their love and attention on their people.

One Pug or Two?

Pugs are like potato chips—it's hard to have just one. Like most breeds, pugs recognize and enjoy the company of other pugs. They can spot another pug two blocks away, and both dogs will be straining at their leashes to reach each other. Having a second pug gives your dog a likeminded playmate with a similar energy level. A pair of pugs will enjoy grooming each other and sleeping together.

▲ Are two pugs better than one? It's essential to carefully weigh the pros and cons of owning two pugs.

But does your pug need a pal? Pugs are companion dogs, and their sole desire in life is to be with their people. That said, most adult pugs are laid-back enough to adjust to being home alone during the day—as long as you spend plenty of time with them in the evening. They will demand your full attention when you're at home. Nonetheless, if your pug must stay home alone during the day, you might want to consider getting him another pug as a companion.

Before you decide that getting two pugs is a great idea, bear in mind that there are disadvantages to a double-pug lifestyle. Two pugs shed twice as much as one—a major consideration for neat freaks. If you get two puppies at the same time, you'll have double the housetraining hassle. There's an economic drawback as well: you'll have greater expenses for equipment, food, toys, training, and veterinary care.

 **Essential**

If you decide to get two pugs, get one male and one female. This is not so you can breed them, but because they're more likely to get along with each other than pugs of the same sex.

Raising two pups at the same time isn't easy, but it's not impossible. Just know that it will take a greater amount of dedication to civilize them than it would a single pup. You'll need to play with them, train them, and spend time with them, both together and separately, so you can build a distinct relationship with each one. If possible, each puppy should have a primary caregiver, and the two should not spend all their time together.

To minimize problems, consider getting one puppy first and take it through puppy kindergarten and basic obedience training. Once the two of you survive the pup's adolescence, you can bring in a second pup. The new puppy will learn a lot by watching your older dog, so training is less difficult, and your first pug will still have plenty of energy to devote to playing with his new friend.

Getting a Show Dog

Purchasing a pug that you plan to show requires an initial investment of time. Go to as many dog shows as you can so you can see pugs in the ring and meet breeders. By seeing which dogs are winning, you'll have a better idea of what to look for when you're choosing a puppy. And when breeders see that you're serious, they'll be more inclined to sell you a pup with show potential.

As you learned in Chapter 2, the pug has a breed standard that describes the perfect dog. If you are interested in showing your pug, you'll want to choose a puppy whose conformation meets the standard as closely as possible. Take a copy of the standard with you when you look at puppies, and ask the breeder to explain why certain puppies are better show prospects than others. Certain things are givens. For instance, check to see that a male puppy has both testicles descended. Don't rely on vague assurances that a missing testicle is sure to drop down later.

Keep in mind, however, that a lot can change as a puppy matures. No reputable breeder will guarantee that a puppy will grow up to be a show-quality dog. He can only promise that a pup has show potential, based on its qualities at the time of purchase. That's one reason to consider purchasing an older puppy if you want a show dog. You'll have a better idea of what you're getting.

A pug puppy with show potential isn't going to come from the backyard litter bred by Joe Blow down the street. For best results, you'll need to find a well-known breeder with a reputation for producing nice show dogs. Finally, expect to pay a premium for a puppy with show potential.

Puppy Primer

Choosing the puppy that's right for you and your family can be the most difficult part of purchasing a pug. All puppies are cute, but each has its own individual personality that sets it apart from the others. In predicting a puppy's adult personality and temperament, you'll want to consider activity level, interactions with littermates, and reactions to people, as well as the breeder's own observations and recommendations.

Your first look at the puppies will probably come when they are six or seven weeks old. By that time, they'll have had their first vaccinations and will be less at risk of infection from outside sources. Observe them closely for clues to their behavior, temperament, and health.

Behavior and Temperament

Predicting a puppy's adult personality and temperament isn't an exact science, but the following tips will give you some grounds on which to make your decision.

Ask how the puppies have been socialized. They should have been exposed to plenty of people outside the breeder's family.

 Fact

Before they reach maturity, dogs go through five stages of development: the neonatal period, when they're just born; the transitional period, starting when their eyes open; the socialization period, starting when their ears open; the juvenile period, starting at ten weeks; and puberty, starting at about six months.

Pug puppies should view all people as a source of pleasure and entertainment. While some may be more cautious than others, in general they should be curious, friendly, and trusting toward people.

Parental Role

To evaluate a puppy's temperament, start by looking at his parents. Are they outgoing or shy? Friendly or suspicious? Loud or quiet? Temperament is heritable. Pug puppies are with their mother constantly from birth until they go to their new homes, so she has a tremendous influence on their development. Dad's temperament plays a role as well, but it's from Mom that puppies take their cues on how to react toward people, other animals, sounds, and other sensory events. The more adult dogs you can meet at the breeder's, the better you will be able to gauge a puppy's future temperament.

Puppy Interactions and Play Styles

Watch the puppies interact as a group. Is one more dominant than the others, jumping on his littermates and taking toys from them? Or is there one that all the other puppies pick on? For most people, a pug that falls between these two extremes is a good choice. Dominant dogs want to run the show and can be difficult to train, while submissive pups may have low self-esteem, which can lead to behavior problems such as submissive urination.

Toss a toy, and see how each puppy reacts. Does he run helter-skelter after it or proceed in a more deliberate fashion? When you take the toy away, does the puppy give it up with a smile or hang on for dear life, growling through his teeth? The reaction you see gives you a clue as to future personality. Prefer the polite puppy to the growler.

Puppies and People

After you've watched the puppies for a few minutes, sit down and see if one or more will come to you. How do they behave? Are they excited to meet you or somewhat submissive? A confident pup has a wagging tail and an alert expression. Offer a treat. The puppy that trusts you enough to come forward and take the treat has good training potential. Avoid a puppy that backs away with an anxious bark. Speak softly. Which puppy cocks his head and listens to you?

Gently roll each puppy on his back. Does he squeal indignantly and struggle to get up or does he relax for a tummy rub? The squealer may become a domineering pug that wants to run the show. You'll need to give plenty of consistent training and strong leadership so this pup will know who's really in charge.

 Alert!

Be sure you differentiate between the pup that's merely high-spirited or assertive and one that's aggressive, fearful, or suspicious. The latter puppy may try to bite, which isn't a good sign. Pugs are known for their sweet, nonaggressive temperaments.

Walk away and see if any of the puppies follow you. Give them a little encouragement if necessary. Some puppies come readily, while their littermates need a little more time to evaluate the situation. Caution isn't a bad thing and shouldn't be confused with shyness. A nice pug with a moderate temperament will be happy to follow you without a lot of wild behavior, such as running in circles, barking, or dashing away.

Next, pick pups up one at a time and gauge their reaction to being held. Does the puppy squirm and struggle or relax happily into your arms? Does he squirm a little and then relax? Being held by a stranger is stressful for puppies, and you want to choose one that reacts to stress by calming down in a reasonable amount of time. The pup that can't control his fear or his desire to be in charge may give you problems in the future.

While you're still holding the pup, walk away from the others. Does he show alarm at being separated from his mother and littermates? Some unease is natural, but if a pug pup trusts people, he should eventually relax and enjoy the ride. You may notice that a quiet puppy becomes more animated and inquisitive on his own, while a bold one becomes a little insecure. A puppy that becomes extremely fearful probably isn't a good choice.

Red Flags

Avoid puppies that act shy or suspicious. You may feel sorry for the pup that's hiding in a corner, but shyness is very difficult to overcome. It's no fun having a dog that runs away from everyone who approaches him or that startles at every unusual sound. A cautious pup stands back at first but eventually approaches you on his own; a shy pup must be coaxed out of a corner or even picked up. Although it might seem as if a suspicious pug would make a good watchdog, this isn't a characteristic that should be evident in such a young dog. An overly suspicious puppy may develop into a fearful adult.

Sound and Touch Sensitivity

Test noise sensitivity by clapping your hands when the puppies aren't watching you. Do the pups look around or run away? If they run away, do they return quickly to investigate? The pup that looks around to see what made the noise or that comes back quickly after running off is a good choice. Avoid the pup that heads for the hills and never comes back. Deafness isn't a common problem in pugs, but if a puppy totally ignores the sound you make, he should be checked by a veterinarian to make sure he doesn't have a hearing disorder.

Properly raised puppies should be used to having all parts of their body touched. Ask the breeder to show you the puppy's teeth and ears. Gently run your hands over his body. Does he enjoy being touched? You want a pup that accepts being handled. It bodes well for future grooming sessions, veterinary visits, and even being judged in the show ring.

Health Indicators

Just as important as temperament and personality is good health. You don't want to take home a sickly puppy. Signs of good or poor health are obvious when you know what to look for. The first thing you might notice is energy level. Healthy puppies are active and enjoy running and playing. Try to schedule your visit before mealtime; puppies can be sleepy after they eat.

Healthy puppies have bright eyes that aren't squinty or watery, clean ears, pink gums, white teeth, and shiny coats. Their ears don't smell bad, and their nose and eyes are free of discharge, never runny or red. Look at the gums. If they're pale, not pink, the puppy may have intestinal parasites such as roundworms.

Hold the puppy close and listen to his breathing. You shouldn't hear any rattling or rasping. Instead, the puppy should breathe easily with his mouth closed. Heavy breathers or pups that must breathe with their mouth open may develop respiratory problems.

Obvious signs of poor health are poor coat condition and loose stools. Missing patches of hair or mottled skin can be signs of disease. A dull coat and a pooched-out stomach that resembles a beer belly are signs of intestinal parasite infestation. Evidence of diarrhea is another red flag. Healthy puppies have small, firm stools.

Think twice about buying a puppy that shows any signs of poor health. Intestinal parasites are easily treated, but the puppy's condition doesn't say much about the breeder's care for her dogs. You can do better.

What Does the Breeder Think?

Listen to the breeder's advice. By the time you see the puppies, the breeder has been watching the litter closely for at least six weeks. She knows each puppy's personality and temperament. Tell the breeder exactly what you're looking for in a pug, and chances are she will match you with the perfect puppy. He might not be the puppy you were thinking of, but you'll be surprised to find that he is indeed just what you wanted. Now you just need to make sure the pup is healthy.

 Question?

What are a puppy's parents called?
The father is referred to as the sire and the mother is called the dam. Both sire and dam should be at least two years old with health clearances before they're bred.

Ask if the puppies have been dewormed and vaccinated. By six to eight weeks of age, the pups should have been vaccinated at least once for distemper and parvovirus. In some areas where the incidence of parvo is high, two vaccinations may have been given.

When Can Pups Leave Mom?

Every breed is different, but pugs are usually ready to make the transition to a new home at nine to twelve weeks of age. They need that amount of time with their mother and littermates to learn everything they should know about interacting with other dogs. It also gives them plenty of time to be weaned and to begin learning how to live in a home. Be wary of a breeder who's willing to let pups go earlier than eight weeks of age. You want a pug puppy that's fully prepared emotionally and physically to meet the world outside the breeder's home.

Choosing an Adult Pug

Whether you're choosing an adult pug from a shelter, a pug rescue group, or a breeder, many of the same temperament tests suggested for use with puppies can also help you choose an adult pug that will be a good fit for your family and lifestyle. For instance, you can encourage the dog to roll over for a tummy rub—a good sign of trust in and submissiveness toward people—and test his sensitivity to sound by unexpectedly dropping your keys or clapping your hands. The most important thing is to spend time getting to know the dog.

 Alert!

Avoid the discredited "alpha roll," which involves pinning a dog by the throat and staring at it. The alpha roll is not only dangerous to you—it could prompt the dog to bite—it's also detrimental to a dog's mental health and well-being.

Evaluating a Pug at a Shelter

Ask if you can take the dog out of the kennel. The way a dog behaves in his kennel is likely to be different from the way he behaves in a less restricted situation. Most shelters have a yard or room where you can spend time with the dog you're considering. Talk to the dog, walk with him on leash, and play with him. Remember that a dog in a shelter is probably frightened, and that may affect his attitude. This may be his first time away from its canine or human family, and that's upsetting for anyone, let alone a sensitive dog that lands in a noisy, unfamiliar place such as a public shelter! A pug separated from his previous owner may go through a period of mourning, so he may seem depressed or withdrawn. Once he's in a less stressful environment, such as a visitation room or an outdoor exercise area, he may perk up. In terms of health, look for the same things you would in a puppy: clear eyes, clean ears, easy breathing, good skin condition, and so on.

Notice whether the dog makes eye contact with you, whether he seems glad to be in your company, and whether he responds when you speak to or move toward him. Any sign that a dog wants to interact with you is positive. Choose a dog that seems to enjoy being with you.

 **Essential**

Most people go into shelters hoping to find a puppy, but don't pass up a grown pug or even one of advanced age. Giving a home to an older dog can be a wonderful experience. Although he may not be with you for as many years as a puppy, the rewards of taking him into your home can far outweigh the pain of the eventual loss.

People who work at the shelter see the dogs every day, and it will be helpful to have their opinion on the dog's temperament as well. Shelter personnel may be able to tell you something about the pug's background, such as how old he is, whether he came from a home with children or other pets, and why he was given up. Questions to ask include whether the dog has a good appetite and whether he came with any health records or other paperwork.

If possible, bring everyone in the family to meet the dog. Many shelters require this before they'll complete an adoption. That's because the way a dog interacts with adults may be different from how he interacts with children. If you have another dog in the home, it can even be a good idea to bring her with you so you can make sure the two of them will get along. (Call to arrange this beforehand.) The neutral setting of the shelter is a great place to introduce them.

Give the dog time to adjust to his new surroundings and provide him with firm, consistent rules and lots of love. Soon, you'll wonder how you ever enjoyed life without Pugsley.

CHAPTER 6

Pug Purchase Paperwork

Y OU'VE FOUND THE RIGHT BREEDER and the right puppy. Now comes the paperwork. Your purchase will involve health certifications, a pedigree, registration papers, a sales contract, and veterinary records. Even if you don't plan to show or breed your pug, this paperwork can be useful throughout his life. The pedigree and health certifications can help you track hereditary problems if they develop later in life, and you'll need the registration papers if you decide you want to participate in AKC-sponsored dog sports.

Health Certifications

You know now that pugs are prone to certain hereditary health problems, some of which can be tested for. Just as the AKC registers purebred dogs, health registries maintain databases of the results of health tests for various genetic diseases or disorders, including hip dysplasia, patellar luxation, eye problems, and more. The best known of these registries are the Orthopedic Foundation for Animals (OFA), the Canine Eye Registration Foundation (CERF), and the Canine Health Information Center (CHIC). The breeder from whom you purchase your pug should provide proof of the parents' health certifications from one or more of these registries. The most important health certifications for pugs are for hip dysplasia, patellar luxation, and eye disease.

Orthopedic Foundation for Animals

The OFA was established in 1966 to help breeders address the problem of hip dysplasia. Since then it has added databases for other conditions, including patellar luxation and Legg-Calve-Perthes disease, both of which can affect pugs. It also has DNA databases. The OFA's goals are to gather and disseminate information about orthopedic and genetic diseases in animals and to encourage and finance research in orthopedic and genetic diseases in animals, so that the incidence of those diseases can be reduced.

Canine Eye Registration Foundation

The veterinary school at Purdue University in Indiana maintains the CERF registry. In addition to registering dogs certified free of heritable eye disease by board-certified veterinary ophthalmologists, CERF collects data on all dogs examined by these ophthalmologists. The foundation compiles this data into a database that helps researchers spot trends in eye disease and breed susceptibility. To maintain their CERF registration, dogs must be re-examined and recertified on a regular basis.

At the CERF Web site (*www.vet.purdue.edu/~yshen/cerf.html*), you can see if the sire and dam of the puppies you're interested in are listed simply by submitting their registered names. You can also search the kennel name of the breeder you're considering to see which of his dogs have been registered. The CERF Web site also provides a directory of board-certified veterinary ophthalmologists and materials on eye disease in dogs that can help you understand the eye problems that might affect a pug.

Canine Health Information Center

The Canine Health Information Center (CHIC) is a relatively new database that's a joint effort by the AKC and the OFA. CHIC's mission is to provide a source of health information for owners, breeders, and scientists. It works with breed clubs to identify health issues that should be included in a central health information system and maintains a centralized database to help researchers investigate canine diseases and provide health information to owners and breeders. Currently, however, pugs are not among the breeds that are included in the CHIC database.

The Pedigree

If you're at all interested in genealogy, you know what a family tree looks like. It starts with one line, showing your name, and branches out to show your parents, grandparents, and earlier generations. A pedigree is your pug's family tree. It usually goes back at least three generations and sometimes five or more.

Reading the Pedigree

When you look at a pedigree, your pug's name, breed, and date of birth appear in the top left corner, as well as its sex, registration number, color, and the breeder's name. Starting from the left, you'll see the sire's name, with the dam's name below. Moving on to the right are the names of your pup's four grandparents, with paternal grandparents on top and maternal grandparents on the bottom. The next column shows the great-grandparents, and so on. Males are always listed on top, females on the bottom.

Titles and Health

The pedigree also shows what titles a puppy's ancestors have earned. In the case of a pug, these will be mostly conformation titles. You're not going to find a lot of pugs with obedience titles, for instance. Titles are good, but they're not everything.

Ask the breeder about the health status of the dogs in your pup's pedigree. Is Grandma Pug still alive? Has she developed any hereditary health problems as she's aged? How old was Great-Grandpa Pug when he died? The more dogs in a pedigree that are known to be free of problems, the better the chance that your puppy will be healthy, too.

A pedigree is not a legal document, but the breeder should sign it, certifying that it's accurate. A pedigree is nice to have, but it's not really important unless you plan to show or breed your pug. The following sections discuss some terms that are useful to know as the breeder explains your pug's heritage.

Question?

What does the CH mean on my pug's pedigree? The AKC title of champion is abbreviated CH. Sometimes the country where the championship was earned is indicated, such as Can. CH (Canadian champion) or Amer/Can CH (American and Canadian champion).

Inbreeding

Inbreeding is the mating of dogs that are closely related, such as father to daughter or brother to sister. When we hear the term "inbreeding," we picture puppies with physical or mental defects, but when done properly, inbreeding is a valid technique that can strengthen a breeder's lines by setting type, or good characteristics. When the dogs used for inbreeding are free of hereditary disease and have excellent conformation and temperament, the result can be a litter of beautiful, healthy puppies.

While inbreeding works well when the dogs involved have superior attributes and few or no defects, it can lead to serious problems if the opposite is true. Inbreeding intensifies good qualities, but it also magnifies flaws. Inbreeding requires in-depth knowledge of the pedigrees of both dogs so that the breeder is prepared for any diseases or defects that could arise from the breeding.

Line Breeding

Line breeding is a form of inbreeding. Like inbreeding, line breeding is the mating of related dogs, but the degree of relationship is not as close. Examples of line breeding would be a bitch to her grandsire or a dog to his granddam. It's another way to enhance good characteristics. Again, dogs that are line bred should be of the highest quality in health, conformation, and temperament.

Outcrossing

An outcross is the breeding of two unrelated dogs. It's used when a breeder wants to introduce a desirable attribute into his line or to correct a fault that has shown up in the line. Outcrosses can help maintain good health and vigor in breeding stock. They have the added advantage of helping to preserve genetic diversity in a breed. The disadvantage of an outcross is that it can bring hidden genetic problems into a breeder's line.

Registration Papers

These are what we usually think of when we hear that a dog has "papers." Registration papers prove that your pug is a purebred and is registered with the AKC. That's it. Papers are nice to have, but they're no guarantee of quality or good health or anything else. They're useful if you plan to show or breed your pug, or you can frame them and hang them above Pugsley's crate, but otherwise they're not really good for anything except paper training.

 Essential

Registration papers serve as proof of ownership in case your pug becomes lost or is being claimed by someone else.

Under AKC rules, any person who sells dogs that are represented as being AKC-registrable must maintain records that give full identifying information with every dog sold. This information may be stated on a properly completed AKC registration application, on the sales contract, or on a written statement—signed by the seller—that gives the dog's full breeding information. This information must include the following:

- Dog's breed, sex, and color
- Dog's date of birth

- Registered names of the dog's sire and dam
- Name of the breeder

When you take your puppy home, the breeder should give you what's known as a blue slip. The blue slip is a form that you fill out with your puppy's name and your name as the new owner. You and the breeder must both sign the blue slip to formalize transfer of ownership. Then you can send the form to the AKC with the registration fee.

Once the AKC receives the form and fee, it transfers ownership from the breeder to you, and you'll be issued an individual registration certificate. It has a purple border and can be framed if you want to show off your pug's "papers." If you were ever to sell your pug to someone else, you would use the back of this certificate to transfer ownership.

Limited Registration

If your puppy is being sold as pet quality, the breeder may check a box on the blue slip that says "limited registration." This means that although your puppy will be registered, any offspring he produces would not be registrable. Nor can pugs with limited registration be shown in conformation, although they can participate in obedience trials and other AKC performance events. You'll receive an orange-bordered limited registration certificate after submitting the form and fee.

What if your puppy develops into a nice-looking pug with a great temperament and you decide you'd like to show or breed him? If the breeder agrees that the dog is of good quality, she can rescind the limited registration and give your pug full registration. You can't do it without her consent, though.

Registration Blues

If you want to register your pug, don't leave the breeder's home without the blue slip. Even the best-intentioned breeder can let things fall by the wayside once puppies are gone. Don't expect the AKC to resolve the dispute if you are promised papers and then don't get them. If the breeder won't give you the papers until your pug is spayed or neutered, be sure that's spelled out in the contract so you have something in writing stating that you are entitled to the papers once certain conditions are met. If the breeder still doesn't send you the papers, you then have evidence you can take to court—if the dispute goes that far.

The Sales Contract

Most breeders have an agreement that you must sign before you can purchase one of their pups. A good sales contract spells out exactly what you're getting, what you can expect from the breeder, and what the breeder expects of you as an owner. For instance, it may require that a pet-quality pug be spayed or neutered at the appropriate age. The contract may state that the breeder will withhold registration papers until she receives proof that the puppy has been spayed or neutered. In the case of a pup with show potential, the sales contract may require that the puppy be shown until it wins a championship or is bred at least once.

 Alert!

Some breeders prefer to co-own dogs. Others demand that you show the dog to a championship and breed it at least once, giving the breeder a puppy back. This can work out well if you're truly interested in showing and breeding, but otherwise, walk away. When these arrangements go awry—and they often do—the results are not pretty.

Some contracts require that the dog be returned to the breeder if for any reason you can't keep him. This may be referred to as a "right-of-first-refusal clause." If the breeder's contract has such a clause, make sure it spells out that the breeder will take the dog back at any time for any reason. You don't want to find out later that the breeder views this clause as optional and refuses to take your pug back if for some reason you must give him up. Be realistic, though. If you're returning your pug after five years because you're getting a divorce, don't expect to get your money back.

As with any contract, read it carefully and make sure you are willing to abide by everything in it. If you're not, don't sign it. A contract is a contract, and you can be taken to court if you breach the agreement.

The Health Guarantee

Some, but not all, reputable breeders offer a health guarantee on their puppies. The health guarantee may be part of the sales contract, or it may be a separate agreement. A guarantee doesn't ensure that a pup will be problem-free, but it does mean the breeder has confidence in his dogs' good health.

The terms of health guarantees vary, from a simple statement that the breeder will take the dog back at any time for any reason to promising a refund of all or part of the purchase price should the puppy develop specified health problems within a given period of time. This time period might be as short as two weeks or as long as two years.

 Essential

Veterinarians must keep up with a lot of different problems in different breeds, and it's impossible for them to know everything that's going on in a particular breed. Breeders see a wide range of health issues in pugs and can be good secondary resources—after your veterinarian—if your dog develops a problem. They often know about the latest treatments and the best specialists for certain problems.

It's important to remember that there are no guarantees in life. Not all health issues are predictable. You can do everything right in finding a breeder, and the breeder can do everything right in screening his dogs, and a puppy can still develop a health problem.

Every situation is different and must be dealt with on a case-by-case basis. If you have fallen in love with your puppy and don't want to give him up, the breeder may offer a second dog at a reduced price, help cover part of the veterinary bills, or offer a partial refund of the puppy's purchase price. Some breeders may pay some or all of the veterinary bills if a puppy develops, for example, parvo after he goes home with you, even though he's been vaccinated.

You need to feel comfortable that the breeder will stand behind her puppies and be a resource for you if things go wrong. You also need to realize that when you buy a living creature, there's always a certain amount of risk. If you have developed a good relationship with the breeder, the two of you should be able to come to a mutually agreeable settlement.

The Puppy Packet

Most breeders send you home with a puppy packet. This folder or envelope usually contains some or all of the following paperwork:

- Breed history
- Breed standard
- Pup's pedigree
- Feeding schedule (including the brand of food the puppy is used to eating)
- Recommendations on feeding and care for the first year of life
- Health certificate for the puppy from the breeder's veterinarian and copies of the parents' health certifications
- Vaccination and deworming records
- Tips on housetraining
- Grooming advice
- Copy of the PDCA code of ethics and educational guidelines

The breeder may also send you home with a sample bag of puppy food, a T-shirt or other piece of cloth that bears the scent of the pup's mother and littermates (to help comfort him in his new home), or a book on the breed. If you're picking up your puppy from a breeder who lives in another town or out-of-state, it's a good idea to bring back a supply of the water he's been drinking. You can mix it with the water at your home over several days so his stomach will have time to adjust to the change.

The vaccination and deworming records should note which vaccinations have been given, and when, as well as the dates the puppy was dewormed. Make an appointment to have the puppy examined by your own veterinarian within forty-eight hours of bringing him home. Take the pup's veterinary records with you so your veterinarian can plan a continuation of the vaccination schedule. You may also want to ask for a copy of the litter's growth record, something most reputable breeders can provide. This will help your veterinarian know if your puppy is growing normally.

Buying Long-Distance

What if you can't find a reputable breeder in your area? It is possible to buy a dog long-distance, especially with the help of the Internet. Ask the breeder to e-mail or mail you photos or videos of the puppies and their relatives. If you know someone in the breeder's town, designate her or him to inspect the breeder's home and dogs. Ask for a written testimonial from the breeder's veterinarian (and be prepared to provide one from your veterinarian). Conduct an extensive phone interview so you're comfortable with the breeder's intentions and trust him to pick the perfect puppy for you. Since the breeder will be selecting the puppy for you, be sure you're clear on what you want as far as personality, color, and gender.

Ideally, you'll be able to go to the breeder's home and pick up the puppy in person. This gives you a chance to meet the breeder and puppy and see the environment the puppy was raised in before you make a final commitment. If that's not possible, try to find someone who's coming your way to bring the puppy in the cabin of the plane. Do your best to avoid shipping your puppy cargo. This flat-faced breed can overheat or suffer respiratory problems.

◀ These mesh crates are perfect for keeping your pug comfortable when traveling.

If someone is delivering your pug pup to you or you're picking him up from cargo, don't forget to bring a collar and leash so you can take him out for a potty break as soon as you pick him up. If the flight was longer than two or three hours, he's sure to be crossing his legs and may even have had an accident in the crate. That's okay. With good housetraining, it's likely to be a one-time incident.

Let the breeder know he's arrived safely and then, if possible, make the veterinarian's office your first stop on the way home from the airport, to be sure the puppy is in good health. You don't want to get attached to him and then find out he has a serious health problem. Never buy from a breeder who sells only on a "no returns" basis. Once you and the veterinarian are satisfied with Pugsley's condition, take him home and start enjoying life together.

Preparing for Your New Pug

THE FIRST DAY WITH YOUR NEW PUG will be a memorable one. By being prepared beforehand with the appropriate equipment and food, a completely pug-proofed home, and an understanding of everyone's responsibilities, you'll enjoy the day even more. What follows is a guide to the necessary preparation and get-acquainted period with your new dog, from ways you can make your home and pug safe from each other to the supplies you'll need—especially if you're a first-time dog owner.

Family Affair

The most important thing you can do before you bring your new pug home is to decide who's responsible for what. Ostensibly, you may be getting the pug for your children, but realistically, the burden of his care falls on the adults in the household. Decide as a family how to parcel out the dog-care chores, put your decisions in writing, and post them where everyone can see them.

As the adult, it's your job to ensure that your pug gets daily exercise, eats right, learns his manners, and stays groomed and well cared for. Your children, depending on their ages, can and should participate in the dog's care, but it's a well-known fact that children have short attention spans and need constant nagging when it comes to dog care. It's great to involve the kids in the dog's care, but an adult needs to ensure that meals are served on time, water dishes are kept filled and replenished daily, and grooming is done. The dog shouldn't suffer because of a child's forgetfulness or activity schedule.

 **Essential**

If you get a pug for your children, it should be because you want and will enjoy having a dog too. It's not fair to the dog to rely on youngsters' promises to take care of him and then get rid of the dog when they don't follow through.

Decisions you must make include where the dog will sleep, whether he's allowed on the furniture, and who is responsible for the various elements of dog care: feeding, training, grooming, and so on. To help keep things running smoothly, make a pug-care checklist with everyone's responsibilities and post it in a prominent area such as the refrigerator or by the front door. That way, no one can say, "I forgot" or "I didn't know it was my turn." Include the following items on your checklist:

- **Mealtime.** As a rule, schedule three meals daily for puppies, switching to two meals daily at six months of age.
- **Potty time.** Puppies need to go out as soon as they wake up in the morning and after naps, immediately after every meal, after playtime, and just before bedtime. Your pug puppy should have an opportunity to relieve himself at the very least every two to four hours.
- **Playtime.** Puppies, including pugs, come in two speeds: full throttle and crash (naptime). Channel your pug pup's energy with several short daily walks or play periods, but hold off on long walks on hard surfaces or activities that involve jumping (including on and off the furniture) until he's eight to twelve months old.
- **Grooming.** Schedule fifteen minutes weekly to brush your pug's coat, clean his ears, and trim nails if needed. Daily,

brush the teeth and check eyes for discharge. Wipe away any "sleepies" that form in the corners.

- **Training.** Training classes usually meet weekly, for a period of five to eight weeks, but your pug also needs daily practice of two or three five- to ten-minute sessions.
- **Health.** Note any upcoming veterinary visits for booster shots or exams, as well as who's responsible for taking the dog to the veterinarian.

Kids' Responsibilities

Children who are at least six years old can perform such tasks as putting food in the dog's bowl, filling the water dish, and brushing the dog. Children who are ten or older can be responsible for taking the puppy out first thing in the morning and last thing at night if the dog sleeps in their room. They can also attend training class with an adult and learn how to handle the dog. The whole family should take turns at home practicing commands so the dog will understand that he should respond to every family member.

Setting Boundaries

Dogs are pack animals that get along by knowing and following the rules. Pugs are no different. They like it best when things stay the same. By teaching your puppy the behaviors you want from day one, you'll establish expectations that he can understand and follow. Before you bring your pug home, decide what's okay and what's not.

Sleeping Arrangements

Whether or not you approve of letting dogs sleep on the bed, it's highly likely that your pug will end up sleeping there at some point in his life. Puppyhood is probably not the best time to introduce this habit, however, since puppies aren't physiologically able to control their elimination habits reliably. (See Chapter 9 for details on housetraining.) Wait until your pug has been housetrained for several months to a year before you let him sleep on anyone's bed. If the kids want the puppy to sleep in their room, he'll need to be confined to a crate, or you'll have difficulty housetraining him. Your child or children should be old enough to take responsibility for taking Pugsley out to potty first thing in the morning, even if that means getting up extra early.

▲ It's important to plan ahead and prepare your home
before you introduce your puppy to his new environment.

If you don't have children or they're not old enough for such an arrangement, Pugsley's crate should be in your room where he can hear and smell you during the night. Letting the puppy sleep in your room aids in housetraining because you'll be able to hear him in the morning when he awakes and needs to go out. It's also easier to reassure the dog immediately if he barks or whines during the night. Sleeping in your room accustoms the pug to your scent and is a good bonding experience.

On or Off the Furniture

Is there really a question here? There's a reason pug people lovingly refer to their breed as couch "pugtatoes." Pugs are lap dogs, bred for centuries to spend time with their people, and that includes being on the furniture with them. Most pug owners enjoy sharing a sofa or chair with their dogs, and frankly, if you don't want a dog on the furniture, you may want to reconsider getting a pug. Still, if you'd prefer that your pug stay on the floor, on his own bed, or on a particular piece of furniture, then be consistent. If you let him up on the "good" sofa "sometimes," he will soon want to be up there all the time and will be confused at not being allowed to stay.

 **Essential**

If your pug puppy barks or whines in his crate at night, don't take him out of the crate. If you just say, "Shhh," he will know you're there and be comforted.

Items Your Pug Needs

Now that you've made all the big decisions, it's time to buy all the stuff a dog needs. Try to have everything on hand before you bring your pug home. It's a lot easier to care for a puppy when you're not constantly running out to the pet supply store for things you didn't realize you needed. You'll need some essentials, but be sure to check out a wide variety of options before settling on things like leashes or crates. Don't forget to look at pet supply catalogs or online pet supply outlets if you can't find exactly what you want. The Appendix B for some catalog and online sources.

Collar, Tag, and Leash

Your pug will need a flat, buckle-style collar that's twelve to sixteen inches in length. A half-inch width is a good size for puppies or small pugs, while a three-quarter-inch width is suitable for most adult pugs. Collars can be made of leather or nylon. Leather has a classic look, while nylon comes in a range of colors and designs. Leather's primary disadvantage is that it smells good, and puppies enjoy chewing on it. Put your pug's leather collar out of reach if he's not wearing it. Whichever material you choose, look for a collar that's well made, with fine stitching and a sturdy buckle. Many collars come with quick-release buckles for easy removal. Check the collar regularly to make sure it hasn't tightened as your puppy has grown, and adjust it as needed. A rule of thumb is that two fingers should fit comfortably between the collar and the puppy's neck.

 Question?

Should I buy a choke chain?
No. The pug can be injured with a choke-chain correction. More and more trainers are moving away from any type of training tool that uses negative reinforcement, such as choking. This is especially true with pugs—they respond better to rewards than corrections.

Of course your pug's collar needs an identification tag. Tags can be made of metal or plastic, and they come in a variety of shapes and colors. You can purchase a tag from a machine at your local pet supply store and have it engraved in the store. There's only so much information you can fit on a tag, so include only the most important: your name and phone number. You might also want to include an additional phone number, such as that of your office, your cell phone, or your veterinarian's office.

You can keep tabs on your pug using more high-tech methods as well. A company called PetTrax sells a transmitter collar that emits a silent signal every two seconds, with a range of a half-mile to three-quarters of a mile. With the purchase of a PetTrax membership, you can call a toll-free number if your dog becomes lost and a technician will come out to do a search for him. For more information, see Appendix B.

A leash is a must for keeping your pug in sight and safe from harm. Buy a lightweight leash that's well constructed. Leather leashes have the same advantages and disadvantages as leather collars.

Nylon leashes are colorful and sturdy and can usually be purchased in matching pairs with nylon collars.

Harness

Some pug owners prefer harnesses to collars because they don't want to restrict the dog's breathing in any way. A collar can pull against the trachea and flatten it out, making breathing more difficult. Walking a pug puppy with a harness until he's at least six months old (or has learned to walk nicely on lead) can help prevent neck injuries. A harness is also useful for restraining dogs that ride in the car. And some pugs' shoulders are bigger than their head. If you put a collar on them, it just slips over the head. In that respect, a harness can be a safer choice.

The disadvantage of a harness is that it encourages pulling. Pugs are notorious for not walking well on a leash unless you spend lots of time working with them. They're very strong, and they want to go where they want to go. It can also be annoying to have to put a harness on and take it off each time you want to go out with your pug. And some people believe that wearing a harness can make the legs develop improperly.

In choosing a harness or halter, take into account the same considerations of durability and type of material that you would in choosing a collar. Take your pug to the store to be fitted. You may need to buy two harnesses: one when he's a puppy and one when he reaches maturity.

Feeding Dishes and Food

You will definitely want substantial dinnerware that can stand up to being pawed or nosed in frustration because it's not full yet. Sturdy metal bowls that are weighted on the bottom are your best choice. You can also buy metal dishes that fit in a stand. This makes it easier for the dog to eat comfortably and less likely that the dishes will move out of place. Metal dishes last forever, don't retain odors, and are easy to throw in the dishwasher. Look for wide bowls with a rounded bottom and low sides.

One drawback of metal dishes is that they can't be used to warm food in the microwave. Some dogs like having their food warmed because it intensifies the aroma and increases flavor. On the upside, puppies can chew on metal dishes all they want without doing any damage.

 Alert!

Wash your pug's food dishes daily so they don't become encrusted with food. You wouldn't want to eat off grungy dishes and neither does your pug!

Ceramic dishes have advantages too. They're heavy, so they stay in place, and they're colorful and attractive. If you want, you can purchase a ceramic bowl personalized with your pug's name. The main drawback to ceramic dishes is that they're breakable. Be sure to choose ceramic dishes that are dishwasher- and microwave-safe. Check the country of origin before you buy as well. Foreign-made dishes can contain high amounts of lead.

Plastic dishes are inexpensive and easy to clean, but your breeder or veterinarian may advise against them because many dogs develop allergies to plastic (like pug zits). Plastic can also retain food odors.

The size and type of bowl you choose often depends on your pug's eating and drinking habits. A pug that inhales his food may do best with a large bowl or something low and flat, such as a pie pan. When the food is spread out over a large area, the dog has to slow down a little to eat it all. A water dish with a guard around it is a good choice for a pug that slurps, so you don't come home to puddles.

Until your pug gets used to you and his new home, he's best off eating what he's used to. Ask the breeder what she's been feeding, and make sure you have a two-week supply of that food before bringing your puppy home. Even if you plan to feed another brand, you'll want to make the switch gradually (over a period of seven to ten days) to prevent tummy upset. To do this, mix in a small amount of the new food with the old brand, and then add a little more of the new and less of the old food each following day.

Grooming Tools

For a pug, all you need are a metal flea comb, a natural bristle brush or a hound glove, a nail trimmer made for use with dogs, and a toothbrush and toothpaste formulated for dogs. The breeder may suggest specific brands he likes. You can find a good selection of most dog grooming implements at large pet supply stores as well as through pet supply catalogs. For more information about grooming, see Chapter 13.

 Fact

Metal bowls help prevent "pug zits," blemishes that can develop between eight and eighteen months of age. These are especially common in dogs that eat out of plastic dishes, because some dogs are allergic to plastic. Using metal bowls that can be easily and frequently washed cuts down on the number of pimples your pug might get.

Using a Crate

A crate is an essential piece of equipment for a pug owner. Your pug will use it as a bed, car seat, and a place of refuge when he's pooped. You'll use it as a housetraining tool (a process we'll discuss in Chapter 9), and as a way of preventing destructive behavior. The pug that is crate-trained has a portable den, allowing him to feel at home wherever he is.

Some people worry that crating a dog is cruel, but dogs are den animals, so they are comfortable curling up inside a crate when it's bedtime or for a nap when you can't be around to watch them. When your pug is in his crate, he can't get into trouble, so you don't have to get mad at him for destroying something. It's a win-win situation.

Your pug's crate should be just large enough for him to stand up and turn around. This provides a cozy feel and—in the case of a puppy—ensures that there's not so much room that he can potty in one corner and sleep in the other. The Varikennel 200 or a similar size in another brand should work well for a pug.

Types of Crates

With the growing number of uses for crates have come innovations in crate design. You can find wire or plastic crates, collapsible soft-sided crates, crates that fit beneath airline seats, and crates that roll on wheels through airports and show grounds. Accessories such as designer covers, cushions, and mats turn them into cozy beds. By taking a few minutes to think about how the crate will be used, you can decide which one best meets your needs.

Wire crates fold easily for storage, and they provide more ventilation than a solid-sided plastic crate. If necessary, they can be covered for warmth or privacy. It's also easy to see inside them to check whether the dog is restless or resting. Plastic crates provide a cozy, denlike atmosphere. Most plastic crates come apart for storage, and some come with wheels for easy transport.

Introducing Your Pug to the Crate

Whatever model you choose, it's important that your pug like the crate. Feed the dog in the crate, and give a treat whenever you put him in the crate. To really encourage your pug to want to go in the crate, place his dinner inside of it a few minutes before mealtime and then shut the door so he can't get inside. That way, he'll be eager to enter the crate.

Place the crate in an area that gives your pug a good view of everything that's going on, such as the living room or kitchen. Move it to your bedroom at night. A pug-size crate is easily portable, so this shouldn't be difficult. If your budget allows, you can have one crate in the family room and one in the bedroom. Some people have a crate in every room. To learn more about the uses for crates, see Chapters 9 and 18.

Toys and More Toys

Pug puppies are just as energetic as puppies of any other breed. An assortment of toys will help keep your pug pup active and entertained. Fleece toys are pug favorites. Many pugs love cuddling up to a soft stuffed toy, while others will aggressively shake it or toss it in the air. Expect to repair or replace soft toys frequently. No matter how well made, sharp puppy teeth can make short work of them. The best soft toys are free of bells, button eyes, or ribbons that can be chewed off and swallowed. If your pug loves squeaky toys, keep an eye on the toy's condition so he doesn't rip it open and remove or swallow the noisemaker inside.

 Essential

Pugs aren't known for chasing balls or playing fetch, although there are a few exceptions. They prefer fuzzy squeaky toys to rubber or latex squeaky toys. As they grow older, toys become less important to them, and toy play often stops by two or three years of age.

Hard rubber chew toys are long lasting and help soothe the aches caused by teething. Stuff a hollow chew toy such as a Kong with peanut butter, or fill it with good-smelling treats to encourage your pug to gnaw on it. Avoid giving rawhides. Dogs tend to chew them up and swallow them in large pieces. The resulting diarrhea or intestinal obstruction is not fun to deal with.

Pug-Proofing Your Home

Dogs are curious by nature, and lacking hands with opposable thumbs, they test anything and everything with their mouths, biting or chewing objects to see how they taste or feel and whether they might be good to eat or fun to gnaw on. Your pug puppy might be small, but he can do a lot of damage if left to entertain himself. Pug mischief includes ripping the cover off the end of a mattress, ripping the carpet away from the wall, chewing up eyeglass frames, shredding bathmats, tearing up throw rugs, and ransacking the bathroom wastebasket in search of used tissues. Prepare your home accordingly before he arrives.

 **fact**

Pug-proofing is important even if you're getting an adult pug, at least until you get to know the dog. Some adult pugs have nice manners, but others are capable of opening cabinets and drawers or getting into other mischief.

Pug-proofing your home involves getting down on your hands and knees and looking at things from a pug-level perspective. This will help you spot all the hazards a puppy might think to investigate. Anything below eighteen inches will catch your pug's eye. Things that will attract a puppy's attention include shoes, shoelaces, electrical cords, and chair legs, especially if they have interesting shapes. Conduct this search in each room of your house and take steps to protect your home by putting things you value—or that would be dangerous to a dog—well out of reach. Let's take a look and see what potential hazards you might find in each room.

Living Room, Family Room, and Home Office

Check for dangling cords from lamps, televisions, stereos, computers, and any other electrical appliances. Wrap cords with tough plastic cable ties and place them out of reach if possible. Otherwise, coat them with Bitter Apple, a bad-tasting liquid that encourages your pug to chew elsewhere. You may also want to place something solid in front of an outlet with a plugged-in cord, such as a chair or a small but heavy chest.

Other items to keep out of reach include toys, knickknacks, glass frames, photo albums, sewing materials, pens and pencils, books, eyeglasses, and cameras. Don't leave anything down low that you don't want tooth marks on or that you don't want to disappear down your pug's gullet. Wrap furniture legs in aluminum foil or coat them with Bitter Apple. Remind your kids not to leave their homework lying in reach.

A number of common houseplants can cause toxic reactions if they're eaten, ranging from mouth irritation or upset stomach to respiratory problems or even death. Among the plants that are known to be toxic are the following:

- Asparagus fern
- Boston ivy
- Caladium
- Calla lily
- Dieffenbachia (dumb cane)
- Elephant's ear
- Mother-in-law plant
- Philodendron
- Pothos

Check with your veterinarian or a local poison control center for a more complete list. Most dogs love nibbling on green things and digging in dirt, so put plants out of reach, even if they're not toxic—unless you don't mind finding piles of dirt on the floor or having your pug throw up the leaves he's eaten.

Bedrooms

Your pug will seek out anything that smells like you. Shoes and dirty clothes on the floor are an open invitation for a puppy to chew on or drag into the living room while your mother-in-law is visiting. Your pug will think it's a fine idea to run through the living room with your underwear on his head while you have company. Keep laundry and shoes behind closed doors or otherwise out of reach. Do you have things stored under the bed? Your puppy will crawl under there to go exploring. Put storage boxes and any breakables or valuables up high.

Kitchen and Bathrooms

Keep cleansers and medications up high or behind cabinets with child locks. Child locks on kitchen and bathroom cabinets will prevent your pug from getting into such items as stored food, cosmetics, paper towels, and toilet paper. Don't leave toilet paper dangling. Your pug is not above grabbing the end of it and running with it through the house or rolling himself up in it like a mummy.

Make sure trashcans are securely covered or located in areas where they can't be tipped over or climbed into. You don't want your puppy eating twist ties, rubber bands, cellophane wrappers, poultry skin, fat trimmings from meat, or bones. Unplug and put away blow dryers and curling irons after use so your pug doesn't pull them down on his head or electrocute himself by chewing on them.

Garages, Basements, and Attics

Garages contain chemical hazards such as antifreeze, cleansers, fertilizer, glue, paint, pesticides, strippers, and turpentine. Put tools away, especially those with a sharp edge, and close or seal boxes tightly so they can't be climbed into. Store chemicals up high or behind closed doors, and clean up any oil spots or antifreeze drips. Antifreeze, which is highly toxic, has a sweet taste that dogs find appealing. It takes less than a tablespoon of antifreeze to kill a pug if he's not treated in time. Suspect antifreeze poisoning if your pug appears disoriented, drunk or wobbly, and vomits or seems depressed. Any time you suspect antifreeze poisoning, rush your dog to the veterinarian. The antidote, if given in time, can save his life.

Automatic garage doors can be dangerous. Before you flick the button to close the door, be sure you know where your puppy is. Dogs can be crushed beneath the door if they don't make it out of the way in time.

Many dogs enjoy snacking out of the cat's litter box. If your cat's litter box is in the garage, consider getting a cover for it or placing the box in an area that's accessible to the cat but not the dog, such as behind a baby gate with a small hole cut in the bottom. Your cat will be able to slip through, but the dog won't fit.

All kinds of things are stored in basements and attics, from old clothes and toys to poisons and traps for pests. It's best to deny your pug access to these areas. If that's not possible, place dangerous or special items out of reach.

 Alert!

Use antifreeze that's labeled pet-safe, containing propylene glycol instead of ethylene glycol. It's still poisonous, but it's less toxic than the other kind. Some brands of antifreeze contain a bittering agent to repel curious pets. Federal legislation has been proposed to require all antifreeze to contain a bittering agent.

Yard

Search your yard for such hazards as poisonous plants, holes in fences, sharp or pointed edges along fencing, poisonous bait laid out for pests, or tools lying around. Repair or board up any holes in fencing that a puppy could wriggle through, and sand down sharp edges. Fix broken locks so gates close securely. Remove or repair loose wire that could entangle a pup or poke him in the eye. Take up bait and put away fertilizers and pesticides. Return hoses, tools, and any toys the kids have left lying around to their proper places.

The bulbs, leaves, and berries of a number of plants commonly found in yards can cause gastrointestinal upset, irritation, respiratory problems, skin reactions, and even death if they're eaten. Remove them or make sure your pug can't get to them. Toxic plants include the following:

- Azalea
- Buttercup/daffodil
- Chrysanthemum
- Delphinium
- Jasmine

- Monkey pod
- Oleander
- Tomato vine
- Wisteria
- Yew tree

Check with your veterinarian or a local poison control center for a more complete list.

◀A fenced-in lawn with secure gates gives your pug a safe space where he can exercise and play.

Some pugs are diggers. To prevent them from digging beneath chain link fence, buy a roll of chicken wire or wire garden fencing with square holes. Cut it into long strips about two inches wide and use wire to fasten them to the bottom of the chain link. Aluminum wire is relatively inexpensive and won't rust. Be sure to clip any rough ends of the wire so your pug doesn't cut himself. Cover the pieces of fence that lie on the ground with several inches of dirt, or use stone for a border. If you use dirt, you can plant grass over the area so it looks nice.

 Alert!

Do you have a pool or spa? A pug is top-heavy and could drown quickly if he falls in when no one is looking. Keep the pool or spa securely covered if you're not there to supervise. Gates to pool or spa areas should latch securely.

Pugs are garden connoisseurs and will happily nibble on your strawberries or tomatoes. To prevent this, place picket fencing, chicken wire, or some other barrier around them. If that's not practical, confine your pug to a wire exercise pen or build a dog run. A good-size yard pen for a pug that will be supervised consists of four-foot-high chain link with a strip of eighteen-inch chicken wire around the outside bottom so he can't dig out. A run where your pug can play without supervision should be long enough to give him plenty of sniffing area and at least six feet high or covered to keep him from escaping. Remember that pugs are sensitive to heat, so place a pen or run in an area that always has shade, and provide a source of water that can't be tipped over. Never leave your pug outdoors for long periods in hot weather. He's just not built for it.

Choosing a "Safe" Place

Your pug is a member of your family and should spend his time indoors with you. When you're not there to supervise, however, you need a safe place he can stay where he won't be able to do much, if any, damage. A suitable safe place usually has a tile or linoleum floor, so it's easy to clean up potty accidents. It doesn't contain much furniture or anything else that can be chewed. Common choices for safe rooms are the kitchen, bathroom, or laundry room.

Question?

How long until my pug can stay alone in the house without being confined? Depends on the individual dog. Some pugs are trustworthy at an early age; others aren't ready to be left on their own until they're one or two years old—or sometimes ever.

If you choose a spot such as the kitchen, laundry room, or bathroom, use a baby gate to block the doorway. That way your pug can still see what's going on. A closed door will only encourage him to whine, bang, and even attempt to chew his way out. If you're concerned that your puppy will chew on cabinetry or baseboards in the room, put him inside a puppy playpen—also referred to as an x-pen—so he can't get to those areas.

A dog-proofed, temperature-controlled garage can also be a good place to let your pug stay unsupervised. Some people turn part of the garage into a dog room, complete with carpeted floor, crate, grooming table, bed, and toys. A dog door leading to the yard lets your pug play outside or potty when he wants.

Keeping Your Pug Comfortable

In areas with hot, humid climates, a pug must live in an air-conditioned home. Pugs that get too hot can have trouble breathing. They begin gulping air, which causes gas, or they develop heat exhaustion or heatstroke, which can be fatal if not treated in time. Always make sure the air conditioning is set at a comfortable level before leaving your pug at home, and never leave him in a car on a hot day, not even for a few minutes. Even with the windows rolled down, he can rapidly develop heatstroke. Schedule walks for cool mornings and evenings, not during the heat of the day.

Bringing Your New Pug Home

THE BIG DAY HAS ARRIVED! Your home is pug-proofed, and it's time to bring your new puppy or dog home. You can help this event go smoothly by planning when and how to introduce your pug to his new surroundings. This includes getting a complete information packet from the breeder, shelter, or rescue group, scheduling a trip to the veterinarian for a health check, and introducing him to the neighbors and other pets.

Take Time Off

Introducing a dog to a new home and family is a big deal for everyone involved, especially the dog. If you can take puppy-leave from work to settle the dog into his new home, you have a better chance of starting him off on the right paw regarding housetraining and learning house rules. A week is ideal, but even a long weekend will help you place this new relationship on a solid foundation.

If you're planning to bring your pug home during the holiday season because you'll have time off, think again. Most breeders and rescue groups prefer not to send dogs to new homes during that period. Any hectic holiday season or birthday celebration is the last time you want to bring a new dog into the home. There's just too much going on—food preparation, relatives visiting, and packages and decorations just waiting to be attacked by an excited dog.

The time to bring the dog home is when the excitement is over.

That way you can focus on supervising and teaching him from day one. If you must bring your new dog home during the holidays because it's the only time you can take off, keep things low-key. Try to schedule family get-togethers at someone else's house or at a restaurant, and let the puppy watch any gift-unwrapping from the calm vantage point of his crate.

 Essential

> Rather than bringing your new pug home to chaos, give the promise of a pug instead: a box containing a collar, leash, and a copy of this book!

Picking Up Your Pug from a Breeder

If you are driving to the breeder's home to pick up the puppy, be sure to bring a crate for him to ride in on the way home. It's fun for a passenger to cuddle the puppy or dog, but inside a crate is the safest place for a squirmy and no doubt confused pug pup. Besides, if your pug is going to throw up because he's carsick or nervous, it's better that he does it inside the crate instead of all over you. Don't forget his new collar, tags, and leash. You'll want to put them on him before you leave the breeder's home. A chew toy will help keep him occupied on the drive back.

Know Before You Go

Before you leave the breeder's home, take notes on the puppy's eating schedule, the amount he eats, and his sleeping habits. Ask if he has any experience with potty training or knows any basic commands, such as "Sit." These same questions apply if you're adopting an adult dog. You can do a better and faster job of teaching your pug pup the more you know about him.

The breeder should provide you with a puppy packet (as

described in Chapter 6). Also, be sure to ask for an item that has the scent of Mom or the littermates on it to help keep your puppy calm during the adjustment.

▲ The perfect time to take a pug pup home is when he's reached eight weeks of age.

Visiting the Veterinarian

Before you leave the breeder's home, give the puppy the once-over to make sure he seems clean and in good condition. If you've chosen a reputable breeder, you're not likely to find anything wrong with him. Your next stop, as soon as possible, should be the veterinary clinic. You'll want to make sure your new pug is healthy before you become so attached to him that you can't give him up. At the very least, schedule an exam within forty-eight hours of acquiring the dog.

The Veterinarian Is Your Pug's Friend
This first visit to the veterinarian should be as stress-free as possible. Ask for a physical exam only, with no painful vaccinations. This

allows your pug pup to gain a positive first impression of the veterinarian, staff, and clinic as a whole. Praise and a treat will reinforce his conception of the veterinary clinic as a good place to go.

The veterinarian will listen to the dog's heart and lungs with a stethoscope, examine the eyes and ears for injury or infection, and palpate the body to ensure that the organs feel normal. He may test the range of motion in the limbs to check for patellar luxation or hip dysplasia. A stool sample, if the dog is obliging enough (or if you bring one with you), allows the veterinarian to check for parasite infestation. Notify the breeder immediately if any problems are discovered.

Your Pug's Health Record

On this visit, you'll be asked to complete a form detailing such information as your pug's age, sex, color, and so on. The veterinarian or technician will fill in the dog's weight and other notes on his condition. This information will become the basis for your pug's medical history. Add the vaccination and deworming records from the breeder to the dog's new file.

Questions you might want to ask at this first visit include the following:

- How much and how often does my pug need to eat?
- What type of diet do you recommend and why?
- How should I care for his eyes and ears?
- What are some emergency situations I might encounter, and how should I deal with them?
- What preventive health routine do you recommend?
- Do you give vaccinations all at once or space them out to lessen the impact on the immune system?

The veterinarian's answers will help you feel confident about your ability to care for your new pug.

Arriving Home

When you get home, walk the puppy around outside first so he can relieve himself. He'll be excited and nervous, so this probably won't take long. Praise him when he performs: "Good go potty!" The sooner he learns this phrase, the better.

Take him inside on leash. Until you're sure he's reliably house-trained and knows the house rules (which will be some months from now), don't allow your pug the run of the house. Keep him on leash, confined to his safe place or crate, in a fenced yard or dog run, in someone's lap, or under a watchful eye.

 Alert!

Your pug's crate is his safe place, where he can go when he wants to rest. Teach the kids not to bother him when he's in his crate, and don't let them climb inside the crate with him.

Use baby gates to prevent wandering when you don't want him to go anywhere. He'll be curious about his new surroundings and will follow you from room to room. Put his crate wherever you want it to be, with the scented towel inside it. Show him the crate so he'll know where to go for a reassuring sniff. Dogs are pretty adaptable, though, and your pug will probably settle nicely into his new home in a day or two.

Busy, Not Bored

Spend plenty of time playing with and training your pug these first few days. You can teach simple commands such as "Sit" and "Come." Your attention and the activity will help distract him from his missing mother and littermates. He may be shy at first, even if he was outgoing at the breeder's home. He was comfortable there, and it may take a few days for him to adjust to you and your home. Take him out every couple of hours so he starts to learn that "outside" is where he needs to go potty. And play, play, play! A tired pug is a pug that's more likely to sleep through the night.

Nap Time

After half an hour of play, your pug will probably be ready to rest. This is a big day for him. All the new sights, sounds, smells, and people he encounters will completely bewilder your pup. Don't overwhelm him with a lot of new experiences all in one day. Walk him outside to see if he'll potty again, then put him in his crate. Give him a treat before you close the door, and tell him he's a good dog. When you're ready to let him out again (he'll let you know when he's ready for more action), take him straight outside on leash for a potty break.

The Kids and Their Friends

If you have children, they'll want to show off their new four-legged friend. That's fine, but make a rule that only one or two friends at a time can come over to play with the new pup. Keep a lid on loud squealing, poking, and prodding, and rule out dressing the dog up in baby clothes or carrying him around unless they're mature enough to do so safely.

 Essential

Teach young children to hold the puppy only when they're sitting down. It's safer for both of them. It's easy for a child to accidentally drop a squirming puppy and although pugs are fairly sturdy, they can be injured by a fall.

Another rule to establish is that your children are never to hit the dog. Many young children like being the dog's "boss" and think it's their job to yell at or hit the puppy if he does something wrong. Explain very clearly that it's never okay for anyone (including adults) to hit the dog. Instead, the children should let you know if there's a problem.

Meeting Other Children

Even if you don't have children, your pug is likely to encounter them in everyday life. Be aware of approaching children so you can control the situation. Hold a toddler or young child's hand to guide her strokes, and suggest that children ask their parents' permission before petting your dog. Explain that dogs have very sensitive ears, so it's not nice to scream around them.

The Neighbors' Dogs

Ask neighbors not to bring their own dogs over to meet the pup. It's important for him to get to know the neighborhood dogs, but right now his immature immune system needs to be protected. Ask your veterinarian what age is appropriate for dog-to-dog meetings. Usually it's advisable to wait until the pup is twelve weeks old and has had two series of vaccinations.

Meeting Other Pets

Your pug and your other pets need to learn to live together amiably—or at least neutrally. A proper introduction will help keep tensions to a minimum and allow all pets to develop friendly relationships. Remember that animals like routine and structure. Begin introductions slowly, rather than just throwing everyone together and hoping they all get along. How you introduce them depends on which species are involved.

Dog Pals

Pugs tend to get along well with everyone, especially other pugs. Nonetheless, whatever breed or mix you have, it's a good idea to introduce them on neutral ground, such as a nearby park or a neighbor's yard. It might help smooth the initial meeting, and it certainly can't hurt.

With each dog on a loose leash, let them sniff and circle each other. This is an essential part of the canine meet-and-greet. Let them take their time. A puppy may show deference to an older dog by rolling on his back. When they seem to be getting along, walk them home. This gives them more time to adjust to each other's presence.

 **Essential**

As a rule, an adult dog is more likely to welcome a puppy than another adult dog. That said, if you're bringing a puppy home, be sure the older dog has a place where he can escape if puppy play becomes too rambunctious.

A meeting on neutral territory isn't always possible. If that's the case, be sure your other dog is confined when you bring your pug home. Let your pug sniff around the yard on leash to get the scent of your other dog. Then put your pug in his crate or in the dog run. Let your other dog out so they can visit through the crate door or kennel bars. Once they've had a few minutes to get used to each other's presence, you can let the newcomer out for a nose-to-tail meeting.

Feline Friends, Not Foes

When you're introducing a dog and cat, start with your dog in a crate, and your cat loose. The cat will feel less threatened than if she were put into a crate with the dog left loose. This allows them to see and smell each other first before venturing a closer inspection. Schedule a cage-free meeting—with the dog on leash—after the pug has had an energetic play session. A tired dog might be less likely to lunge at Kitty.

A smart pug will approach a cat somewhat cautiously. Praise him and give a treat if he ignores the cat or offers a gentle sniff. Be ready to restrain him with the leash if he lunges at the cat. This is especially true with a puppy that might not know to be respectful of a cat's claws.

It can take a couple of weeks for cats and dogs to become used to each other. Be sure the cat has a place to go where she can escape the dog if necessary. This can be a room closed off with a baby gate or a tall cat tree she can climb. Pugs have been known to chase cats obsessively, but most learn soon enough that it's wise to leave cats to their own devices.

Helping an Older Pug Feel Welcome

The move to a new home is stressful for a dog of any age, but most adjust well given a little time. Treat an older pug the way you would a puppy. Give him attention and playtime, but if he prefers to sit back and observe for a while, that's okay, too. Don't overwhelm him with a lot of new people all at once, but give him plenty of opportunities to do things he enjoys, such as going for walks. This will help him relax.

He may feel a little confused at first in your home. If you know what his previous routine and environment were like, it may help to make things as similar as possible. This means using the same food, the same type of food dishes, and the same type of bedding. Whenever you can, make changes slowly.

Give the dog a place he can call his own, such as a crate or bed. Like a puppy, he should sleep in your bedroom. Even though you're sleeping, the time together will help begin the bonding process.

Avoiding Separation Anxiety

With a puppy or an older dog, accustom him right away to short periods of your absence. Start by leaving him for a few minutes in a room on his own. Gradually extend the amount of time you're gone until he learns that there are times when he's alone or when you aren't going to give him attention. You can also give the dog a signal to indicate that this isn't "his" time. He'll learn to recognize and associate this with being left to his own devices. Turn on a radio or jingle your keys. The trick is to give the signal every time, even for short periods, and make sure the dog sees you doing it.

Another way to decrease the possibility of separation anxiety is to reduce the amount of attention you give just before you leave the dog. When you return, don't make a big fuss over him. Greet him calmly and don't feed him or start any fun games until you've been home for a few minutes.

Naming Your Pug

Classic pug names play to the breed's heritage of pet to nobility and royalty. Some pugs are named for their comical behavior or personality. Favorite literary and television personalities are good sources for names. And some pug owners take a leaf from the names in the dog's pedigree. Whatever name you choose, it should sound good and be easy to call.

 **Fact**

> The top ten dog names for males are Sam, Max, Jake, Rocky, Buster, Buddy, Charlie, Rusty, Bear, and Jess. The top ten female dog names are Lady, Princess, Maggie, Ginger, Daisy, Lucy, Zoe, Missy, Tasha, and Molly. You'll notice that all of these names are short and sweet. Of these, Rocky, Buster, Zoe, and Daisy are especially good pug names.

It's best to select a name of only one or two syllables or that can be easily shortened. Avoid names that rhyme with "No" so you don't confuse your dog during training. The following names are well suited to pugs:

- **Bogart**—an old French word meaning one who is strong; a good choice for a strong, silent, handsome pug
- **Chloe**—a Greek word, meaning flowering
- **Cosmo**—a Greek word, meaning world
- **Dempsey**—an Irish name, meaning one who is wise and proud
- **Emma**—an English word, meaning energetic
- **Lulu**—a slang word, meaning remarkable or wonderful; for a female pug with an attitude

- **Sophie**—short for Sophia, a Greek word meaning wise
- **Stella**—a Latin word, meaning star
- **Vincent**—after actor Vincent Price, who loved pugs
- **Winston**—after England's famous prime minister, who was also a pug fancier

If you're still stuck on what to name your pug, look in pet name books, baby name books, and check out the Web sites listed in Appendix B.

Your Pug's First Night

After a busy first day, it's finally bedtime. Take the dog out to potty one last time. Praise him and give him a treat when he does. Put his crate in your bedroom so he'll be reassured by your presence. It also allows you to take him out first thing in the morning (or in the middle of the night, if necessary) so he doesn't have an accident in the crate or in the house.

Line the crate with a pad, towel, or blanket. He's used to cuddling with his littermates, so providing a stuffed animal or the scented towel you brought from the breeder's home can offer comfort. When you put him inside the crate, give him a treat and say good night. Don't make a big production out of it.

Some puppies settle down and sleep through the night right away. If you get one of these, congratulate yourself on your good luck. More likely, your pup will cry or whine the first few nights. Grit your teeth and ignore it. He'll fall asleep eventually. When he's older, if he hasn't wormed his way into your bed, your pug will appreciate a comfy bed where he can relax after a busy day of lap-sitting, eating, and low-riding.

CHAPTER 9

Housetraining

THIS IS ONE OF THE MOST IMPORTANT lessons your pug needs to learn. Unfortunately, for this breed, it's also one of the most difficult. Pugs can be cavalier about where they eliminate—indoors, outdoors, what's the difference? The keys to successfully housetraining a pug are using a crate, establishing a routine, recognizing elimination behavior, understanding dog physiology, offering consistent positive reinforcement, having plenty of patience and, above all, maintaining a good sense of humor.

Crates and Housetraining

What does a crate have to do with housetraining? Pretty much everything! For starters, it prevents your pug from having accidents in the house. Dogs are den animals, and their instinct is never to soil their den—in this case, the crate. Put your pug in his crate when you can't watch him. That way he won't have an accident in the house. It's as simple as that.

Crates Aren't Cruel

Some people worry that it's mean to confine a dog to a crate. Nothing could be farther from the truth. Your pug will appreciate having a place where he can relax and feel safe. What is mean is not preventing him from making mistakes and then punishing him when he does something wrong. Teaching your pug in positive ways—by showing him what you want and preventing him from doing the wrong thing—is much more effective than yelling at him after he makes a mistake.

A Happy Place

To help make the crate special to your pug, associate it with things your dog likes. In the case of a pug, this is best done with food. Feed your pug in his crate. Every time you put him in the crate other than mealtimes, give him a small treat and say "Crate" or "Bed" or whatever word you choose. Use a happy tone of voice. Pretty soon, every time he hears the magic word, your pug will scramble to get to his crate to receive that yummy snack. It's a nice way to say goodbye to him when you're leaving or good night at bedtime, and it makes him feel good about being in his den. Be aware, though, that your pug may go on strike if you ever stop giving him a treat when he goes in the crate.

 Alert!

The crate isn't a place for punishment. Never put your pug in the crate in an angry manner. You want him to feel safe and secure there. Give him a soft toy to snuggle with when he's in the crate.

Don't expect to lock your pug up in the crate while you're at work all day. That would be cruel. Except at nighttime, never confine your pug to the crate for more than four hours at a time. For one thing, if you leave him there too long, he will have an accident in it, which negates the purpose of the crate as a housetraining tool. For another, he needs exercise and attention.

During the Day

When you must be gone for longer than four hours, your pug can't comfortably stay in a crate, so leave him in his safe room instead. Put his open crate, a fleece toy, a Kong stuffed with peanut butter, and food and water dishes in one part of the room. Cover the floor with papers, so any accidents will be easy to clean up. If you notice that your pug consistently potties in a particular area, you can gradually remove the papers, leaving only a few in the preferred potty spot. Another option is to arrange for a neighbor or pet sitter to come by and take him out at the appropriate time.

◀ Your pug's crate should be a safe place for him that carries good associations with it.

Establishing a Routine

It's easy to predict when puppies will need to go to the bathroom. You can count on a potty trip first thing in the morning when they wake up, after every meal, after a nap, and after an energetic play session. Use this knowledge to set up a housetraining schedule that will reduce or eliminate accidents in your home.

When you take your pug out at specific times, he learns when and where it's okay to go potty. Use a timer or alarm clock to remind yourself to take the dog out at set intervals. A good rule of paw is to base the frequency of trips on the dog's age in months. A two-month-old might need to go out every two hours, a three-month-old every three hours, and so on. Remember that each dog is an individual. Your pug may need to go out more or less frequently.

Take Him out on Leash

Why take your pug out to potty on leash? Because you need to make sure he really does potty, and you need to be there to praise him when he does. Too often, people put their dogs out in the back yard and just assume that they've peed and pooped. Then the dog comes in, potties on the carpet, and earns himself a scolding he doesn't understand. Your pug doesn't know why he's outside, so you need to be there to "explain" it to him by praising his actions.

If your dog doesn't eliminate after ten or fifteen minutes, take him inside and put him in his crate. Try again in half an hour. Follow the same routine after every meal, after every playtime, and before bedtime. Try to take the dog to the same spot every time. Spend some time playing with him before you go back inside—but only *after* he potties.

 Fact

A pug puppy's holding capacity varies. Some need trips outside every hour on the hour, while others can make it for two or three hours. Sample schedules that you see in books are just that—samples! You need to figure out your own schedule based on your pug's needs.

Change this routine only if your pup needs to go out in the middle of the night. As soon as he potties, take him back inside and put him in his crate. You don't want him to start demanding playtime at two in the morning.

Mealtimes and Housetraining

Part of your pug's routine should be eating his meals at the same time every day. If you know when he has eaten, you can better predict when he'll need to eliminate. On the other hand, if you leave food out for him all the time, you won't have any idea that he ate just before you got home from work and needs to go out now!

Feed your puppy breakfast after he eliminates in the morning. Space meals about six hours apart, so if breakfast is at 6:00 A.M., lunch will be at noon, and dinner at 6:00 P.M. Most puppies need to potty half an hour to an hour after they eat. Start by taking your pug out ten minutes after he eats. If he doesn't do anything, continue taking him out at ten-minute intervals until he performs. This will help you figure out how soon after eating he needs to pee and poop.

Elimination Association

Pay attention to the way your pug behaves before he starts to potty. Many dogs circle, whine, or sniff first. Others assume a particular expression. Some pugs just stare at the door. Know the signals so you can hurry your dog outside when you see them. Get his attention and say, "Do you want to go out?" Don't wait "just until the next commercial." By then it will be too late.

On the other hand, some dogs just squat and go the instant they feel the urge. If you have this kind of dog, you're going to have to take him out frequently. Keep him crated when you're not watching him unless you don't mind cleaning up puddles.

You can teach your puppy to let you know when he needs to go out. To do this, hang a bell on the doorknob. Every time you take him out, ring the bell before you open the door. It won't be long until he starts to ring the bell himself when he wants to go out.

You may find a puddle or pile right in front of the door. This is a good thing! It means your dog tried to potty as close to the outdoors as he could. He just didn't have anyone to open the door. Of course, you shouldn't praise your dog if you catch him eliminating in front of the door, but you should acknowledge that he's trying.

Should You Paper Train?

Teaching a puppy to go on papers inside the house has certain benefits. People who live in condos or high-rises without access to a yard can find it easier to use this method. It's also great for anyone who gets a puppy in the dead of winter and doesn't want to venture outside and stand around shivering eight times a day. That said, many trainers see dogs that find it difficult to make the transition from paper training to going outside. If you have access to a yard, you may want to skip paper training altogether.

The Paper-Training Process

Lay down papers in the area where you want the dog to go. When your dog shows signs of needing to potty—circling, sniffing, whining—take him to the papers. If he moves off them, put him back. When he performs, praise him. Help your puppy remember what the papers are for by using a sponge to capture some of the urine. Use it to scent a clean set of papers. The next time you take your dog to the papers, the scent of the urine will prompt him to go again.

Housetraining Pads

These pads are specially scented to attract a dog and encourage urination and defecation. The benefit is that their water-resistant backing makes them easier to clean up than papers. The drawback, besides expense, is that these pads may or may not work. Some dogs use them for their stated purpose; others chew them up or carefully avoid them. You can find housetraining pads at pet supply stores.

Litter Box Training

Litter boxes and litter specially made for dogs are now available. Litter box training is a good alternative for pugs that are home alone during the day. A litter box allows your pug to potty any time he needs to instead of having to "hold it" until you get home. It's also great for cold or rainy days when neither of you wants to go out.

What You'll Need

You can use a large cat-litter box or purchase one made specifically for dogs. If you use a plastic cat litter box, cut an opening in
the side to make it easy for your pug to walk into the box. (Pugs
aren't quite as agile as cats.) Use a Dremel tool or rough sandpaper
to smooth the edges. To fill the box, you can use shredded newspaper, the above-mentioned housetraining pads, or commercial dog
litter (available at pet supply stores). Purchase a large litter scoop to
remove waste. You can dump it in a trashcan, diaper pail, or even
down the toilet as long as you're using flushable litter.

 Alert!

If you find a puddle or pile after the fact, simply clean it up. It's too
late to scold. Never use the long-discredited practices of rubbing the
dog's nose in the mess or swatting him with a newspaper.

Teaching Your Pug to Use the Box

Put the litter box in an easy-to-clean area, such as a bathroom
or laundry room with a tile or linoleum floor. Your pug's safe place is
an ideal spot for it. As you would with paper training, take your pug
to the box any time you notice preliminary elimination behaviors. As
he potties, say "Go potty" or "Do your business" or whatever phrase
you choose. Praise him for using the box, and make sure he always
has easy access to it. Again, you can scent the box filler with urine
or leave a small bit of feces inside it so your pug will be prompted to
potty inside the box.

The Accidental Puppy

No matter how careful you are, accidents are bound to happen.
That's just the way it is with puppies. If you catch your pug in the act,
it's okay to say "Outside!" but avoid saying "No!" or "Bad dog!" It's the
place he chose that's bad, not the act itself. Anger and punishment

only increase your dog's stress level and make him fearful, which in turn leads to a greater likelihood of accidents.

Cleansers

Keep a good enzymatic cleanser on hand for cleaning up after an accident. These products contain enzymes that break down organic debris and waste. Products that do a good job include Resolve carpet cleaner, OdorMute, Nature's Miracle, and Simple Solution. Look for them at your grocery store or pet supply store. Before using any such product, test an inconspicuous area of the carpet (or other fabric surface) first to make sure it's colorfast.

Avoid using any cleansers that contain ammonia. It's one of the components of urine, and the scent of it will draw your puppy back to the same spot. Stick to cleansers made specifically for cleaning up dog accidents.

The Cleanup Process

When you find a puddle, use an old towel to soak up as much of the urine as possible. Then saturate the area with the cleanser of your choice. Spread a clean towel over the spot and cover it with some heavy books or another heavy item. This helps wick the moisture out of the carpet.

Pick up a pile of poop with a plastic bag or a towel. Spray the area with the cleanser and use a clean towel to blot up any remaining stool. Then follow the same steps as if it were a puddle. When the area dries, it should be odor-free.

How Long Does Housetraining Take?

It's important to remember that your pug puppy is still a baby. Just as it takes months to potty train a toddler, it also takes months—and often up to a year—to reliably housetrain a pug. Pugs can be stubborn about learning where they should and shouldn't "go." If you've owned other breeds, you may not be prepared for just how hard-headed a pug can be. Some pugs are never reliably housetrained, and this is something you should be aware of and willing to accept before you get one.

Be patient during the process. Yelling at your dog when you find an accident only teaches him to sneak around and find secret places to potty. He may even avoid peeing or pooping in front of you at all, which really slows down the process.

Remember, too, that until he's at least six months old, your pug isn't physiologically capable of controlling his bladder or sphincter for long periods. The muscle control just isn't there yet. It's not something that can be hurried along. That's why you need a crate and a schedule.

 Alert!

If you're having an especially difficult time housetraining your pug, have him checked for a urinary tract infection. That can make it impossible to housetrain any dog. Suspect a urinary tract infection if your puppy is constantly peeing in the house or if you notice pink staining where the puppy peed, indicating blood in the urine.

Never assume that your pug is fully housetrained until he's been reliable in the house for months without an accident. He may have occasional setbacks. If that occurs, make sure you still have him on a regular schedule. See if there are changes you can make to give him more opportunities to go outside when he needs to.

Housetraining an Adult Pug

The same techniques you'd use with a puppy are effective with adult dogs. The advantage is that an adult dog doesn't have to go out as often. The main thing he needs to learn is where you want him to go. A schedule is still important, simply to give him some structure in his new life. Dogs, especially older ones, appreciate routine. Going out, eating, and playing at set times will help your new pug adjust more quickly to living in your home.

You can also crate train an adult pug. Use the same techniques described for crate training puppies. Again, a crate will keep your pug out of trouble and in your good graces.

Pet-Store-Puppy Problems

Puppies that come from a pet-store environment are often difficult to housetrain. That's because they're accustomed to eliminating in a cage, so crate training doesn't always work with them. Sometimes they even wait to eliminate until they're put in a crate, because that's all they've ever done. Working with this puppy requires an extra dose of patience, as well as some creative thinking.

If you're faced with a puppy that doesn't understand that he's not supposed to potty in his crate, try keeping him leashed by your side all the time. That way you'll be right there if he shows signs of needing to go out. Take him out as often as possible until he potties outside, and then heap praise on him.

 Essential

Don't give up! It can take months before a pug realizes that outside is the place to go. By learning his schedule and understanding his body language, you can help teach him.

One way to teach a dog to potty outside is to reward the action in a way he'll remember. Take a clicker and some treats outside with you. As the dog urinates or defecates (not before, not after, but during), click once. The idea is for him to associate the sound of the click with the act of eliminating. When he's finished, give him a treat. He'll soon be very anxious to potty for you when you go outside.

If he potties in his crate at night, take him outside as late as possible before you go to bed. If he doesn't go then, wait a few minutes and try again. Even if you have to go out several times, do your best to get him to go potty before you put him in his crate for the night.

Relapses in Housetraining

What do you do if your pug suddenly starts having accidents in the house after months of being reliable? The first step is to take him to the veterinarian. Many health problems such as bladder infections cause housetraining lapses. A physical exam and possibly a urinalysis or fecal exam can rule out any health problems.

If your pug gets a clean bill of health, study the circumstances surrounding the accidents. Has your routine changed? Is there a new pet or baby in the home? Are you pregnant? Dogs can smell a difference in your body chemistry. Insecurity often causes housetraining lapses. Make any reasonable changes you can to help your pug feel more comfortable, such as providing extra playtime or giving additional attention. You may need to go back to a strict routine of going out at specific times and confining him as needed until he's back on track.

Practice, Practice, Practice

Housetraining takes time. If your pug is having lots of accidents, review your schedule to see where you might be going wrong. Take him out more often, and don't forget to crate him or put him in his safe room when you can't watch him.

If the amount of time you have to housetrain your pug is limited by work or school, accept that the process will take longer. Be willing to back up to a point where he was being successful, and stay there for a while before you start asking him to wait longer intervals to go out. Patience and a positive attitude will get you successfully over the housetraining hurdle.

Basic Nutrition

PUGS LOVE FOOD. It's an intrinsic part of being a pug. In one sense, that's good, because it means your pug will probably eat whatever you set in front of him. On the other hand, you'll need to think about nutrition for him. The quality of dog food ranges from "barely-qualifies-as-food" to "good-enough-to-eat-yourself." To figure out which food is best for your pug, it helps to know some nutrition basics, how to read labels, and your pug's nutritional needs at various life stages.

Pug Eating Habits

First, let's get the important stuff out of the way. Food is very important to pugs, and they'll let you know if they think you're taking too long to feed them. If you've forgotten a meal or are a little late serving it, your pug may give you a hint by staring meaningfully at you. If his dish is in the vicinity, he'll stare at you, then at the dish, and back again until you take the hint. When that doesn't work, a pug may take matters into his own paws, giving you a nudge with his nose or a push with his paws. More verbal pugs will "bap"—a loud, persistent, sharp, obnoxious sound—until their mealtime needs are met.

Every pug is an individual. Don't be afraid to experiment until you find a food and amount that suits your particular pug. How can you tell if your pug is eating right? Simply take a look. He'll have bright eyes, good muscle tone, nice breath, a shiny coat, and healthy skin.

Vital Nutrients

Nutrients promote growth, provide energy, and help the body perform metabolic functions, such as maintaining and synthesizing tissues and regulating temperature. Dogs are omnivorous, meaning they can obtain these nutrients from a variety of foods: meats, grains, fruits, and vegetables. Providing high-quality nutrients in the correct amounts is the best way to ensure that your pug leads a long and healthy life.

 Alert!

Your pug may have a nutritional deficiency or a food allergy if he has chronic ear infections, loose stools, scratching, a dull coat, or dry, flaky skin. Ask your veterinarian for advice on changing his diet.

Dogs need protein, carbohydrates, fats, and water to maintain good health. Meat, eggs, fish, grain, or a combination of meat and grain all provide protein. Common meat proteins you might see listed on a dog-food label include beef, chicken meal, and meat by-products. Protein that comes from animals is of higher quality than protein from grain.

The Label Breakdown

Besides providing the most concentrated form of energy of all the nutrients, fat has the benefit of being highly digestible. The downside is that foods high in fat taste so good that dogs—especially pugs—tend to eat too much of them. That's one of the reasons you need to exercise portion control, because your pug won't do it for himself. The main sources of carbohydrates in dog foods are grains such as corn, oats, rice, and wheat. They provide the body with complex carbs in the form of starch and are cooked to enhance digestibility and flavor. Fiber comes from sources such as beet pulp and rice or wheat bran. As with most things, moderation is key when it comes to fiber in the diet. Too much leads to puggy flatulence, which you definitely want to minimize.

Water is the most important nutrient in a dog's diet. It makes up 60 to 70 percent of a dog's body and is important for cell and organ function. Dogs can go for long periods without food—although this would make for a very unhappy pug—but without water they can die within days.

▲ Making sure your pug gets plenty of water, in addition to the right food, is essential for maintaining good health.

Vitamins and Minerals

Vitamins are organic molecules that serve an essential function in many of the body's metabolic processes. With a few exceptions (such as vitamin C), most vitamins can't be synthesized by the body, so they must be provided in the diet. Vitamins are powerful, so the body requires only a tiny amount of each one. Vitamins fall into two categories: fat-soluble and water-soluble. Fat-soluble vitamins—A, D, E, and K—can be stored in the liver, while water-soluble vitamins are excreted in the urine if the body doesn't use them right away. Among the vitamins you might see on a dog-food label are thiamin, riboflavin, niacin, pyridoxine, pantothenic acid, biotin, folic acid, and choline.

 **Fact**

Be wary of adding vitamins and minerals to your pug's diet. More is not always better. During puppyhood, an overdose of certain vitamins and minerals can cause problems in musculoskeletal development. Fat-soluble vitamins stored in the liver can quickly reach toxic levels if dogs are given them too frequently.

Like vitamins, minerals are essential for life, although the body needs only tiny amounts to function. Minerals provide skeletal support and are involved in nerve transmission and muscle contractions. Macrominerals, which include calcium, phosphorus, and magnesium, account for most of the body's mineral content. Microminerals, also called trace elements, are present in the body in very small amounts. Microminerals include zinc, manganese, iodine, and selenium.

What Is a Balanced Diet?

A balanced diet contains all the nutrients dogs need in appropriate proportions to one another. The nutrients are also balanced to the energy level of the diet. For example, a diet formulated for older dogs provides a lower energy level than one formulated for puppies.

Read the Label

You can find out whether a food is complete and balanced simply by looking at the label. Manufacturers must state whether their foods meet the nutrient profiles set by a group called the American Association of Feed Control Officials (AAFCO). Puppy food and adult food have different nutrient profiles. Some foods are labeled for "all life stages," but a puppy should eat a food labeled for growth. Beyond that, look to see whether the manufacturer conducted feeding trials to test the food's adequacy. Look for a nutritional adequacy statement that says something like, "This food is complete and balanced for maintenance [or for growth] based on AAFCO feeding trials."

Is there a balanced diet that's right for every dog? No. Dogs are individuals. A majority of them might thrive eating a particular diet, but there will always be a few that have special needs. A dog's nutritional needs can be affected by stress, environment, and other factors.

 **Question?**

Can a pug be a vegetarian?
Commercial vegetarian diets exist for dogs, but they don't contain the high-quality protein provided by meat.

When you wheel your grocery cart down the aisles at a pet supply store or grocery store, you may be overwhelmed by the variety available. You'll see foods for puppies, large-breed puppies, overweight dogs, and dogs with allergies. While it's nice to have a selection, it can be difficult to decide which food is right for your pug. Knowing the pug's special needs will help.

Watch Those Calories!

One thing to consider is growth rate. Although the pug is a small breed, it is prone to hip dysplasia. Your breeder or veterinarian may recommend starting your pug pup on adult food as early as ten to twelve weeks of age. That helps slow the growth rate and reduces the amount of calcium in the diet. Veterinary researchers have discovered that when they reduce calcium and control calories, puppies grow less quickly and develop fewer musculoskeletal problems.

An adult or aging pug usually has a lower activity level and metabolic rate than a young dog. He can eat less food and still maintain a good body weight. He still needs the same amount of nutrients, though, so it's important that he get a high-quality, nutrient-rich food.

The Label Breakdown

The label must list ingredients by weight in decreasing order. Ideally, the first ingredient is some form of animal protein. None of the other ingredients can weigh more than that first ingredient. Manufacturers have been known to get around this requirement by a practice called split-ingredient labeling, which involves spreading out, or splitting, ingredients of the same type so they appear farther down the label. For instance, a grain such as corn, rice, or wheat might appear on the label in several different forms, such as flour, flakes, middlings, or bran. A food labeled this way might end up containing more protein from plant sources than from animal sources.

When you find a food you like, check the label regularly to make sure the ingredients remain the same. The best manufacturers use a fixed formula, meaning that the ingredients don't change from batch to batch. Some manufacturers change ingredients based on availability and market price. Dogs often have sensitive stomachs and can suffer digestive upsets from this kind of unexpected change in ingredients.

Name Calling

Can you tell anything from a food's name? Surprisingly, yes. Strict regulations govern what a food can be called. Let's say that you're looking at a can that reads "Grandma's Chicken for Pugs." That food must contain 95 percent chicken, excluding the water used for processing. Once the water is accounted for, the food must still contain at least 70 percent chicken. If the name includes a combination of ingredients—"Grandma's Chicken and Beef for Pugs"—chicken and beef must make up 95 percent of the total weight (excluding water), and the food must contain more chicken than beef.

A food name that contains a qualifying term such as "dinner," "entrée," "formula," "nuggets," or "platter" must contain at least 25 percent of the named ingredient—beef, for instance. So "Grandma's Beef Dinner for Pugs" contains at least 25 percent but less than 95 percent beef. What if Grandma makes a Beef and Chicken Dinner? The beef and chicken together must make up 25 percent of the product, with at least 3 percent being chicken.

Sometimes you'll see a label that highlights a particular ingredient; for instance, "Grandma's Chicken Dinner for Pugs 'With Cheese.'" The label can read this way only if the added ingredient makes up at least 3 percent of the food. If it says "with cheese and bacon," it must contain at least 3 percent of each ingredient.

Feeding Guidelines

The label also suggests amounts to feed. The operative word here is "suggests." Each pug is an individual, so you'll need to experiment to find the right amount of food for your dog. Let your pug's condition be your guide. If he's a chubby puggy, cut back. If he looks too thin, add more. Remember that a growing or active pug needs more food than one that just lies around the house all day while you're at work. Ask the breeder how much your pug pup has been eating at each meal, and go from there.

What Type of Food Should You Buy?

Most dog food comes in bags (dry) or cans (wet), but you can also find frozen and semi-moist foods. Each has advantages and disadvantages. The choice you make depends on your pug's nutritional needs, whether he likes the taste of the food (palatability), your own desires regarding convenience and quality, and your budget.

Canned Food

Dogs love canned food. It gets that good flavor from its high fat content. For old pugs that have lost teeth, canned food is easy to eat. It's also easy to serve; just plop it into a bowl.

The disadvantages are several. For one, canned food is expensive. Its water content is high—as much as 78 percent—so you're not getting a lot of meat for your money. Canned food sticks to teeth and is a factor in the formation of plaque, which leads to periodontal disease. Although canned food has a long shelf life while it's still in the can, it must be refrigerated after it's opened, and it can't be left in your pug's bowl for long periods without spoiling.

Dry Food

Pricewise, dry food has it all over canned food. It costs much less, which is something to consider if you're on a budget or feeding more than one pug. Dry food has a long shelf life and won't go bad if it sits in your pug's bowl all day (not likely unless he doesn't like the taste). Don't forget to choose a small kibble size for your pug's eating comfort.

Dry food has a reputation for helping to prevent the buildup of plaque and tartar on teeth, although it's not as beneficial as you might think. Dry foods and dog biscuits can help chip off small amounts of tartar (the hardened form of plaque), but they don't affect the gum line area, where the real problems start. The exception to this is veterinary foods that are designed to have a cross-hatch effect on teeth, scrubbing them all the way to the gum line.

On the downside, kibble usually contains less fat and more carbohydrates than canned food, so it doesn't taste as good. If you have one of the rare finicky pugs, you can tempt his taste buds by mixing a little canned food in with the dry food.

Frozen Food

Frozen dog foods are made with fresh ingredients and contain no artificial preservatives. They're mixed, formed into loaves, rolls, or cubes, and flash-frozen to preserve freshness. Consider a commercial frozen food if you like the idea of fresh ingredients but don't have time to cook for the dog yourself.

The disadvantage is that frozen dog food is available only in limited distribution. You're more likely to find it at mom-and-pop pet supply stores rather than at big pet supply chains. It must be kept frozen until you're ready to use it, and you have to remember to defrost it before feeding. While cubes can be fed frozen, it's unlikely that this sort of cold meal would appeal to your pug. Any unused portion must be refrigerated. If you're traveling with your pug, it's difficult to bring frozen food along unless you have some means of refrigeration or of finding it in pet supply stores along the way. Check the manufacturer's Web site before you leave so you can note the addresses and phone numbers of stores that carry the food.

Semi-Moist Food

This type of diet is softer than dry food but not as messy as canned food. The amount of water it contains ranges from 15 percent to 30 percent. Ingredients include fresh or frozen animal tissues, grains, fats, and sugars.

Other than convenience and palatability, there's not much to be said in favor of semi-moist foods. They contain high amounts of sugar, putting them squarely in the junk food category. In cost, they fall somewhere between canned and dry food, although single-serve packets usually compare in price to canned foods. This type of food is best given in small quantities as a treat.

Premium Foods

Some dog foods are described as "premium." This term, which is not regulated by law, generally refers to products that contain highly digestible ingredients with good to excellent availability of nutrients. The difference between premium and nonpremium foods is density per volume. That is, a cup of a premium food usually has more usable nutrients than a cup of nonpremium food. You can see the difference in the amount of poop your pug produces. In the long run, it can cost less to feed a premium food because your pug eats less of it and gets more out of it.

Homemade and Raw Diets

More and more dog owners today are preparing homemade or raw diets for their animals. The draw of this type of diet is the ability to control the quality of ingredients and the desire to provide what seems to be a more natural diet for dogs. People who feed raw diets or homemade diets believe they provide better nutrition. They say their dogs have better health, beautiful coats, few or no skin problems, and great dental health. However, these are anecdotal claims, and no controlled scientific studies have been done to prove these benefits. Your pug may benefit from a homemade diet if he has food allergies, is sensitive to artificial dyes or preservatives, or has a particular health problem that requires a special diet. Factors to consider before feeding a homemade or raw diet include nutritional balance, time, expense, and safety.

 Essential

Rotate the proteins, vegetables, and fruits you use so your pug receives a variety of nutrients. This will also keep him interested in his meals.

One of the concerns about homemade diets is that they aren't always nutritionally balanced. As you've learned, if ingredients aren't provided in proper proportions, the diet may not meet your pug's needs. It's possible, however, to design a nutritionally complete homemade diet for dogs if you use appropriate recipes from valid sources. There are a number of books on natural diets for dogs written by veterinary nutritionists or laypeople trained in nutrition (see Appendix B for suggestions).

Cost

If you choose to feed your pug a homemade diet for the health benefits, be prepared to use only the best and freshest ingredients, not leftovers from your own meals or scraps from the butcher. High-quality ingredients are expensive. This is especially true if you prefer to use organic meats and vegetables, which have the benefit of being grown without the use of potentially harmful antibiotics, hormones, and pesticides. Expect to spend as much as or more than you would for a premium commercial food.

Time Is Money

Commercial dog foods come ready to go in bags or cans. They're easy to measure out and feed. When you feed a homemade diet, you must purchase fresh ingredients on a frequent basis and prepare meals daily or every few days if you make a large batch and refrigerate or freeze it. Of course, this isn't a problem if you enjoy cooking and have plenty of time to spend in the kitchen. When time is a factor, an alternative is to purchase a commercial natural or raw diet from a pet supply store or by mail.

Safety

If you are considering feeding your pug a raw diet, you may be concerned about bacterial infection, either in yourself or in your dog. Infection from E. coli, salmonella, staphylococcus, listeria, and toxoplasmosis is possible, but following safe handling practices reduces the risk immensely. Remember that many of these bacteria live naturally in the intestinal tract of people and dogs.

 **Fact**

Most meats purchased from the grocery store have bacteria present on or in them. That becomes a problem only when specific strains of specific disease-causing bacteria proliferate, usually because of unsafe handling practices.

If you're preparing a raw diet for your pug, follow these safe-handling practices:

- Defrost meat in the refrigerator, not on the kitchen counter.
- Wash your hands before and after touching raw meat.
- Use hot, soapy water to clean and disinfect dishes, utensils, cutting boards, grinders, and other equipment used to prepare meals.
- Refrigerate or freeze raw food if you don't plan to feed it immediately.

Making the Choice

Feeding a dog is all about choices. There's nothing wrong with feeding a commercial food if your pug is happy, active, and healthy on it.

It's convenient to feed, and it obviously meets your dog's nutritional needs. If your pug has health problems or allergies, or you'd simply like to have more control over what goes into his body, then you may want to consider a premium, natural, raw, or homemade diet.

How Often, How Much, and When to Feed

How frequently you should feed your puppy for optimal growth depends on his age. Most puppies start with four meals a day after they're weaned. By the time they're ten to twelve weeks old, they're down to three meals a day, one every four to six hours. At four months (sixteen weeks), they can start eating twice a day, a schedule that should be continued for the rest of the dog's life.

If you're a working owner, though, it's not always convenient to fit in that third or fourth meal. When that's the case, it's perfectly fine to feed a puppy only twice a day—morning and evening. It won't make any difference in his activity level or behavior. Just divide the amount of food he needs daily into two meals instead of three or four.

Controlling a pug puppy's growth rate is important. A puppy needs lots of calories to fuel his rapid development, but too many calories simply make him fat. That excess weight is often the determining factor in the development of orthopedic problems such as hip dysplasia or luxating patellas. Try to keep your pug pup lean. Pugs are cute when they're roly-poly, but it's not a healthy condition for them.

 Fact

Within a single breed, gender, and age group, energy requirements can vary by about 30 percent, so it's easy to overfeed one dog, while underfeeding another, even if they're getting the same amount and same kind of food.

Young puppies up to sixteen weeks of age usually eat one to one-and-a-half cups of food each day. It's a good idea to switch him to an adult food at ten to twelve weeks of age. This allows slow, steady growth, and may help prevent the development of orthopedic problems. Active adult pugs usually eat ¾ cup to 1 cup of food each day, divided into two meals. Base the amount you feed on your pug's appearance.

A routine is important. Try to feed your pug at the same time every day. Feeding meals at set times ensures that you know how much your pug is eating and whether he has a good appetite. Free-feeding (leaving food out all the time) is not a good idea as it promotes obesity.

Why Do Dogs Get Fat?

Obesity is the most common health problem veterinarians see in dogs. Diabetes and orthopedic conditions such as hip dysplasia and luxating patellas are just a few of the problems that are linked to obesity. Obese pugs often develop knee problems and are predisposed to intervertebral disk problems, which are aggravated by excess body weight.

Among the reasons for the canine predisposition to obesity are the appetizing flavors of commercial pet foods, owners who leave food out all the time, and a sedentary lifestyle. All of these factors, plus the ability to sniff out food wherever it can be found, are applicable to pugs. They are extremely persistent when it comes to getting what they want, and what they usually want is food. It's not unusual for pug owners to find themselves mindlessly handing the dog potato chips just because he's giving them that special pleading look.

Is My Pug Fat?

A fat pug is neither a pretty sight nor a healthy one. He waddles when he walks and has difficulty going very far or jumping up into a lap. A pug's ideal weight depends on his size and frame. Eye your pug objectively and give him the hands-on test. Can you feel his ribs (but not see them), or are they well padded with fat? As you look down from above him, your pug should have a visible waist behind his ribs. A rounded or bulging abdomen and no waist are clues that your pug has been eating a little too much and not exercising enough. If you're still in doubt, your veterinarian can confirm whether your pug needs to go on a diet and exercise program.

Preventing Obesity

If your pug is a chowhound—and most of them are—take steps now to keep his weight at an appropriate level. Long before little rolls of fat start appearing around his middle, you should have an obesity prevention plan in place. Puppyhood is not too soon to begin. Dogs are very much like people. If they're allowed to become fat when they're growing, they're going to be more predisposed to obesity later in life.

 Essential

Pugs can't get on counters, but they can learn to open cupboards and drawers. Consider getting child-safe locks for any cabinets or drawers that hold food and any areas where garbage is stored.

The bottom line is that pugs must be prevented from gaining weight. That comes down to feeding the dog, not the food bowl. It's very easy to overfeed this breed, especially when he's looking longingly at you with those big pleading eyes. Don't look at the amount in the bowl, look at your pug. If he weighs too much, feed him less.

A Pug Diet and Exercise Plan

There's no way you can exercise a pug enough for him to lose weight, so exercise must be combined with feeding fewer calories. The simplest way to start is to reduce the amount of food you give. If you usually measure out a heaping cup of food, level it off. That alone can help.

If reducing the amount of food isn't practical, switch to a brand with fewer calories. You can find any number of diet dog foods at the grocery store or pet supply store. Look for a product that says "lite" or "less active."

Introduce a new food gradually, over seven to ten days, to avoid stomach upset. And don't switch to a type of food that your pug isn't used to eating. For instance, if you feed him canned food, the new food should be a reduced-calorie canned food, not a dry diet. If that's not possible, mix the canned food with the dry over a period of several weeks so he has time to become used to the change.

If your schedule allows, feed several small meals a day rather than two large ones. Eating more frequently will help your pug feel more full and less deprived. Another way to fill him up is by adding more fiber to his diet. Canned green beans, raw baby carrots, and canned pumpkin (plain, not the sweetened pie filling) are high in fiber but low in calories. Most dogs gobble them down. (Rinse canned green beans before feeding to reduce the level of sodium.)

Finally, be sure your pug gets daily exercise. Throw a soft toy for him to chase, and take longer walks. If he's seriously overweight, start slowly and work up to longer periods of exercise. As he loses weight, you can increase the length of walks or playtime.

Treat Talk

What kind of treats do pugs like? You name it, and they'll eat it. Fruits and vegetables fill the bill nicely. Many pugs love chopped baby carrots, apples, or bananas. Fruits and veggies are low in calories, so you can give them without a guilty conscience. Frozen baby carrots can help numb the sore gums of a teething puppy.

Keep treats small. Break a biscuit into several pieces and give them one at a time. Your pug is more interested in getting something—anything—than in how much he gets.

Limit treats to 5 to 10 percent of your pug's daily intake. That's one-and-a-half to two tablespoons, depending on how much your pug eats each day. Cut back a little on his food in the evening if you had an extra-long training session with treats or a special event such as birthday with doggie cake.

What Not to Feed

Are there any foods your pug shouldn't eat? Absolutely! Chocolate, onions, grapes, raisins, and alcoholic beverages are among the items your pug should never get.

It may be the food of love, but chocolate doesn't love dogs. A chemical in chocolate called theobromine is toxic to dogs and can cause vomiting, diarrhea, panting, restlessness, and muscle tremors. Too much chocolate can even kill a dog. Dark chocolate and unsweetened baking chocolate contain more theobromine than candy, which is adulterated with sugar and other ingredients. Keep any form of chocolate out of your pug's reach.

Raw or cooked, onions are off-limits to dogs. A particular chemical in onions can destroy a dog's red blood cells. The result is a serious or even fatal case of anemia.

Grapes and raisins (dried grapes) have been reported to cause acute kidney failure in some dogs. If your pug does snack on some grapes or raisins, you'll know there's a problem if he vomits or has diarrhea within a few hours of eating them, loses his appetite, or becomes lethargic and seems to have a stomachache. Activated charcoal helps prevent absorption of toxins, and your pug may need hospitalization with intravenous fluids for at least two days. The veterinarian will monitor the dog's blood chemistry to ensure that kidney failure doesn't develop.

Getting a dog drunk isn't funny—it's dangerous. Alcoholic beverages can be harmful or even fatal to dogs. Don't offer your pug even a sip.

CHAPTER 11

Basic Health Care

PREVENTIVE MEDICINE is the best way to keep your pug in good health. By taking steps to prevent problems or recognize them before they become serious, you'll save money as well. Preventive health care includes spay/neuter surgery, vaccinations, and regular home health checks.

Spaying and Neutering

Sometimes referred to as "altering," spay (ovariohysterectomy) or neuter (castration) surgery is the removal of a dog's reproductive organs (the uterus and ovaries in a female and the testicles in a male) to prevent the dog from producing puppies. Spaying is the procedure used for female dogs, and neutering generally refers to the procedure used for male dogs. Both surgeries offer health benefits beyond the prevention of unwanted puppies.

Why You Should Spay or Neuter Your Pug

One of the greatest health benefits of spay surgery for females is the reduced risk of mammary (breast) cancer, especially if the surgery is performed before the first heat cycle. Spayed females also run no risk of developing uterine or ovarian infections or cancer. Spaying also prevents behavioral and physiological changes associated with estrus (heat), such as bloody discharge from the vulva and attraction of male dogs. Neutering of males results in a lower risk of testicular and prostate cancer, less desire to roam, and a reduced incidence of aggressive behavior.

 **Fact**

Spaying a female before her first heat can reduce the risk of mammary cancer to as little as 0.5 percent. The risk increases to 8 percent if she goes through one heat cycle and 26 percent if she goes through two or more heat cycles.

Despite these benefits, many myths exist about spay and neuter surgery that may make you reluctant to have it performed. Among these myths are "My pug will get fat," "My pug's personality will change," "My pug should have a litter before she's spayed," "Anesthesia is dangerous," and "Surgery is painful and I don't want to put my pug through it unnecessarily." Let's take a look at each myth realistically.

Myth Number One: My Pug Will Get Fat.

Studies have documented a reduced metabolic rate in female dogs after spaying, but remember that spay or neuter surgery is usually scheduled when a dog is six to nine months old, just when growth is beginning to slow and hormonal balances change, influencing appetite. Young animals naturally start to put on weight during this time, especially if they're still getting the same amount of food and not enough exercise. It's understandable that you might associate spay/neuter surgery with weight gain, but it's not the surgery that causes the problem. Adjust your pug's diet and provide plenty of exercise to prevent obesity.

Myth Number Two: My Pug's Personality Will Change.

Yes, for the better! Altered dogs are more bonded to their people, less likely to roam, less given to marking territory by lifting a leg and spraying urine around the house, and less likely to develop aggressive behaviors.

Myth Number Three: My Pug Should Have a Litter Before She's Spayed.

Having a litter has no positive effect on a female's emotional state. Dogs don't dream about someday having puppies, and they don't feel deprived if they don't have them.

Myth Number Four: Anesthesia Is Dangerous.

The risk from anesthesia is much less than it used to be. The drugs used today are very safe, and many veterinarians use high-tech equipment to monitor heart rate and breathing during surgery. If you're concerned, ask if the clinic uses reversible gas anesthesia and a heart monitor. These safety features are more expensive but worth the money.

Myth Number Five: Surgery Is Painful.

Surgery is performed under full anesthesia, so your dog doesn't feel a thing. Soreness is normal after surgery, but veterinarians today are much more knowledgeable about pain prevention in dogs than they were just five years ago. Use of pain relief before and during surgery is the mark of a progressive veterinarian. In fact, if your veterinarian doesn't believe in pain relief for routine surgery, you're better off finding another one.

When to Spay or Neuter

Most veterinarians recommend that spay or neuter surgery be scheduled at four to nine months of age. Some clinics schedule spay/neuter surgery to coincide with a puppy's final series of vaccinations. This makes things convenient for you and the veterinarian, since your puppy is coming in anyway.

The Food and Drug Administration (FDA) approved the first product for chemical sterilization of male puppies. Neutersol Injectable Solution is an alternative to surgical neutering, although it doesn't provide the same benefits. It may not significantly reduce testosterone production, which means it doesn't necessarily eliminate behaviors such as marking, roaming, or aggression. Nor does it protect against diseases associated with male hormones, such as prostate disease or testicular or perianal tumors.

 **Fact**

Costs for spay/neuter surgery vary regionally. The cost for neutering a male generally ranges from $80 to $150. The cost for spaying a female ranges from $100 to $250, depending on whether it takes place before or after the first estrus cycle. Some veterinarians charge according to the size of the dog, since a larger dog requires more anesthesia than a smaller one.

In females, it's best if spaying takes place before the first estrus (heat) cycle. If your female puppy starts urinating more frequently, acts "antsy," flirts with male dogs, or acts shy or wild, she may be approaching estrus. The age at which a female first goes into heat varies within and across breeds. In general, small breeds such as pugs come into heat at a younger age than large dogs. Plan to spay your female pug at four to six months of age. Young dogs are resilient and recover quickly from surgery.

Preparing for Surgery

Your veterinarian may recommend running a blood panel before spay/neuter surgery. This is most commonly done if your pug is middle-aged or older, has a previous history of health problems, or has a current health problem such as obesity. A blood panel helps ensure that no underlying problems will cause trouble during surgery. If your pug is young and healthy, a blood panel probably isn't necessary.

Withhold food and water twelve hours before surgery. This generally means not feeding your pug after 8:00 to 10:00 P.M. Withholding food and water helps ensure that your pug doesn't vomit and aspirate (breathe in) food into the lungs while under anesthesia. Your veterinarian will let you know if there's anything else you need to do beforehand. Feel free to ask any questions you might have about the procedure so you're fully comfortable with it. Most dogs can go home the same day of surgery, but some veterinarians like to keep animals overnight for observation. The choice is yours to make.

Recovery

Spay/neuter surgery is one of the most common surgeries performed by veterinarians and is generally low-risk. Recovery takes about a week. Keep your pug quiet during this period. Sedate walks on leash are fine, but hold off on any rambunctious play. The easiest way to limit your pug's activity is to keep him or her on leash and at your side for the next week. When you can't supervise, the crate is the safest place for your pug.

 Alert!

Don't be alarmed if your puppy has some swelling at the incision site. That's normal, especially with absorbable sutures. Swelling can take weeks or even months to go away.

If your pug tries to bite at the stitches, you may need to acquire an Elizabethan collar, a cone-shaped device that fits around the neck and prevents the dog from reaching the stitches. When the incision heals, usually in a couple of weeks, the veterinarian will remove the sutures (unless they're self-dissolving).

Vaccinations

Vaccination is the process of exposing a dog's immune system to specific heat-killed germs, live germs rendered incapable of causing disease, or toxins, and germ products. Once the immune system encounters these disease-causing agents, it manufactures antibodies against them. Antibodies are protein substances that neutralize the effects of an antigen, a disease-causing foreign substance in the body.

Today's dogs are fortunate to have vaccinations against a number of killer diseases, including parvovirus and distemper. Before the development of vaccines for dogs, many died every year because their immune systems weren't strong enough to fight off the diseases.

When dogs are naturally exposed to disease, immunity often lasts a lifetime, but immunity stimulated by vaccination can be limited. That's why booster shots are necessary. With the exception of rabies, no data exists to indicate just how long the immunity provided by vaccination lasts, although studies in this area are being performed.

Vaccination Frequency

While vaccinations have been a boon to dogs, too much of a good thing can be just as bad as not having it at all. Veterinarians are currently rethinking the requirement that dogs be vaccinated every year. Over-vaccination has been associated with autoimmune hemolytic anemia in dogs, a disease that can be fatal.

Many schools of veterinary medicine now recommend a standard three-shot series for puppies to protect against parvovirus, adenovirus 2, parainfluenza, and distemper. The first vaccination is given at six to eight weeks of age, the next three to four weeks later, followed by the final shot in another three to four weeks. A rabies shot is given after sixteen weeks of age. After the initial three-shot series, they recommend that dogs receive booster shots for these diseases at one year of age and every three years after that. Note that some states require annual rabies vaccination instead of triennial (every three years) vaccination.

Types of Vaccinations

Three types of vaccinations are used in dogs: killed virus, modified live virus (MLV), and recombinant. Killed vaccines cannot cause disease and are stable during storage, but they are often associated with vaccine reactions and require more frequent booster shots. Modified live vaccines are stronger and provide longer-lasting protection against disease. In a dog with a weakened immune system, however, they have the potential to cause disease.

Recombinant vaccines are a new development. They're made by splicing gene-sized fragments of DNA from a virus or bacteria, and they work by delivering specific antigen material to the dog on a cellular level. This cuts out the risk of vaccination reactions that sometimes occur when vaccinating with the entire disease-causing organism.

Recombinant vaccines cannot cause disease. It's not known yet how long the immunity they provide lasts, but there's a good chance they will soon replace MLV and killed-virus vaccines. Recombinant vaccines are available for distemper, rabies, and Lyme disease. The future may also bring more nasal vaccines, which may be less likely to cause adverse reactions.

Vaccine Reactions

It's not uncommon for pugs to have reactions to vaccinations. Their lips and eyes may swell, or they can develop hives. In rare cases, the dog can go into potentially fatal anaphylactic shock. Most reactions occur within twenty minutes after the injection, but it's a good idea to schedule your pug's vaccinations for early in the day and monitor the dog for hives or other problems. Ask your veterinarian to spread out individual vaccinations instead of giving a five-in-one combination shot, and avoid scheduling a rabies vaccination at the same time as other vaccinations. If you know your pug reacts to vaccines, you can ask your veterinarian to provide allergy medication before giving the injection.

Which Vaccines Are Really Necessary?

Core vaccines—those for distemper, adenovirus 2, parvovirus, and rabies—are essential for all dogs. These viral diseases are serious (and can be fatal), common, highly contagious among dogs, or are a threat to humans (rabies). Distemper, adenovirus 2, and parvovirus can be treated only with supportive therapy such as intravenous fluids.

There's no medication that can cure the diseases, although antibiotics can help ward off secondary bacterial infections. Rabies is fatal once signs develop.

Other vaccines can be given based on the amount of risk the dog faces. Vaccines for coronavirus, Lyme disease, parainfluenza, leptospirosis, bordetella, and giardia fall into this "noncore" category. The risk of infectious disease varies throughout the country. Your veterinarian can help you tailor a vaccination program that's appropriate for your pug, based on his current health and the incidence of infectious disease in your area.

▲ Excellent health care, playtime, and activity
help to keep pugs strong and happy.

How to Examine Your Pug

You can help prevent problems or catch them before they become serious by giving your pug a home health check on a regular basis. Doing so helps you get to know your dog and sharpen your observation skills. Even slight changes in behavior or condition can signal a health problem. By getting things checked out early, you can protect your pocketbook and your pug.

Schedule a weekly health check as part of your pug's routine, and consider keeping a written "pug diary" so you'll notice patterns or changes more quickly. Things to note in your pug diary include eating and potty habits. The average pug skips a meal only rarely, so a steady decrease in appetite—or a more ravenous appetite than normal—is cause for concern. Stools should be small and firm. Loose stools or diarrhea may indicate a health problem or the need for an improved diet.

When your pug is a puppy, get him used to being touched all over his body. He should let you look at his teeth and inside his ears, handle his paws, lift his tail, and roll him over for a tummy rub and belly check. By accustoming your pug to being handled, you'll ensure that he's always willing to let you—and the veterinarian— examine him when necessary.

Mouth Check

"Say aah." Use this phrase (or another of your choosing) to teach your pug to open his mouth on command. Lift his lips to check the teeth for tartar buildup. While you're at it, make sure the gums are nice and pink. When you push on the gums, they should go white and then regain color rapidly. Pale gums are a sign of many serious problems, including bloat, poisoning, and parasite infestation.

Eye Care

Eye problems can run the gamut from irritation or injuries to allergies, inflammation, or infection. A swipe from a cranky cat or a brush with sharp-edged foliage can scratch your pug's cornea. Eyes can also be injured by blowing dust, dirt, or debris when a dog hangs his head out the car window. Grass seeds or particles can enter the eye when a dog runs through tall grass. During the pollen season, many dogs have mild allergies, which are manifested in red, itchy, watery eyes.

Irritation

When irritation occurs from a speck of dust or dirt, blinking usually produces tears that clean the eye. You can also bathe the eyes with preservative-free saline solution, like that used for rinsing contact lenses.

 Alert!

Never use any ointments or eye drops without checking first with your veterinarian. Drops containing any type of steroid that are put on an eye with a scratch or puncture can permanently damage the eye.

A normal eye is bright and shiny. If your pug is squinting and the eye appears painful, red, or cloudy, your veterinarian needs to have a look right away. Early diagnosis and treatment could save your dog's vision.

Discharge

Goopy eyes are a common affliction of dogs. Like people, dogs produce tears—a combination of mucus and water—as a way of cleansing and lubricating the eye. As the tears drain, the result is a watery or mucus-like discharge that can be clear, whitish, cloudy, light yellow, brownish, or reddish. This type of discharge is normal and can simply be wiped away with a dampened tissue, paper towel, or soft washcloth (use warm water but no soap).

Some eye discharge, though, can signal injury or disease. Thick, greenish gunk or heavy amounts of normal discharge are a clue that a visit to the veterinarian is an order. It's especially important if the eye is red or swollen or the dog is squinting or pawing at his eye.

Dealing with Eye Problems

If an irritated or runny eye doesn't improve within a day, take your dog in for a veterinary exam. Be sure you don't clean the eyes before the visit. The veterinarian needs to see the discharge to get an idea of the disease and treatment course. If you treated the eye with saline solution or some other mixture, be sure to tell the veterinarian what you used. All the information you can provide is helpful. Once the problem is diagnosed, your veterinarian will prescribe eye drops or ointments containing antibiotics or anti-inflammatories.

The Rest of the Body

Run your hands over your pug's entire body to check for lumps, bumps, sores, or painful areas. Some dogs are stoic, so a barely distinguishable flinch may be the only reaction you get if you touch a sore spot. Lift the paws to check for stickers between the toes or in the footpads. In winter, clean your pug's feet after he's been outside to remove any de-icing chemicals, salt, snow, or ice. Make sure toenails are at a comfortable length. A healthy coat is shiny with no patchy areas or hot spots.

What's Normal?

Heart rate, respiratory rate, temperature, and urination and defecation are all physiological signs that can tell you about your pug's health. Like people, dogs have ranges for normal temperature, heart and respiratory rates, and elimination. The following values can help you assess your pug's condition.

Body Temperature

The normal temperature range for a dog is 100 to 102.5 degrees Fahrenheit, with the average at 101.3. If your pug has a fever, he could be suffering from heat exhaustion or heatstroke (common in this breed), infection, or pneumonia. Take your pug to the veterinarian any time his temperature goes above 103.

To take your pug's temperature, use a rectal thermometer. Lubricate it with petroleum jelly or K-Y Jelly. While someone else holds the dog, lift his tail and gently insert the thermometer one to three inches into the anal canal, using a twisting motion. Don't force it. Leave the thermometer in for the amount of time recommended by the manufacturer, or for two minutes. Don't let your pug sit down while you're taking his temperature or the thermometer may break. If this happens, take him to the veterinarian to have it removed.

 **Fact**

Dogs lower their body temperature by panting. Panting allows water to evaporate from the mouth, tongue, and lungs, and exchanges warm air in the body for cooler air from the environment.

Heart Rate

The normal heart rate for adult dogs at rest ranges from 60 to 160 beats per minute. Heart rate varies depending on such factors as a dog's size and activity level. For instance, toy breeds tend to have higher heart rates than large breeds. A puppy's heart rate is as high as 220 beats per minute. The heart beats faster with exertion, fright, and high temperatures.

You can feel the heartbeat by pressing against the rib cage over the heart (it's on the left side), along the inside of the thigh where the leg joins the body, or just below the left elbow joint. To take your pug's pulse, count the beats per minute. An easy way to do this is to count the beats for fifteen seconds and then multiply that number by four.

Respiratory Rate

The average respiratory rate—the number of breaths per minute—for a dog at rest is twenty-four breaths per minute. A normal range is ten to thirty breaths per minute. Rapid breathing—as distinguished from panting—or labored breathing can signal serious problems, including fever, pain, anxiety, heatstroke, and heart or lung disease. To estimate respiratory rate, watch your dog's chest rise and fall. Count the breaths for fifteen seconds and multiply by four to get the breaths per minute.

How to Give Your Pug Medication

Even with the best of care, most dogs experience illness at some point in their lives. When that happens, they'll more than likely have to take pills or liquid medications or be treated with drops or ointments for their eyes or ears. Knowing the best way to give a pill, get liquids down the throat, or apply topical medications will help ensure that your pug gets well soon.

The most important thing to know about giving medication is that your pug needs all of it, even if he seems to be better before the medication is used up. To ensure a complete recovery, give all of the medication prescribed instead of saving it "for the next time."

Pills

Mary Poppins had it right when she sang that "a spoonful of sugar helps the medicine go down." The easiest way to give a pill is to hide it inside something yummy. Cream cheese, peanut butter, canned dog food, soft cheese, and liverwurst all qualify—in a pug's mind—as "a spoonful of sugar." Most pugs swallow doctored food so quickly they don't even notice the pill going down. Before you try this method, check with the veterinarian to make sure it's okay to give the pill with food. Some medications work best on an empty stomach.

If your pug turns up his nose at the "Trojan pill" or must take his medicine without food, you'll need to make a bit more of an effort. Holding the pill in your dominant hand, gently pry the mouth open by using one thumb to press upward on the roof of the mouth and the other to press down on the lower jaw. Slip the pill in and place it on the back of the tongue. Close the mouth and rub the throat to encourage swallowing. If your pug licks his nose, that means he's swallowed the pill. Pugs are champion pill-fakers, capable of hiding a pill in the side of the mouth, appearing to swallow two or three times and then spitting the pill out later, so don't be fooled.

Liquids

When your pug needs liquid medications, a plastic syringe (the kind without a needle) or eyedropper is your best friend. Draw the required amount of medicine into the syringe and place the delivery end into the pouch formed by the cheeks. Hold the lips closed with your fingers, and slowly press the plunger to dispense the liquid.

If you aren't able to get the medicine into your pug this way, ask your veterinarian if you can mix the medicine with the dog's food. This method has drawbacks, however. Many dogs are suspicious of food that tastes or smells unusual. It's also a less accurate way of giving medication, because you can't be sure the dog takes in all of it. Using a syringe to give medicine to a squirming pug can be difficult, but it's a good skill to master.

Are there any ways I shouldn't give a pill?
Yes. Unless your veterinarian okays it, don't pulverize pills into a powder and sprinkle it on the dog's food. Powders can have a nasty taste, and some pills have protective coatings that are necessary for delayed release.

Eye Drops and Ointments

A pug playing outdoors may suffer an eye injury from running through foliage or underbrush, so it's important to know how to administer eye drops and ointments. Eye drops are usually dispensed straight from the bottle. Hold the bottle in one hand, and tilt the dog's muzzle upward with the other. Squeeze the required number of drops into the eye. Try not to touch the applicator tip to the eye.

To apply ointment, hold the head still with one hand, using your thumb to pull the lower eyelid down. With the ointment applicator in your dominant hand, slowly squeeze out a line of ointment. Release the eyelid and close the eye, gently rubbing the surface to distribute the ointment. If possible, have someone help you hold the dog so you don't poke him in the eye.

Ear Drops and Ointments

Ear medications often come in plastic bottles with long, narrow applicators to help ensure that the medicine gets deep into the ear. To avoid spreading infection, use separate applicators if you're treating more than one dog. It may cost a little more upfront, but you'll save time and money by not having to treat repeated infections.

Hold the head still, insert the applicator into the ear, and dispense the appropriate amount. Your pug will try to shake his head, but don't let him. Massage the cartilage at the base of the ear to make sure the medication is well distributed. Then he can shake all he wants.

Parasite Prevention

KEEPING YOUR PUG FREE of internal and external parasites is imperative for good health. Worms, fleas, and ticks are not just irritating, they also spread disease between dogs and sometimes to humans. Parasite infestation results in physical problems such as bloody diarrhea and secondary bacterial infections, and some parasites can even transmit other parasites. If your pug goes outdoors—as he surely will—he might come in contact with these minuscule pests, so it's important to take precautions against them.

Internal Parasites

One of the more unpleasant aspects of being a dog is the potential for internal parasites that can infest your pug if they're not kept at bay with preventive medication. Intestinal worms take a toll on dogs by leaching nutrients from the body. They can cause internal bleeding, dull fur, and a potbellied appearance. Heartworms can be fatal if left untreated. And some worms can be transmitted to humans.

How do you know if your pug has worms? A fecal exam is usually necessary to determine the presence and type of worms that have invaded your pug's body, although tapeworms can occasionally have more obvious signs. Tapeworms can cause your dog's rear end to itch, and you may see him scooting his bottom on the ground in an attempt to get more comfortable. Tapeworm segments, which resemble grains of white rice, can sometimes be seen in feces or clinging to the fur around the anus.

In any case, a diagnosis is important because different worms require different medications to kill them. Don't assume that an over-the-counter product or a folk remedy such as raw garlic will take care of the problem. It's best to treat the infestation appropriately the first time and get rid of it. It's even better to prevent worm infestation in the first place by giving a regular course of heartworm medication, which also prevents most intestinal parasites.

Roundworms

The scientific name for roundworms is *Toxocara canis*. These are the most common worm parasites seen in dogs. The microscopic roundworm eggs can live for months or years in the soil. They infect dogs when they're ingested (dogs eating grass, dirt, or some interme-diate host). Once roundworm eggs enter a dog's system, they hatch in the stomach. The larvae make their way to the intestine, where they develop to maturity. The adults lay eggs that are passed in the dog's feces, falling to the ground and continuing the roundworm's life cycle. Unborn puppies can become infected if their mother has worms. Newborns can become infected through their mother's milk.

 Alert!

Roundworms can be transmitted to people. This usually occurs when young children eat dirt or put their hands in their mouths after touching dog feces. Teach young children to wash their hands after petting any animal and not to put dirt or sand in their mouths.

Roundworm infection is toughest on puppies. Adult dogs usu-ally develop a resistance to the parasites. Young puppies with round-worms look unhealthy, with dull fur and a pooched-out stomach. They may vomit or have diarrhea. Safe dewormers for puppies (and adult dogs) are available from your veterinarian. Most heartworm preventives also protect against roundworms.

Hookworms

Technically known as ancylostoma, hookworms are commonly found in the southern United States, where they thrive in the hot, humid conditions. These worms use their sharp mouthparts to latch onto the small intestine and suck blood and tissue fluids. Dogs with a heavy load of hookworms can suffer severe blood loss and malnutrition.

Like roundworms, hookworms can infect unborn puppies if the mother is infested or newborn pups through the mother's milk. They may also penetrate the skin—usually through the paws—or enter the body when the dog eats dirt, grass, or an intermediate host that contains eggs. Serious hookworm infestations are most common in puppies younger than two months of age. Suspect hookworms if your pug puppy has diarrhea that looks bloody, dark red, or black and tarry. Without treatment, the progressive blood loss can cause a puppy's death.

Hookworms can be difficult to diagnose because eggs may not show up in the feces for two or three weeks. Sometimes it takes a couple of fecal exams to confirm the presence of hookworms. Several dewormers from your veterinarian are effective against hookworms. You may be advised to repeat the treatment in a couple of weeks to make sure all the adult worms are eliminated. Certain heartworm medications are effective against roundworms and hookworms.

Tapeworms

Dipylidium caninum is the scientific name for this parasite, which uses hooks and suckers on its head to attach to the intestinal wall and feed on the nutrients that should be nourishing your pug. Tapeworms can sometimes be diagnosed visually, because body segments containing eggs are often seen wriggling in a dog's feces. They resemble grains of white rice.

Fleas and lice are intermediate hosts for tapeworms. This means that the tapeworm eggs live inside the flea (that tells you how small they are). If a dog (or person) swallows an infested flea, the eggs can then hatch inside him. The most common sign of tapeworms is an itchy behind. Suspect tapeworms if your pug frequently scoots his bottom on the ground. Your veterinarian can prescribe a dewormer that's effective against tapeworms.

Heartworms

This parasite—*Dirofilaria immitis*—lives in the right side of the heart and is spread by mosquitoes. It's most common in humid areas that attract mosquitoes, but it's found throughout the world. Left untreated, heartworms are killers, and the treatment is difficult and expensive. It's best to prevent them altogether.

The heartworm life cycle begins when infective larvae enter the dog's skin through the bite of a mosquito. The larvae burrow beneath the skin and eventually develop into immature worms. These immature worms enter the bloodstream where they're carried to the heart. They reach adulthood approximately six months after entering the dog's body. Adult heartworms can reach lengths of four to twelve inches. They are long and threadlike, with small mouths. Heartworms take only six months to grow to maturity and can live for as long as five years. If male and female worms are present in the heart, they reproduce, giving birth to live young known as microfilaria. The microfilaria can remain alive in a dog for up to three years. The next time a mosquito bites the dog, it ingests the microfilaria with the blood it takes in and the life cycle continues.

Heartworm Effects and Signs

What do heartworms do? They clog the pulmonary arteries of the heart, obstructing blood flow. They can entwine around the heart valves and interfere with the heart's pumping action. Some heartworms migrate to the veins of the liver, causing liver failure.

The signs of heartworm disease depend on the number of worms infesting the dog. A dog with few worms may not show any signs at all. A heavy load of worms can cause fatigue, a soft, deep cough, weight loss, and rapid breathing.

Diagnosis, Treatment, and Prevention

A blood test is required to diagnose heartworm disease. A chest x-ray helps the veterinarian determine the severity of the problem. Heartworms can be prevented with daily or monthly pills, as well as with a monthly topical (applied to the skin) preventive. Once the worms develop, however, a drug must be administered to kill the adult worms, followed by a second medication to kill any circulating microfilaria. In severe cases, the worms must be removed surgically.

Your pug can begin taking heartworm preventive at six to eight weeks of age. He'll need a blood test first to make sure no worms are present. Dogs that live in areas where mosquitoes are endemic should take heartworm preventive year-round, even if they spend most of their time indoors.

▲ It's important for your pug to see a veterinarian
on a regular basis, even if he's problem-free.

Other Internal Parasites

Whipworms, threadworms, and lung flukes can also affect dogs. Whipworms fasten to the walls of the intestines and can cause bloody diarrhea. Dogs with a heavy infestation lose weight and become anemic. Whipworms are difficult to get rid of, and a dog may need two or three treatments before they're eradicated. Certain heartworm preventives also control whipworms.

Threadworms, or strongyloides, as they're technically known, live in the small intestine. They can affect both people and dogs and are most common in humid regions such as the southeastern United States. Most commonly seen in young puppies, they cause watery or bloody diarrhea, which can be fatal to a young dog. Threadworms are diagnosed through a fecal exam and can be treated with a dewormer prescribed by your veterinarian. A follow-up treatment in one month is a good idea.

Lung flukes are flat worms that are hosted by aquatic snails and crawfish. When a dog eats the host, the worm finds a new home in the dog's lung. Lung flukes are a regional parasite, found in the Great Lakes area, the Midwest, and the southern United States. They can be treated with a dewormer prescribed by your veterinarian. Unless your pug lives in a coastal area and is fond of snarfing up these creatures, you probably don't have to worry about them.

External Parasites

Besides the nasty internal parasites, there are several external parasites that would enjoy dining at the Pug Café. Fleas, ticks, and mites not only cause your pug to scratch miserably, they also spread infection and disease. Fortunately, thanks to new pharmaceutical developments, it's easier than ever to control external parasites.

Fleas

Fleas are wingless insects that feed on blood. Among the flea species (nearly 2,000 species of fleas have been identified) that prefer dogs as their diner of choice are *Ctenocephalides felis*, more commonly known as the cat flea, and *Ctenocephalides canis*, the dog flea.

More than 50 percent of the skin problems seen by veterinarians are flea-related. Fleas live in the environment, hopping onto your dog only when they need a meal, so just because you don't see fleas on your pug doesn't mean they're not there.

Recognizing a Flea Problem

You'll know if your pug has fleas. You might not see them, especially on a black pug, but the constant scratching and biting at the body will announce the fleas' presence. Flea saliva, which is deposited into the dog's skin when the flea bites, contains substances that cause severe itching. A single bite from a flea can cause a hypersensitive dog to go into a frenzy of scratching and biting. If fleas aren't controlled, the dog can develop crusty stores, thickened skin, hair loss, and bacterial skin disease.

 **Essential**

Some topical treatments also protect the dog against other parasites, including ticks, heartworms, ear mites, and mosquitoes. Be aware, however, that products labeled for control of mosquitoes do not prevent heartworm disease.

To confirm a flea infestation, place your pug on a white towel or piece of paper. Run a flea comb through his fur and see if small amounts of black debris fall onto the surface. Moisten them. If they turn red, what you've got is flea dirt, the blood excreted by a flea after it feeds on your dog.

Flea Control

Flea control used to mean an endless cycle of bathing and spraying a dog, as well as spraying and flea-bombing the home and yard. Happily, flea control is much easier, safer, and more effective these days. A number of treatments or combinations of treatments can render your pug and home flea-free. Flea-control products for dogs include dispersing liquids applied to the skin and tablets given orally.

Topical, or spot-on, treatments kill adult fleas on contact and prevent flea eggs from hatching. They're applied monthly on the skin between the shoulder blades and absorbed by the body.

Tablets work in a couple of different ways. One type of tablet sterilizes female fleas when they feed on your dog. Another type of tablet begins to kill adult fleas in as little as thirty minutes. Both can be used in conjunction with spot-on products. One tablet combines flea control with heartworm preventive and is also effective against roundworms, hookworms, and whipworms.

Treating the Home

In addition to using flea preventives on your pug, you can treat your home and yard with sprays or powders that contain insect growth regulators, which prevent flea larvae from developing to maturity. Insect growth regulators work by preventing the formation of chitin, which makes up the flea's exoskeleton. It's also a good idea to steam-clean your carpets to kill larvae and eggs. Be sure to move the furniture so you clean as much of the carpet as possible.

Your veterinarian can help you choose appropriate products for use on your pug and in your home. Some flea-control products shouldn't be used on young puppies. Others are effective even if a dog is bathed frequently. While the products available are fast-acting and effective, it's important to remember that it still takes a certain amount of time before your dog and home can be considered flea-free. Don't expect overnight success.

Ticks

Shaped like a teardrop with eight legs, the tick is cousin to the spider. Often no larger than a poppyseed (except when they're engorged with blood), ticks use forearm hooks to snag onto fur and a pair of sharp mouthparts to dig into skin and feed on the blood they need to mature and reproduce. That's disgusting enough, but ticks also carry diseases that affect dogs and people, including Lyme disease, Rocky Mountain spotted fever, and ehrlichiosis.

Tick-Borne Illnesses

Lyme disease is the most common tick-borne illness in the United States. It's caused by *Borrelia burgdorferi*, a spirochete bacteria that's spread by the bite of an infected tick. In dogs, Lyme disease is characterized by sudden lameness, with one or more joints becoming swollen and painful. Treatment requires two to four weeks of antibiotics. Be sure to wear gloves when removing ticks from dogs.

Rocky Mountain spotted fever is an infection characterized by fever, depression, vomiting, diarrhea, enlarged lymph nodes, discharge from the eyes and nose, and muscle or joint pain. It's caused by *Rickettsia rickettsii* and is spread by several species of ticks. The disease was discovered in the Rocky Mountain area, but now most cases occur in the southeastern United States, the Midwest, the Plains states, and the Southwest. Suspect Rocky Mountain spotted fever if your pug has suffered tick bites during tick season—April to September. Your veterinarian can confirm it with a blood test. It's treated with antibiotics and supportive therapy.

 fact

Rickettsiae are small parasites about the size of bacteria that live within cells.

Ehrlichiosis often resembles Lyme disease or Rocky Mountain spotted fever. Signs include fever, lack of appetite, eye and nose discharge, and swollen limbs. It's caused by the rickettsial organism *Ehrlichia canis*, spread by the bite of the brown dog tick. Ehrlichiosis is usually seen in the Gulf Coast area, the Eastern seaboard, the Midwest, and California. Unlike most tick-borne diseases, it can occur year-round. It's treated with antibiotics and supportive therapy.

Pugs At Risk

Your pug is most at risk for ticks if he enjoys spending time out-doors. Favorite tick environments are wooded areas or yards that have lots of leafy debris where the tick can lie in wait for its prey. Check for ticks any time your pug has been outdoors or has been for a walk in tick-infested areas.

Removing Ticks

Ticks can attach anywhere on the body, but they're especially fond of the head, neck, ears, and feet (between the toes). The blood of ticks is dangerous to people, so put on gloves before you start your tick hunt. If you find a tick on your pug, remove it with tweezers. Grasp the tick at the head and use steady pressure to pull it away from the skin. Old wives' tales suggest smothering the tick with petro-leum jelly, covering it with alcohol, or applying the tip of a burned match to its body, but these techniques are more harmful than help-ful. Once the tick is removed, drop it in a jar containing alcohol or flush it down the toilet. Certain flea-control products kill ticks as well, another good reason for a flea-control program.

Mites

These microscopic members of the arachnid (spider) family cause itchy skin problems in dogs. Some mites are contagious to other ani-mals, but in most cases they don't cause problems in humans. Four species of mites are known to infest dogs: *Demodex canis, Sarcoptes scabei var. canis, Cheyletiella,* and *Otodectes cynotis.* Skin diseases caused by demodex and sarcoptes mites are often referred to by the general term "mange."

Demodicosis

Cigar-shaped demodex mites usually live harmlessly inside a dog's hair follicles, but every once in a while the demodex population runs amok, often in response to stress or illness. The result is canine demodicosis, also known as demodectic mange or red mange.

Demodicosis can be localized—limited to the head and front legs, for instance—or generalized, covering the entire body. Demodicosis is most commonly seen in dogs three to twelve months of age (localized demodicosis) or younger than eighteen months of age (generalized demodicosis). Pugs are among the breeds known to have an increased incidence of juvenile-onset demodicosis.

Skin scrapings or a skin biopsy by the veterinarian can confirm the presence of demodex mites. Treatment requires a series of baths with medicated shampoo, topical medication, and antibiotics. Demodicosis isn't contagious, but it may be heritable. It's best to spay or neuter a puppy that develops it.

Scabies

Canine scabies, also known as sarcoptic mange, develops when the sarcoptes mite tunnels beneath a dog's skin, resulting in intense itching, crusty sores, hair loss, and wounds caused when the dog bites or scratches at the itchy areas. Sarcoptic mange can be confirmed with skin scrapings. Treatment requires a course of medicated baths over a six-week period. Short-term use of corticosteroids can help reduce itching. Scabies is highly contagious, so if your pug has it, any other pets in the household should also be treated, even if they don't show signs. Canine scabies can also cause temporary itching in humans (usually on the waist, chest, and forearms) and cats.

Cheyletiella

This mildly itchy skin disease is sometimes called "walking dandruff" because the mites that cause it are large enough to be seen with the naked eye. They look like small white specks marching along the dog's back. These mites can be spread to other animals and people, but they're not common in households with a good flea-control program. The usual treatment is a series of medicated baths and dips.

Ear Mites

These mites love warm, moist areas, such as your pug's ear canal. Suspect ear mites if your pug has dry, reddish-brown or black earwax and often shakes his head or paws at his ears. Unless you check the ears regularly, you might not notice an ear mite infestation until it's at the serious stage. Dogs with a bad case of ear mites have bald spots around the ears from scratching at them, often accompanied by bleeding sores. The mites can grow numerous enough to block the entire ear canal.

To treat ear mites, the veterinarian will clean the ear canal and prescribe eardrops to kill the mites. It will take at least a month of treatment before you can be sure all the mites are gone. Give your pug a bath to help speed them on their way.

CHAPTER 13

Basic Grooming

GROOMING DOES MORE than keep your pug looking dapper. It's a great way to build a trusting relationship with your dog and to stay on top of his physical condition. With routine grooming you can catch problems such as ear infections, skin disease, parasite infestations, and tumors before they become serious. And a pug that's groomed regularly is more willing to be handled by a veterinarian, professional groomer, dog trainer, pet sitter, or dog show judge. Grooming serves a psychological function, too; a pug that looks good feels good.

Accustoming Your Pug to Grooming

Whether your pug loves being groomed or runs and hides when you pull out a brush or the shampoo depends on early conditioning. Teach your pug pup to enjoy being handled by stroking ears and paws while the two of you are sitting together. Practice opening his mouth to look at his teeth, and praise him for not fussing about it.

Establish a weekly routine, grooming the dog the same way and at the same place each time. Groom him before he eats, so his tummy isn't full, and take him out to potty before you start. Grooming is easiest when you can place your pug on an elevated, nonskid surface, such as a picnic table, a washer or dryer with a rubber mat or towel placed over it, or a professional grooming table. Keep grooming sessions short and sweet so he learns to enjoy the attention.

Grooming Supplies

Pugs are a wash-and-go breed, with no need for fancy trimming or tedious detangling. They don't drool a lot or have a distinctive body odor. You can complete a pug's grooming needs in about twenty minutes a week with a good brushing, a quick wipe of the ears, and cleaning of the facial wrinkles. Additional grooming needs are monthly toenail trimming and a bath as needed. Here's a list of equipment you'll need:

- Soft bristle brush, rubber curry brush, or hound mitt
- Wire slicker brush, shedding comb, or shedding blade
- Steel metal comb
- Mineral oil or nondrying liquid ear cleanser
- Nail trimmers
- Styptic powder
- Toothbrush and toothpaste made for dogs
- Shampoo formulated for dogs
- Coat conditioning spray

Remember, the earlier you expose your pug to the grooming process, the easier it will be to keep him at his sweet-and-clean best.

Brushes

A bristle brush has natural or nylon bristles and a handle for an easy grip. Choose one with short, natural bristles. Use a soft bristle brush so you don't irritate your pug's skin. Rubber curry brushes are square- or oval-shaped so they fit comfortably in the hand. They have short, nubby bristles that quickly remove dead or loose hair and dirt and give the coat a polished appearance. This type of brush also provides a massaging action your pug will love. Choose one with a strap that you can slip your hand beneath for a better grip. Variations on the rubber curry brush include a nubbly hound mitt that fits over your hand like a glove and rectangular hard rubber brushes with teeth or knobs (like the Zoom Groom).

A wire slicker brush is rectangular in shape with thin, curved wire bristles on the pad and a handle that makes it easy to hold. It's useful for removing dead hair and stimulates the skin to promote blood circulation and new hair growth.

 **Fact**

Shedding is seasonal. In fall, dogs shed to make way for the thick winter coat. In spring, they trade the heavy winter coat for a lighter summer one. Dogs that spend most of their time indoors, such as pugs, are exposed to long hours of artificial light and tend to shed small amounts year-round.

Combs

Your pug will need a metal comb for regular grooming sessions and a shedding comb or blade to prevent those hair-everywhere times. Purchase a steel comb with fine- and wide-spaced teeth. Use the fine-tooth side to remove dirt from the dog's coat and to search for fleas if necessary. The wide-tooth side is useful for removing loose hairs after a bath. A high-quality metal comb should last your pug's lifetime and beyond.

Going over your pug with a shedding comb or shedding blade every month can help keep loose hair to a minimum. Use it after first brushing with the curry. Stroke it over the body as if you were peeling a potato. A shedding blade has sharp edges, so don't bear down too hard. Avoid using it on the dog's legs or any other vulnerable areas. With the help of a shedding blade, you can get enough hair off the typical pug to build a whole new one!

Nail Care Tools

Most pugs need their nails trimmed monthly, but some individuals need nail trimming more or less often. A dog's thick, tough toenails require a specific type of nail trimmer. Look for pliers-style nail trimmers at the pet supply store. Nail clippers can have two cutting edges or a single blade that works like a guillotine to slice off the nail tip. Most groomers and dog experts like the clippers with the orange handles (made by Millers Forge), which are easy to grasp and have a sharp blade to slice off nail tips.

 Essential

> To restrain your pug during any grooming procedure, place your hand beneath the chin and on the chest rather than holding the top of the head. This helps prevent injury to the eyes.

Styptic powder stops bleeding if you accidentally cut into the quick of the nail. You can find it in the grooming section of your pet supply store.

Dental Equipment

Toothbrushes and toothpaste made specifically for dogs are available at pet supply stores or from your veterinarian. For young puppies, use a gentle finger brush (one that fits over your index finger), a piece of moistened gauze, or a damp soft washcloth. When your pug's permanent teeth come in, you can purchase a soft dog toothbrush with a large head at one end and a small head at the other end. This makes it easy to get to all areas of the mouth. Toothpaste for dogs is often meat– or peanut butter–flavored to make it more palatable. Toothpaste made for people can upset a dog's stomach, so don't share your Crest.

Shampoos and Conditioners

A dog's skin has a different pH level than that of a human. Shampoos for dogs are formulated so as not to strip away the beneficial oils that keep the skin and coat healthy. Choose a gentle, tearless deodorizing or conditioning shampoo that won't dry out your pug's coat. For puppies, choose a mild, tearless shampoo.

Unless your pug has parasites or other skin problems, avoid shampoos that contain flea- or tick-fighting insecticides. The fewer chemicals your pug is exposed to, the better. If you do have a problem with fleas, you may want to try a shampoo that contains natural flea-fighting ingredients such as citrus, eucalyptus, tea tree oil, pennyroyal, or citronella. Note that pennyroyal oil, tea tree oil, and other essential oils are toxic when applied directly to the skin or taken internally.

Conditioners leave the coat shiny. You can apply one after the dog is shampooed, rinsing it out after letting it soak in for the required amount of time, or you can use a spray-on conditioner after the dog is dry.

Yes, Pugs Shed

Despite what you may have heard to the contrary, pugs shed like buffaloes. Pugs have double coats—a top coat with long, straight hair and an undercoat with soft, fluffy hair—measuring about three-quarters of an inch in length. Although this coat looks short and smooth, it's really rather long, albeit horizontally instead of vertically. Because pugs shed so heavily, weekly brushing is a must if you want to keep loose hair under control. Pugs shed year-round, and weekly brushing will help keep fallen hair off your clothes and furniture. If shedding gets to be too much, you can help keep it under control with frequent bathing and daily brushing. Monthly use of a shedding blade also helps remove excess hair. Avoid using the shedding blade too often or you'll strip out too much of the coat, leaving your pug with a flaky appearance.

Question?

How much shedding is too much? Bald patches can be caused by hypothyroidism or other hormonal diseases. Hair loss caused by stress or illness usually occurs in specific areas, such as the rear or flanks.

If your pug has an especially heavy shed, give him a warm bath, then brush the coat while blowing it dry (as described on page 174).

Be sure you dry him completely or you won't remove enough hair. Then go over the coat with a shedding blade.

Even with regular and thorough grooming, expect to live with hair. If you don't accept the fact that pugs shed before you acquire one, you're sure to be disappointed. Don't assume you can "cure" shedding with supplements, sprays, or frequent grooming. It just won't happen.

Brushing and Combing

Brushing loosens and removes dirt, dead hair, and old skin cells. It also distributes the skin's natural oils through the coat. Brush your pug weekly to keep his coat and skin in good condition. While you're brushing, check for signs of potential problems, such as itchiness, hair loss, redness, tenderness, or lumps. Keep an eye out as well for evidence of flea infestation. Start at the head and brush back toward the end of the body. Brush all the way down to the skin, not just over the surface of the coat. This helps loosen and remove dead hair and dandruff flakes. Don't skip the stomach area, even if your pug protests. Firmly insist that he allow you to groom every part of his body.

 Alert!

If your pug's coat tends to be dry, spray him before brushing with an antistatic coat conditioner to prevent a shock from static electricity.

To keep hair from flying everywhere, brush your pug outdoors in nice weather or in the garage or laundry room if you need protection from the elements. Place the dog on a sheet or towel that you can just throw in the washing machine after the grooming session. This will help keep hair from getting in your carpet, on your bed and other furniture, or lodged in corners.

When you're through brushing, use the wide-tooth side of your comb to remove any remaining loose hairs. Spray the coat with a leave-in conditioner to add shine. Your pug's coat will be gleaming.

▲ These coats are kept shiny and beautiful thanks to daily grooming.

Caring for Ears and Eyes

A pug's button or rose ears can trap moisture and debris, making the dog prone to ear infections. Check ears weekly to see if they need cleaning. A small amount of honey-colored wax is normal, but if you see a dark, heavy buildup of dirt or wax, the tissues appear swollen and tender, or the ear smells bad, your pug may have an ear infection. Clean the ears only when you see an accumulation of wax, dirt or debris. Cleaning ears too frequently is just as bad as cleaning them too little or not at all.

To clean the ears, moisten a cotton ball or cosmetic pad (never a cotton swab) with mineral oil, a 2 percent solution of acetic and boric acid, or a nondrying liquid ear cleaner recommended by your veterinarian. Gently wipe them out, going no deeper than the first knuckle on your finger. Start in the deepest part and wipe outward. That way you don't push bacteria and dirt farther into the ear canal where they could cause infection or itching. When the ears are clean, dust them with antiseptic powder to help prevent infection.

 **fact**

Ear diseases make up 20 percent of the average veterinary practice. The most common canine ear problem is otitis externa, an infection or inflammation of the outer ear canal. Ear infections are usually caused by parasites, microorganisms such as yeast, or foreign bodies lodged in the ear canal.

Avoiding Ear Problems

Don't clean the ears with alcohol or cleansers that contain alcohol. Alcohol can sting if there's a slight abrasion in the dog's ear, making your pug reluctant to sit still for future ear cleanings. It also dries the ear, masking problems that need treatment. If your pug's ear is oozing, there's a reason for it. Drying the ear up without discovering and treating the underlying problem simply begins a cycle of ear problems.

Eyes Right

Pugs have large, round eyes that are prone to injury. They're also sensitive to chemicals or other irritating substances. Check them daily for redness or other signs of irritation that might indicate a problem, and use a tearless shampoo for baths. Healthy eyes are bright and clear, with a white eyeball. It's normal for your dog to have a small amount of clear discharge in the corners of the eyes. You can wipe it away with a damp tissue or cloth to prevent stains beneath the eyes.

Caring for Wrinkles and Nose

The wrinkle-faced pug needs a little extra facial cleansing to prevent moisture from building up in the wrinkles. Each pug is an individual, and some retain more moisture than others. Wipe out the wrinkles daily or weekly as needed, using a dampened tissue or cotton ball, a small, dampened cosmetic sponge, or baby wipes. You can also use mild hydrogen peroxide as a cleanser, being careful not to get it in the eyes. Then thoroughly dry the wrinkles. There's no need to use powder; it will just cake in the wrinkles, which can irritate the skin.

Neglecting the wrinkles, especially in pugs with a deep nose roll, leads to infection from trapped moisture and bacteria. This condition is often referred to as swamp face and requires veterinary treatment. Keep your pug's face clean.

 Essential

> The easiest way to do anything involving a pug's face is to sit the pug on your lap with the back of his head against your chest. Pugs seem to dislike it if you approach them "face on" to clean them up.

Sometimes your pug's nose may seem dry or crusty. You can prevent this by applying petroleum jelly or baby oil every once in a while. Place a small amount in the fold over the nose and wipe away the excess.

Dental Hygiene

Like most toy breeds, pugs have small mouths into which all forty-two teeth are crammed, making them prone to dental problems. If you want your pug to have healthy teeth and fresh breath, don't ignore his dental hygiene. Periodontal disease caused by tartar buildup is a common problem in dogs, but regular brushing (and baby carrots as treats) helps keeps the dentist at bay. Hard dog biscuits and dry dog food can help chip off small amounts of tartar, but brushing is the only way to provide the thorough cleaning your pug's teeth need. The American Animal Hospital Association recommends brushing a dog's teeth at least three times a week. Daily is better.

How to Brush the Teeth

Pugs tend to dislike having their mouths examined, so accustom your puppy to having his teeth brushed while he's still young. Puppy teeth are too sensitive for a toothbrush, but you can gently rub the teeth with a soft gauze pad or washcloth that's been moistened with water. Wipe all of the teeth, stroking upward from the gumline to the tip of the tooth.

 **Fact**

You don't have to brush the inside of the teeth. Simply getting the outside is beneficial for overall dental care. To make brushing easier, hold the mouth shut with one hand, use your thumb to lift your pug's lip, and brush with the other hand.

When the permanent teeth come in, you can start using a toothbrush and toothpaste made for dogs. Brush the front teeth first, then move to the upper and lower teeth in the back. Get down into the crevices where teeth and gums meet, because this is where food is most likely to lodge, causing odor and infection.

Veterinary Cleanings

If your pug's teeth develop a heavy coating of tartar, he may need a veterinary cleaning. When the veterinarian cleans your pug's teeth, she removes tartar with a hand scaler, probes beneath the gumline to check for pockets where periodontal disease might start, cleans above the gumline with a mechanical scaler, cleans and smoothes the teeth beneath the gumline, polishes the teeth to create a smooth surface, and washes them with an antibacterial solution to help delay the buildup of tartar beneath the gumline and on the crown of the tooth. A fluoride treatment helps strengthen your pug's teeth, desensitize exposed roots, and decrease infection. To ensure a thorough cleaning without stressing your dog, the veterinarian uses a short-acting anesthetic so that your pug is asleep during the procedure.

Bath Time

How often you bathe your pug depends on the individual dog. Some pug owners wash their dogs every two weeks, especially if the dog sleeps in bed with them, while others find that quarterly bathing is sufficient. Bathe your pug any time he smells like Puppy LePew or develops a dull coat. If your pug enjoys rolling in bird droppings or other stinky, dirty substances, you'll want to bathe him more frequently than if he's a couch potato that goes outdoors only to do his business.

Preparation

When it's time for a bath, your pug will fit nicely in the kitchen sink, saving your back from the aches caused by bending over a bathtub. Gather everything you need beforehand: shampoo, conditioner, towels, and cotton balls to place in the ears to help keep water out. Read the directions on the shampoo bottle; you may need to dilute it before use. Brush the dog to remove loose or dead hair.

 Alert!

When bathing your pug, take precautions to keep shampoo out of his eyes. A little mineral oil around them will help form a barrier. Afterward, make sure he's thoroughly dry. Leaving the skin—especially the wrinkles—moist can lead to hot spots and fungal infections.

In the Suds

Place a rubber mat in the sink to provide good footing, put your pug in the sink, and wet him thoroughly with warm water, starting at the head and working your way to the end of the body. Use a sprayer if your sink is equipped with one (test the temperature first so your dog doesn't get a blast of hot or cold water), or pour water over him from a large plastic measuring cup or other container. This ensures that he's not standing in dirty water during the bath.

Lather with a gentle dog shampoo, again starting at the neck and working back. Keep shampoo away from the eyes; instead, use a washcloth to clean the face and head. If you're using a medicated or flea shampoo, leave it on the skin for fifteen minutes, or as directed on the label or by your veterinarian. Rinse thoroughly with warm water to get all the shampoo out of the coat. The residue can make a dog's coat look dull and flaky. To help remove shampoo residue, use a fifty-fifty mixture of cider vinegar and water as a final rinse.

Getting Dry

Towel-dry the dog thoroughly, removing as much water as possible. Your pug will assist you with this process by shaking frequently. (For bonus points, see if you can teach him to shake on command.) Now you can place him in a warm, draft-free place until he's completely dry. This prevents chills and helps ensure that he doesn't immediately run outside and roll in the mud or dirt.

If you want to speed the drying process with a blow dryer, use a low, gentle setting—never a hot setting. Hold the dryer at least a foot away from the dog so you don't burn the skin. As you blow the coat dry, brush with a bristle brush, in the same direction the coat grows. This helps remove excess hair, but only if you brush until the dog is completely dry, not damp-dry. Take special care to thoroughly dry the chest, the neck, and behind the ears. These are areas where the coat is thick or lies in folds and may retain moisture.

Trimming Nails

Frequent walks on pavement will help wear down your pug's nails, but they'll need to be trimmed at least monthly, more often if you want to accustom the dog to having it done. If you can hear the nails clicking on the floor, it's time to give them a trim. Overgrown nails snag easily on carpets, upholstery, and bed coverings. If they get too long, they can grow right into the footbed, which is painful and can even impair the dog's ability to walk.

Most pugs hate having their nails trimmed, and when pugs don't want to do something, they turn into fifteen pounds of pure, squirming muscle. Your pug won't try to bite you when you trim his nails, but don't count on him to hold still for the procedure. You know the saying that it takes two to tango? Well, it takes two or more to trim a pug's nails. Don't try this alone!

To get started, have your assistant hold the dog securely. A good way for your assistant to immobilize the dog is to place him between the knees, facing outward, with the left hand supporting the dog's chest. It can be useful to have a third person on hand to feed treats to distract the dog.

Once your pug is under control, you're ready to trim. As your assistant firmly grips one of the legs at the elbow so the dog can't pull it back, grasp the paw and clip just at the curve of the nail. Avoid clipping past the curve. You don't want to hit the quick (the blood vessel inside the nail). If your pug has light-colored nails, it's easy to see the quick, which looks like a dark line running through the nail. If you can't see the quick because the nails are dark, a good rule of paw is to trim the nails parallel to the toe pads. As you clip, praise your pug if he's behaving nicely, and give a firm "No" to put a stop to squirming.

When you're through, smooth rough edges with a metal nail file and give your pug a treat for enduring such a terrible ordeal. Before you let him go, examine the footpads for foreign objects or injuries. In winter, clean your pug's feet after he goes outside to remove de-icing chemicals, salt, snow, and ice.

Alert!

If you accidentally hit the quick, stop the bleeding by applying pressure with a cloth or cotton ball or putting styptic powder on the injured nail. If you don't have any styptic powder on hand, flour or cornmeal will work in a pinch.

If you can't stand the fuss your pug puts up—and if your budget allows—simply take the dog to a groomer or veterinarian for a nail trim. You'll both be happier.

Anal Sacs

Now we're getting to the end of the grooming process. The anal sacs, or glands, are located on each side of the anus. If your pug's rear were a clock, you would—in most cases—find the anal glands at the 5:00 and 7:00 positions.

The anal sacs produce a fluid that's excreted when a dog defecates. Sometimes the sacs become clogged. If your pug is scooting his rear on the ground or frequently biting and licking at it, he may have intestinal parasites or impacted anal sacs. Stinky, slimy spots on your clothing or furniture also indicate an anal gland problem.

Impacted anal sacs require veterinary intervention in the form of emptying, or expressing, the sacs. The veterinarian can show you how to do this at home should the situation recur, which it often does. It can be a smelly job, though, so if you're squeamish you may prefer to just take the dog in whenever the glands need to be expressed.

Sometimes impacted anal sacs become infected. Antibiotics and hydrotherapy can treat the infection and soreness. In a few cases, more exercise and a change in diet can also bring about improvement. Surgery is a last resort for dogs whose anal sacs are constantly infected.

Dealing with Skunk Odor

Face it—if you live in a rural, or even suburban, area there's a good chance your pug will meet a skunk someday. And he's going to come out on the losing side of the encounter. Before you let him back in the house, you'll want to eradicate that awful, disgusting scent he's sporting. Lots of remedies for removing skunk odor exist, from bathing dogs in tomato juice to dousing them with Massengill douche. The following homemade solution will also work, and you can find the ingredients at most drugstores or grocery stores.

Mix one quart of 3-percent hydrogen peroxide, a quarter-cup of baking soda, and one teaspoon of liquid soap. Wet your pug to the skin, then apply the mixture. Work it through his coat and leave it on for several minutes. Rinse thoroughly. Don't let your pug drink or lick any of the solution. Throw out any of the mixture you don't use. It's not safe to bottle and store this chemical combination.

Grooming for the Show Ring

Pugs don't need much work before you walk into the ring with them. A bath is the only thing that's really necessary. Bathe your pug a couple of days before the show. Bathing gives the coat a fluffy feel that many judges don't like, so doing it ahead of time gives the coat a couple of days to regain its proper texture.

Many handlers also trim the whiskers and any stray hairs on the chest or rear legs. This is to give the pug a cleaner look. It's not a must, however. Before you go in the ring, go over your pug's coat with a stiff natural bristle brush. Then rub your hands over the coat to bring out the natural oils. That's all there is to it!

End any grooming procedure or bath with a nice massage and a treat. Clean equipment thoroughly so it's ready to go for the next time. And if you're ever tempted to skip a grooming session, think about how you'd feel (and look and smell) if you didn't bathe, brush your hair and teeth, and wash your face on a regular basis.

CHAPTER 14

Common Illnesses, Injuries, and Emergencies

ANY DOG CAN SUFFER AN ILLNESS or injury at some time in his life. Your pug may itch and scratch from allergies, hot spots, or flea bites; experience the unpleasantness of diarrhea or vomiting; or develop lumps or bumps that should be examined by a veterinarian. Knowing what to look for and what to do in case of these potential problems will help you deal with them if and when they occur.

When Do You Need to Visit a Veterinarian?

Your pug needs a veterinary exam every year. Even if you choose not to vaccinate him annually, he still needs a physical exam to make sure his overall health is good. Here's what the veterinarian might do during a normal physical exam:

- Listen to the heart and lungs.
- Check temperature, pulse, and breathing rate.
- Check weight.
- Examine eyes, ears, and skin for infection or parasites.
- Look inside the mouth for tartar buildup on teeth or other dental problems.
- Check for patellar luxation or other orthopedic problems.
- Palpate (feel) the body to ensure that organs don't seem enlarged.

- Palpate the body for suspicious lumps or bumps that might indicate infection or tumors.

The annual exam is also a good time to take in a fecal sample to make sure your pug doesn't have any intestinal parasites. That's not necessary, of course, if he's on a heartworm medication that also kills intestinal worms.

Unless a wound is deep, there's no need for a trip to the veterinarian. Simply clean it with chlorhexidine (Nolvasan), and then apply an antibiotic ointment, available from your drugstore, to prevent infection. Signs of infection are redness, tenderness, and swelling.

Following are some of the common illnesses or injuries your pug might encounter and what to do about them.

Allergies

Common allergens include medications, insect bites or stings, grasses, pollens, molds, and foods. Dogs can acquire allergies or inherit allergic tendencies. Eventually, the dog may begin reacting to all kinds of allergens, from dust and feathers to molds and wool.

Atopy is characterized by an itch-scratch cycle that's usually triggered by pollens. Pugs with atopy itch and scratch constantly, especially on the face, feet, and legs, as well as in the external ear canal. The result is thick, flaky skin, hair loss, and scabbing. It's not unusual for dogs with atopy to develop frequent ear infections or secondary bacterial infections (infections that develop as a result of the wounds caused by scratching).

Allergic skin disease is an inherited condition common to pugs. It usually appears in young dogs, from one to three years of age. It takes a lot of testing, including skin scrapings, bacterial and fungal cultures, and intradermal skin testing, to determine whether a dog is suffering from allergic skin disease or some other type of allergy. A good flea-control plan is also important, because flea allergy dermatitis can resemble atopy. Once atopy is diagnosed, there are several ways to manage it:

Change the dog's environment as much as possible by limiting exposure to known allergens.

Antihistamines, essential fatty acid supplements, and medicated shampoos can help control itching and scratching.

Severe cases may need intermittent low doses of corticosteroids to relieve itching.

Allergy shots (hyposensitization) as a last resort can sometimes help.

Flea Allergy Dermatitis

A single bite from a single flea can trigger flea allergy dermatitis (or FAD). The allergy occurs because many dogs are sensitive to a particular substance in flea saliva. FAD is a common skin disease in all dogs, but its incidence has decreased with the advent of better flea-control products.

Dogs with FAD itch like crazy. Their skin becomes inflamed, red, and bumpy. Depending on where you live, FAD can be seasonal or year-round.

 Essential

Flea collars aren't very good at fighting fleas and can often irritate skin. Spend your money instead on a good flea-control program recommended by your veterinarian.

The best treatment for FAD is a good flea-control program. Ask your veterinarian to recommend appropriate products. Until fleas are under control, itching can be controlled with antihistamines and—if necessary—short-term doses of corticosteroids. Some dogs develop skin infections from chewing at the itchy spots. These can be cleared up with topical and oral antibiotics.

Food Allergies

Dogs with food allergies suffer severe itching, and they develop red, bumpy, or raised patches of skin. This rash usually appears on the ears, feet, stomach, and back of the legs. Wheat and corn are common food allergens.

Alert!

Feeding your pug a hypoallergenic food won't prevent allergies from developing. It will just make it more difficult to find a food that contains a type of protein to which he hasn't been exposed.

If your veterinarian suspects a food allergy, she will recommend putting the dog on a hypoallergenic diet for a certain period of time—usually six to ten weeks. A hypoallergenic diet contains unusual ingredients that the dog is unlikely to have encountered. It's also free of artificial colors, flavors, and preservatives, to which pugs can be sensitive. If the food allergy disappears while the dog is on the hypoallergenic diet, it's necessary to add ingredients back to the diet until the allergenic culprit is identified.

Bacterial Skin Problems

Thanks to their wrinkly skin, pugs are prone to bacterial skin diseases. These usually develop in response to other skin conditions that cause the dog to scratch, chew, bite, or lick at his body. Bacteria settle in the abraded area, worsening the original problem. Bacterial skin diseases your pug can develop include hot spots and pyodermas.

Hot Spots

Also known as acute moist dermatitis or pyotraumatic dermatitis, hot spots are warm, moist, sometimes oozy areas of redness and hair loss, usually occurring along the lower back or the inside of the thighs. Painful and bad-smelling, they develop where the skin has been broken from scratching or biting, allowing bacteria to proliferate. Hot spots are frequently seen in pugs that have fleas or other itch-causing external parasites, especially during hot, humid weather. They're treated by cleaning the area and giving topical or oral antibacterial drugs to fight the inflammation. Instituting a good flea-control program is the best way to keep hot spots at bay.

Pyodermas

Like hot spots, pyodermas are secondary to other skin diseases. They're bacterial skin infections that develop in response to the trauma caused by scratching and biting. Types of pyoderma that might affect pugs are acne, folliculitis, and skin fold pyoderma.

Teenage pug pups from three to twelve months of age can also develop blackheads or pimples on the chin, lower lip, or sometimes the genital area. This mild surface skin infection usually occurs when hair follicles are blocked by skin scales and sebum. Medicated shampoos can help clear up mild cases, but deep-seated cases of acne may also require a course of oral antibiotics effective against staphylococcus bacteria. Acne usually disappears as the dog matures.

Sometimes referred to as superficial pyoderma, folliculitis is an inflammation of the hair follicles. It's said to be the second most common skin disease in dogs. It often develops as a complication of scabies, demodectic mange, hypothyroidism, or other skin problems. Vigorous grooming can also damage the hair follicles.

Dogs with folliculitis have small pimple-like bumps (pustules) with a hair shaft protruding through each bump. The infection can then spread deep into the skin, forming large pustules that rupture, disgorging pus and crusting over. Folliculitis is most common in the armpits, abdomen, and groin. A pug with folliculitis may have patchy hair loss, giving him a moth-eaten appearance. Mild cases of folliculitis can be treated with medicated shampoos, but deep folliculitis requires oral antibiotics as well, for a period of six to eight weeks.

When skin folds rub together, the skin can become damp and inflamed, ideal growing conditions for bacteria. Skin fold infections, or pyodermas, can occur in a pug's facial wrinkles, in the vulvas of obese female pugs, and in the folds of a pug's curly tail. The moist skin is irritated and inflamed and has an unpleasant smell. Skin fold pyodermas are treated with medicated shampoos. Topical steroids used for a brief period can help if itching is severe. Your veterinarian may recommend using a benzoyl peroxide gel to prevent recurring infections. In chronic cases, the most effective solution is surgery to eliminate skin folds.

Yeast Infection

A type of yeast called *Malassezia pachydermatis* is commonly found on the skin and mucous membranes of healthy pugs. Normally, the yeast doesn't cause problems, but for unknown reasons it sometimes proliferates and causes a skin disease known as cutaneous malassezia or malassezia dermatitis. It's most often seen in dogs that live in humid areas and is characterized by greasy, itchy skin, increased pigmentation, and thickened or blackened skin, often in conjunction with ear infections or atopy. Affected areas usually include the face, ears, and paws between the toes.

Malassezia is diagnosed through microscopic examination of a skin scraping and treated with antifungal agents and medicated shampoos. Malassezia dermatitis is often mistaken for pyoderma. If your pug has been treated with antibiotics for a supposed case of pyoderma and still has problems, he may have malassezia instead.

Diarrhea

If your pug's stools appear loose or liquid instead of firm and compact, he has diarrhea. If you suspect that your pug's diarrhea results from anxiety or excitement, or because he snarfed some spicy or fatty food and is suffering the consequences, withhold food for twenty-four hours, but provide plenty of fresh drinking water (diarrhea can lead to dehydration). For the next couple of days, feed him a bland diet of boiled skinless chicken with white rice or cottage cheese. Other easily digestible foods you can give are boiled hamburger meat, cooked macaroni, and soft-boiled eggs. Gradually replace the bland diet with his regular food.

If diarrhea continues for more than twenty-four hours, take the dog to the veterinarian. Diarrhea that's bloody, black, or tarry looking or that's accompanied by vomiting, weakness, or fever calls for an immediate visit to the veterinarian.

Vomiting

Like diarrhea, vomiting can be caused by any number of problems, including anxiety or excitement, eating too quickly, or eating something that doesn't agree with the digestive system. Vomiting is also a sign of some infectious or chronic diseases.

If your pug is healthy and you suspect the vomiting is related to eating something that gave him an upset stomach, withhold food and water for twelve hours, then feed a bland meal such as boiled chicken and rice. Give only one or two tablespoons at first to make sure your dog can keep the food down. If he can, gradually return him to his regular food.

Take your pug to the veterinarian if he has projectile (violent) vomiting, if the vomit smells like feces, if the vomiting is accompanied by diarrhea, if the vomiting continues even though the dog hasn't had any food, or if the vomit contains blood or worms.

Lack of Appetite

This is generally a sign that your pug isn't feeling at all well. A pug might skip a meal once, but any more than that is something to worry about. Not wanting to eat can have any number of causes, from poor dental health (it hurts to chew) to viral diseases such as distemper or infectious canine hepatitis (not infectious to humans).

Any time your pug loses interest in food—especially if he's less active than usual, his tail is uncurled, or he shows other signs of not feeling well—take him to the veterinarian. This is a situation where your pug diary can come in handy. You'll be able to tell the veterinarian when your dog stopped eating and about any other unusual behaviors you may have noticed.

Lumps and Bumps

Dogs can develop all kinds of lumps and bumps on or beneath the skin. Some are harmless while others require veterinary intervention. Look (and feel) for lumps and bumps every time you groom your pug. Lumpy skin problems include abscesses and hematomas, various types of adenomas, warts, and cysts.

Abscesses and Hematomas

A soft, painful lump may be an abscess or hematoma. An abscess is an infection that occurs at the site of a bite or puncture wound. A hematoma is a blood clot beneath the skin. Ear hematomas are common in dogs, especially those that have ear mites or infections that cause excessive scratching at the ear. Abscesses are drained by the veterinarian and the infection treated with antibiotics. Some hematomas disappear on their own, but others must be drained by the veterinarian.

Adenomas

Your dog may develop small, smooth, pink warts on the eyelids or legs. These benign (harmless) tumors are sebaceous adenomas and are commonly seen in older dogs. If tumors on the eyelids are large, they should be removed to prevent damage to the cornea.

Ceruminous gland adenomas are dome-shaped, pinkish-white tumors of the wax-producing gland that develop in the ear canal. Sometimes they become ulcerated or infected. Small tumors of this type are usually harmless, but large ones can become invasive and must be treated with surgery and radiation therapy.

Warts and Cysts

More commonly known as warts, papillomas are caused by a virus and can grow on the skin or inside the mouth. They're usually harmless and don't need to be removed unless they're causing a problem because of their location on the body. Warts in the mouth often go away on their own, but they can be removed by your veterinarian either surgically (cutting) or cryogenically (freezing).

Cysts are firm lumps beneath the skin. They form when hair follicles become blocked with hair and a cheesy material called sebum. Cysts are generally harmless, but they can become infected and may need to be surgically drained or removed.

Skin Cancer

Dogs can develop several types of skin cancer, including mast cell tumors, melanomas, and squamous cell carcinomas. None of these conditions is especially common in pugs, although mast cell tumors are often seen in short-nosed breeds as a whole. With your pug's smooth coat, signs of skin cancer can sometimes be obvious in the early stages, so pay attention to anything unusual.

Mast Cell Tumors

Mast cell tumors make up 10 to 20 percent of the skin tumors seen in dogs. Mast cell tumors have many nodules and usually look red, hairless, and ulcerated. They can be benign or malignant (harmful) and should be removed surgically. Dogs with malignant mast cell tumors may also need radiation or chemotherapy.

Melanomas

Melanomas develop from cells in the skin that produce melanin, which is what gives your pug the dark pigment on his nose and skin. Melanomas look like brown or black nodules and can occur on the eyelids, lips, in the mouth, on the nail beds, and elsewhere on the body. Skin melanomas are usually harmless, but melanomas in the mouth and nail bed are usually malignant. They can and should be removed surgically, but they often recur. Dogs with melanomas in the mouth don't have a good prognosis.

Squamous Cell Carcinoma

Squamous cell carcinomas are caused by exposure to the ultraviolet radiation in sunlight. They're usually found on lightly pigmented areas of the body. Appearance ranges from a firm red patch to a cauliflower-like growth to a hard, flat, grayish-looking ulcer that doesn't heal. They can be removed surgically or treated with radiation therapy if surgery isn't possible.

Emergencies

If you're lucky, your pug will never suffer an emergency, but it never hurts to be prepared. The purpose of first-aid is to keep the dog alive until he can receive veterinary help. By dealing with emergencies quickly and calmly, you can greatly increase your pug's chances of survival.

 **Essential**

Signs of internal bleeding are bleeding from the nose, mouth, or rectum; coughing blood; blood in urine; pale gums; and collapse. Keep your pug warm and get him to the veterinarian as soon as possible.

A first-aid kit for dogs is much like one for humans. You can probably use the same one you keep on hand for your family, or you can put together a separate one for your pug. Keep the first-aid kit in your bathroom or on top of your pug's crate, so it's easily accessible when you need it. Make sure everyone in the family knows where it is.

Besides your first-aid kit, other useful items to have on hand are a blanket to keep the dog warm in case of shock, and clean towels or cloths for putting pressure on wounds that are bleeding. A penlight is helpful for examining eyes, mouth, and ears. By your telephone or in the first-aid kit, keep the phone numbers for your veterinarian, your veterinarian's on-call pager or home, the nearest animal emergency hospital, and a local or national poison-control center.

▲ Pugs can get into trouble easily; make sure
you're prepared in the event of an emergency.

How to Move an Injured Dog

As you probably learned at some point in your life, it can be dangerous to move a person with an injury. The same is true for dogs. If
your pug is injured and must be moved out of harm's way or trans-
ported to a veterinary hospital, you can take steps to reduce the risk
of potential injuries from moving him.

- Cradle him in your arms, with the injured side away from
  your body.
- Support his rear with one arm.
- If necessary, hold the front and rear legs to prevent kicking.
- If he appears to have a back, neck, or spinal injury, transport him on a firm, flat surface such as a cookie sheet (for a
  puppy) or a sturdy board of some kind.

On the way to the veterinarian, keep the dog as still and warm
as possible. Cushion him with pillows, towels, or rolled blankets.

Keeping him warm with a blanket or towel will help ward off shock.

Most emergencies are pretty obvious. Heavy bleeding, broken bones, choking, electrocution, heatstroke, and poisoning all qualify. Insect stings, deep cuts and lacerations, and animal bites might not be immediately life-threatening, but they can turn into big trouble if they're not dealt with appropriately. The following tips will help you recognize and handle most emergencies your pug might encounter.

Bleeding

No matter what kind of injury your pug has, if he's bleeding, that's what you need to deal with first. You need to put pressure on the wound and keep it there until bleeding stops. Using sterile gauze bandages (ideally) or any type of clean cloth, apply firm, consistent pressure to the wound. It may take five to ten minutes for bleeding to stop completely. Tourniquets can do more harm than good, so use them only as a last resort.

Broken Bones

Assume that a bone is broken if your pug can't stand on a leg, if a bone is protruding through the skin, or if the dog can't move—which may indicate a spinal injury. Stabilize the dog and then get immediate veterinary care. A compound fracture is one in which the bone sticks out through the skin. If the break has caused an open wound, cover it with sterile gauze pads or a clean cloth, wrapping the cover loosely with a bandage to keep it on. Don't try to set a broken leg. It's most important to keep the dog warm and get him to a veterinarian quickly. Broken bones take eight to twelve weeks to heal.

Choking

Pawing at the mouth, gagging or retching, or having difficulty breathing are all signs of choking. If coughing doesn't dislodge the object and your pug is conscious, get him to the veterinarian to have it removed. Trying to get your fingers around it to pull it out can push it farther into the throat.

If your pug loses consciousness because he can't breathe, lay him on his side, open his mouth, pull his tongue forward, and sweep your fingers through the mouth to see if you can grasp the object and remove it. If you're successful, perform rescue breathing or CPR as needed. If the object doesn't come out easily, move on to the Heimlich maneuver. To perform the Heimlich maneuver, hold your pug upside down in your lap with his back against your chest and your arms around his waist. With your hands at the dog's upper midabdomen (just behind the last rib), make a fist with one hand and grasp it with the other hand. Quickly thrust up and in with the fist four or five times. This forces a burst of air through the larynx, which should dislodge the object. Keep in mind that you are doing this on a very small animal. There is no need to use as much force as you would on a human.

If the Heimlich maneuver doesn't work, try holding the dog's hind legs in the air and thumping his back between the shoulder blades with the heel of your hand. When the object is dislodged, perform rescue breathing or CPR as needed. Take the dog to the veterinarian for an exam to make sure he's okay.

Deep Cuts or Lacerations

First, stop the bleeding. Then clean the area around the wound with povidone iodine or chlorhexidine to reduce the risk of tetanus or other infection. Don't touch the wound with either product, as they can sting and irritate the skin. Then flush the wound with tap water until it looks clean. Don't rub the wound with anything, not even a gauze pad, or you could start the bleeding again. A gaping wound or a cut that's more than half-an-inch long should be closed with stitches.

Electrocution

If you find your pug unconscious near an electrical outlet, *don't* touch him. Shut off the main power, then pull the plug. Administer rescue breathing or CPR as needed. If CPR is effective, take the dog to the veterinarian as soon as possible for further treatment. A dog that is shocked but doesn't lose consciousness may cough, have difficulty breathing, drool, or have a strange odor in the mouth from electrical burns. Take him to the veterinarian.

Heat Stroke

Too much activity on a hot day, or too much heat at all, being left in a car on a hot day—even with the windows rolled down—or going without shade or water on a hot day, especially on a concrete or asphalt surface, are all causes of heat stroke. Pugs are not outdoor dogs and *must* stay in air-conditioned comfort on hot days. Signs of heat stroke are heavy panting and difficulty breathing. The tongue and mucous membranes look bright red. Your pug may drool thick saliva or start vomiting. His body temperature can climb to 104 degrees Fahrenheit or higher. If left untreated, he'll go into shock, collapse, and die.

At the first signs of heat stroke, move your pug into an air-conditioned area and take his temperature. If it's above 104 degrees Fahrenheit, begin cooling him by immersing him in cool water for up to two minutes. You can also place the wet dog in front of a fan to help lower his temperature. Take his temperature every ten minutes. When it falls below 103 degrees Fahrenheit, you can stop cooling the dog and dry him off. Take your pug to the veterinarian as soon as possible after heat stroke. It's associated with breathing problems, seizures, and other serious conditions, which can develop hours after the dog has seemingly recovered.

Hypothermia and Frostbite

Pugs aren't any more suited to cold weather than they are to hot. If exposed to extreme cold, they can develop hypothermia (excessively low body temperature) or frostbite, which occurs when a part of the body—usually an extremity such as a paw or ear—freezes. Frostbite often accompanies hypothermia.

Signs of hypothermia include shivering, lethargy, and a body temperature below 95 degrees Fahrenheit (remember that a dog's normal temperature range is 100 to 102.5). To treat hypothermia, warm the dog by wrapping him in blankets. Dry a wet dog thoroughly. Take the dog to the veterinarian if his temperature is below 95 degrees Fahrenheit.

Alert!

You may have heard that it's a good idea to massage frostbitten areas or to rub them with snow or ice, but that's an old wives' tale. It can actually cause more damage to the dog's body tissues.

Suspect frostbite if your pug's skin looks pale white or blue. Apply warm compresses to the frostbitten area until the tissue begins to regain color. Take the dog to the veterinarian as soon as possible.

Insect Bites and Stings

Allergic reactions to stings or bites can include hives (raised circular areas on the skin), swelling, rashes, itching, and watery eyes. A bite or sting on the face or neck of a pug can cause dangerous swelling that closes off the dog's airway. Anaphylactic shock is a system-wide reaction characterized by agitation, diarrhea, vomiting, difficulty breathing, and collapse. Any time your pug has these signs, rush him to the veterinarian.

Minor reactions such as a rash or itching can be treated with calamine lotion or a paste made of baking soda and water. A topical steroid can reduce swelling, and ice packs help reduce pain and swelling.

Poisoning

Snail bait, putrefying animals, garbage, medications, rodent poisons, antifreeze, plants, and insecticides are all sources that can poison your pug. Sometimes even your best efforts at pug-proofing your home fail. If you see your pug eat something that you know or suspect is toxic, check the ingredients. Look on the label or call the National Animal Poison Control Center (see Appendix A).

Depending on the substance, you may be advised by your veterinarian or a poison control center to induce vomiting by giving the dog hydrogen peroxide. The usual dose is one teaspoon for every ten pounds the dog weighs. Give the appropriate amount every twenty minutes, up to three times, until the dog throws up. After he vomits, give a five-gram tablet of compressed activated charcoal (you may want to keep this handy in your first-aid kit). The activated charcoal prevents absorption of any remaining poison in the dog's stomach. Take your dog to the veterinarian for further treatment.

Signs of poisoning may not become apparent for several days. Suspect poisoning if your pug is weak or shows signs of internal bleeding such as nosebleeds or bleeding from the mouth or rectum. Take him to the veterinarian immediately. If you suspect what the poison might be, bring the packaging with you.

Common Poisons		
Poison	**Symptoms**	**What to Do**
Antifreeze	Depression, vomiting, seizures, stumbling as if drunk.	Take to veterinarian immediately.
Bacterial	Stomachache, bad breath, vomiting, and diarrhea.	Take to veterinarian immediately.
Contact poisons	Absorbed through skin by coming into contact with toxin.	Flush with water for thirty minutes. Bathe dog to ensure he does not ingest poison orally.

Puncture Wounds and Animal Bites

Puncture wounds are caused by sharp, pointed objects such as nails, barbed wire, or jagged pieces of wood. Bite wounds are serious because they're chock-full of bacteria from the other animal's mouth. Treat bite and puncture wounds the same way. First, stop any bleeding. Then thoroughly clean the injured area with povidone iodine or chlorhexidine. If a bite is severe, your pug may need stitches. A course of antibiotics can help ward off any infections. Signs of wound infection are swelling, redness, heat, and pain. If you suspect that the animal that bit your pug was rabid, notify your veterinarian immediately.

Choosing a Trainer

PUGS HAVE A REPUTATION for being untrainable, a reputation that they have carefully cultivated over the centuries. It's true that they typically prefer to follow their own pug path, but pugs are smart, and they are perfectly capable of learning with the right motivation—usually food. A good trainer, then, can be your best friend in the quest to teach your pug what he needs to know.

Going It Alone: Pros and Cons

Dozens of dog-training books and videos are published every year. With those resources available at your nearest bookstore or library, why should you spend money to attend a dog-training class? Books and videos can certainly assist you in the training process, but with a mind-of-his-own breed such as a pug, the personalized help a trainer can provide will help you and your pug learn more quickly.

Besides the basic behaviors a pug should know—sit, down, come, stay, walk nice—a trainer can help you understand what's normal and what's not, and what behavior to expect at different stages of your pug's puppyhood and adolescence. She can also help you learn to teach tricks and advise you on getting involved in animal-assisted therapy or activities such as freestyle or agility. A good trainer will help you elicit your pug's positives, using training techniques that make learning fun. You'll gain the following advantages from attending a class:

1. Trainers have experience with large numbers of dogs, so they can call upon a variety of tricks and strategies to see what works best with your pug.
2. Training class provides socialization opportunities so your pug can become accustomed to meeting and interacting with other dogs and people.
3. Training class helps your pug learn to pay attention to you even in the face of distractions.

Finding the Right Trainer

Dog training is often a do-it-yourself career. No special licensing or certification is required before a person can claim to be a dog trainer, although some trainers attend dog-training schools or obtain a university degree in behavioral psychology or ethology (the study of animal behavior). No matter what their educational background, or lack thereof, the most successful trainers have excellent communication skills; a thorough understanding of learning theory and training techniques; and a deep knowledge of breed characteristics, general dog behavior and physiology, and human nature. Why human nature? When all is said and done, the trainer's real job is to teach *you* how to teach your dog.

 Essential

A good dog-training program has well-organized classes, helpful instructors, small class sizes, and provides written information for study at home.

To find a trainer, start by contacting one of the professional dog-training organizations. A trainer who belongs to one of these organizations has an interest in continuing education, staying informed about advances in behavioral knowledge, and learning from others in the field. Professional organizations in the dog-training field are American

Pet Dog Trainers (APDT), the International Association of Canine Professionals (IACP), and the National Association of Dog Obedience Instructors (NADOI). See Appendix A for contact information.

▲ The right trainer can make all the difference in your pug's performance.

Meeting the Trainer

You should be able to find at least two or three trainers in your area that belong to one or more of the above organizations. Call each trainer to see if you can attend a class as an observer. This allows you to make sure you'll be comfortable with the trainer's teaching style.

Talking to the trainer should give you a good idea of her experience and background. Ideally, she'll have had some experience with pugs or, at the least, with other toy breeds. Here are some questions to ask:

- How long have you been training dogs?
- Do you belong to any professional organizations?
- How did you learn to train dogs?
- How many pugs have you trained?

- What training techniques do you find work best with pugs?
- What will my pug and I learn in this class?
- Can my children attend class too?

Observing a Class

It's easy to tell when you're dealing with an experienced trainer. He goes through a number of steps to ensure that everyone, human and canine, understands what's being taught and how to do it.

A good trainer explains and demonstrates each behavior before teaching it, usually using his own dog. Then he explains and demonstrates how to teach the behavior, providing written materials if necessary. He allows time during class for everyone to practice and spends time with students to work on specific problems. Last but not least, he treats people and dogs with respect and courtesy.

 Alert!

Never allow anyone, and certainly not a trainer, to mistreat your dog. Hitting, hanging, kicking, or shocking are all unacceptable under any circumstances. No training method should ever be harmful to the dog!

Pay attention to whether people and dogs are having fun in the class. Your pug is not going to do well in a boot-camp atmosphere. Choose a class where the trainer uses positive, humane training techniques such as clickers, praise, and food rewards.

It's important to choose a class where your training needs and goals will be met. Ask the people attending the class if they're satisfied with the progress they've made. A six- to eight-week class should give you basic skills to work competently with your dog at home.

If your pug is a family dog, everyone will need to know how to train him. Note whether the class permits children. Well-behaved children of appropriate age (six years or older) should be welcome. Good trainers encourage the entire family to participate.

Once you find the right trainer, sign up for the next class. Your pug is smart (smart enough to make you think he can't learn anything), and he can begin learning as soon as you bring him home.

Training Classes

Teaching your pug can take a lifetime. You'll want to reinforce the basics throughout his life, of course, but more than that, you'll want to keep his brain sharp and his little pug-self entertained so he doesn't get bored. From puppy kindergarten to animal-assisted therapy, there's a class for just about anything you might want to teach your pug.

Puppy Kindergarten

An old wives' tale has it that dogs aren't ready for training until six months of age, but that's far too long to wait, especially in the case of the wily pug. Your pug pup is capable of learning basic commands at the tender age of eight weeks. The earlier you begin training him, the more successful you'll be. In puppy kindergarten, you'll learn positive reinforcement techniques that will help you maintain a modicum of control over your new pug. The most important benefits your pug should take away from puppy kindergarten are increased confidence and an enjoyable experience.

What You'll Learn

Puppy kindergarten teaches the basics—sit, down, come, stay, off, and walk nicely on a leash—in a fun, positive fashion. While your pug pup is learning these must-know behaviors, you'll be learning how to communicate effectively with him. In a typical class, the instructor will show you how to train your dog and watch you practice in the class setting. Your homework will be to practice what you've learned in the week following class and to demonstrate it at the next session.

A good puppy kindergarten trainer will also help you deal with typical puppy behaviors such as barking, chewing, digging, jumping up on people (something you'll probably never break a pug of), play biting, and stealing food or trash (another lifelong struggle). In addition, your trainer may cover such issues as spaying, neutering, grooming, health care, safety, and tattooing or microchipping for identification.

What to Look For

Most puppy kindergarten classes require dogs to be at least ten weeks old and not more than six months old. Your pug must be vaccinated and flea-free before attending class. Most trainers will ask you to bring written proof of distemper and parvo vaccinations.

The puppy kindergarten class you choose should have a manageable number of people and puppies. Avoid one that seems too crowded. The trainer should have time to give you and your pug (and everyone else) individual attention during each class period.

 Essential

Your local pug breed club may offer training classes. If this is the case, it's a great way for you and Pugsley to meet other pugs and pug people. Contact the PDCA to see if there's a pug breed club in your area.

Most puppy kindergarten classes allow a period of free play for all the pups. Look for a class that divides puppies by size during playtime. Dogs play rough, and it's all too easy for a big dog to injure a small one without meaning any harm.

Puppy High School and College

Basic obedience classes reinforce what was learned in puppy kindergarten or introduce the basics to pups that didn't have the benefit of puppy kindergarten. The class may emphasize more difficult behaviors that require a longer attention span, more precision, or an instant response, such as stay, heel, and come. Even at six months of age, however, your pug still lacks the maturity to be consistent and reliable, so basic obedience training should be a continuation of building confidence. As in puppy kindergarten, the trainer should use positive training methods, but she'll also teach you how to reduce and eventually phase out food rewards, with the goal of teaching your pug to respond only to verbal commands and hand signals. Remember, your pug will not respond well, if at all, to jerking, yelling, or scolding. Train in small steps and praise like crazy for even the smallest successes.

Advanced Obedience

If your pug has enjoyed learning the basics, you may want to teach him more advanced skills that he will need if you decide to participate in obedience trials. In an advanced obedience class, your pug can learn to walk off lead, retrieve on command, and complete jumping and scent discrimination exercises. He can also start learning to recognize and respond to hand signals. Even if you don't plan to compete in obedience trials, teaching your pug these skills will help keep his mind sharp and his body active.

 Essential

Your pug shouldn't train over any but the lowest jumps until he's twelve to fourteen months old, which is when the growth plates close. Repetitive or concussive activity such as jumping over obstacles can lead to orthopedic problems.

Training for Sports

Pugs aren't particularly athletic, but they are hams and can do well in canine sports such as agility and freestyle. You can find classes for agility and freestyle through your trainer or through a local community college. Agility and freestyle both have national organizations (see Appendix A) that can direct you to trainers or clubs in your area.

 **fact**

Hand signals aren't just for the obedience ring. You can use them in other dog sports and at home. For example, if Pugsley is barking while you're talking on the phone, simply give him the hand signal for "Quiet" (finger moving across your throat) and follow it with the hand signal for "Down" (palm up, toward his face). With practice, he'll learn to be quiet and still during your phone conversations.

Don't sign up for a class in your favorite dog sport until you're sure your dog is ready for it. This means he should know and respond to basic obedience commands. If you have to call him several times before he comes or if he won't sit or lie down the first time you tell him to, take him to a refresher obedience class first, and get in lots of practice at home.

Animal-Assisted Therapy

With their comical nature and love of people, pugs are perfect for animal-assisted therapy (or AAT). You can't just waltz into a nursing home with your pug and let him start visiting people, though. The two of you must first become certified as a therapy team. You can find certification programs through the Delta Society, Love on a Leash, and Therapy Dogs International (see Appendix A).

Training Tips and Techniques

The dark ages of dog training had people swatting their dogs with newspapers or rubbing their noses in the mess from an accident. Trainers and dog people alike now know that positive reinforcement and prevention are the best ways to teach a dog—especially a pug— what he needs to know.

As a new pug owner, you'll find that praise, rewards, and a clicker to signal correct behavior are your most effective tools during training sessions. All of them help to motivate your pug to perform the behaviors you want. The idea is to communicate with your dog rather than force him.

Praise

Remember how good you'd feel when your teacher or parent praised the way you solved a problem or performed a task? Just like people, pugs respond better to praise than to criticism. Saying "Good dog!" in a happy, high-pitched tone of voice lets Pugsley know that you like what he's done.

Praise isn't limited to formal training sessions. Use it any time you catch your pug doing something right. Is he playing with a toy? Say "Good toy!" or "Good play!" Is he in a down position? "Good down!" Every time you see him doing something you like, give it a name and praise it. This is much better than the old method of scolding him every time he does something you don't like.

Rewards

Praise is good, and pugs love it because it means they're getting attention, but they'll work even harder if food is involved. A reward can be anything your pug likes, from a special toy to a favorite game, but most of them prefer food, glorious food. Rewards can take two forms: instant gratification (you give your pug a bit of cheese when he sits on command) and delayed gratification (you give him a bite of hot dog or pull out a favorite toy after he finishes a fabulous freestyle routine). Both types of rewards work, and both should be used so your pug doesn't learn to expect only one thing from you.

Types of Treats

Training treats have specific characteristics. First, use something that your pug doesn't get every day. You want the reward to be special, something he'll really want to work for. Choose a treat that has a strong aroma and is easily swallowed. You don't want to stand there all day while he chews it up. So rawhides and jerky are out; cut-up hot dogs, small cubes of cheese, dried liver, and cat treats such as Pounce are in.

Click, Click, Click

A signal that means "That's it; here comes a reward" is called a conditioned reinforcer. Behaviorists in the 1940s and 1950s used conditioned reinforcers, and in the 1960s marine mammal trainers began using the sound of a whistle to train whales, dolphins, seals, and polar bears. Dog trainers popularized the method in the early 1990s, substituting clickers for whistles. Today, clicker training is a positive force in dog training.

Using a Clicker

Clicker training, also known by the technical term "operant conditioning," is based on the tendency to repeat an action that has a positive result. The sound the clicker makes is paired with a reward such as a treat. By clicking exactly when your pug does something you like and then following the click with a treat or other reward, you can teach him any number of behaviors, from a simple sit to the complicated moves of a dance routine.

 Fact

A clicker is a small plastic box with a metal strip that makes a clicking sound when pressed. If you don't have a clicker, you can instead snap your fingers or jingle a chain. Any such sound can serve as a bridge between the dog's action and a reward.

A clicker works by instantly reinforcing your pug's action. Timing is everything in training, and giving a click is much faster than saying "Good dog!" A clicker also allows you to shape specific behaviors that might otherwise be difficult to teach, such as tilting the head or giving a high-five. It's a great way to teach your pug tricks to perform in his therapy work, routines for freestyle events, or even just to sit pretty for the camera.

Loading the Clicker

Before you can use a clicker effectively, you need to teach your pug that "treat" follows "click." This is called "loading the clicker." To do it, simply click, then give your pug a treat. Repeat twenty or thirty times in a row. Your pug will soon make the connection.

 Question?

When my pug does something really good, should I click several times to encourage him? No. Click only once, at the exact instant your pug is doing what you want. The click tells him that he's been successful and will be rewarded.

You can start to click and treat every time your pug does something you like—sits, lies down, comes toward you, potties outside—even if it's something he's done on his own and not at your command. Carry a clicker and treats with you so you can always reinforce the behaviors you want.

Clicker Tips

Once your pug understands a particular behavior and starts doing it on his own, you can give the action a name: sit, down, roll over. Give the cue word, and click if your pug responds correctly during or after the time you say it. This works for hand signals as well as verbal commands.

As your pug's skills improve, ask him to try a little harder. Click and treat only for a straighter sit, a longer down, or a come from farther away than usual. This allows you to shape the exact behavior you want. With a clicker and the help of a trainer or a good book on clicker training, such as *The Only Dog Training Book You'll Ever*

Need, by Gerilyn J. Bielakiewicz, you can teach your pug all kinds of things. For more dog-training resources, see Appendix A (groups and organizations) or Appendix B (books and magazines).

Training Success List

- Always use positive motivational training.
- Pugs work best for food rewards and praise.
- Never force or bully your pug unless you just want him to become stubborn.
- Give your pug lots of opportunities to please you by showing him what you want.
- Your level of commitment and the amount of time you spend working with your pug determine how successful you'll be.

Basic Obedience and Manners

PUGS ARE TOO CUTE TO NEED MANNERS, aren't they? Absolutely not! If anything, you need to teach your pug manners simply so he won't run roughshod over you and the rest of the household. Manners make the pug, and you'll be glad to have a dog that you can take anywhere, secure in the knowledge that his charm and behavior will win friends for both of you.

Basic Commands

All pugs should know the six magic words: sit, down, come, stay, and walk nice. Start teaching these behaviors the first day you bring your pug pup home. He's more than capable of learning them at eight weeks of age, and early practice will give him a head start in puppy kindergarten. Before you get started, here are a few simple rules for training your pug:

- Keep training sessions short—no more than five or ten minutes in length.
- Train when you're in a good mood.
- Use tone of voice to guide your pug—low and firm for commands; high-pitched and happy for praise.
- Train where you won't be interrupted by the kids, television, or phone.

- End training before you get frustrated, and always after your pug has done something successfully.

Include the entire family in the training process. Everyone should understand how to give commands to the dog, and your dog should respond to anyone in the family who gives him a command. This also helps ensure that your pug fully understands each command.

Sit

The sit position is one of the most natural things for a dog to do, and it's easy to teach. The sit command has any number of uses, from preventing your pug from jumping up on people to waiting politely instead of mauling you while you prepare his meal. You'll also need it if you plan to compete in obedience.

 Essential

At mealtime, ask your pug to sit before you put his dish down, and praise him when he does. He will learn to respect and love you as the person who provides his food. As a bonus, he'll develop polite eating habits, a must in this breed.

How to Start

Before you start, make sure you have some training treats on hand. Take one treat and hold it just above your pug's nose. Slowly raise your hand straight up. He should automatically go into a sit position as he looks up to see where that treat is going. As soon as he's sitting, say "Good sit!" in an enthusiastic tone of voice, and give him the treat. Repeat these steps three to five times, then stop. You don't want your pug to lose interest in the game. You can schedule several of these five-minute training sessions throughout the day.

Once your pug starts to understand what you're asking, tell him to sit without the accompanying hand signal. It's okay if he doesn't respond. Just walk away, and try again later. There's no need to scold him; withdrawing your attention is punishment enough.

Teaching Sit with a Clicker

Using a clicker to teach the sit command is as easy as pie. Any time you see your pug sitting, click, then give him a treat. Add the verbal command "Sit!" or a hand signal (a raised hand, with fingers closed) once your pug starts to sit every time he realizes you have a treat in your hand. Give the command just before he moves into the sit position.

When your pug understands that the word "Sit" and the action of sitting are linked, begin rewarding only the sits that you ask for. Again, if he doesn't perform on the first try, don't repeat the command. Walk away.

 Fact

Another way to correct your dog is to teach him a word or sound that means "Wrong. Try again." You can use the words "Wrong" or "Cold" or a game-show-buzzer sound, such as "Aaack!" Whatever you choose, say it in a neutral, not angry, tone of voice. Avoid using the word "No," which has a negative tone and can discourage your pug from trying again.

Practicing the Sit Command

When your pug starts getting good at the sit command, ask him to work a little harder. Reward only the fastest sits or the straightest sits. Step away from him and expect him to remain in place. Gradually increase the distance you move from him until he remains sitting even if you are across the room. (This helps you work into the stay command.)

Practice sits in different parts of the house so your pug doesn't think he only has to sit in the training area. Good places to teach him to sit are at the front door, in the kitchen before giving a meal, and out in public (the checkout line at the pet supply store, for instance). To increase the length of a sit, pause before you click. Gradually increase the amount of time between the sit and the click.

 **Essential**

Always give praise when your pug does something good, regardless of whether you give a treat. Eventually you will be able to phase out the treats, and your pug will respond just to the praise.

To Sit or Not to Sit?

If you plan to show your pug in conformation, some handlers advise against teaching the sit. Dogs aren't supposed to sit in the show ring, and some dogs make that very mistake because they're used to sitting when their people are otherwise occupied. On the other hand, some trainers teach the dog to differentiate when it's okay to sit and when it's not by using a different lead for obedience training and conformation training or simply by practicing in a ringlike setting so the dog learns that it's not okay to sit in that situation.

Down

The down command is a little more difficult to teach than the sit. It puts the dog in a submissive position, which many dogs prefer to avoid. Nonetheless, down has the same benefits as sit, and it's a must if you plan to compete in obedience trials.

The traditional way to teach the down command is by placing a treat in front of the dog's nose and then lowering it between the legs and pulling it forward. With a dog as low to the ground as a pug, it helps to sit on the floor when you do this. The theory is that the dog will automatically go into the down position in an attempt to follow the treat. If he does, say "Good down!" and give the treat. Follow with the same techniques you used to teach the sit command.

◀ This pug demonstrates his ability to sit, a command every pug should master.

Teaching Down with a Clicker

If the previous approach doesn't work, move on to the clicker method, which usually works very quickly. Click and treat every time you see your pug in a down position. Then start to add the verbal command "Down!" or a hand signal—a downward sweep of the hand. Give the command or hand signal as he moves into the down position. Again, once your pug understands that the word "Down" and the action of lying down are linked, begin rewarding only the downs that you ask for.

Practicing the Down Command

When your pug knows the down command, gradually increase the length of the down, just as you did for the sit. Any time he breaks the down and comes toward you, put him back in the same place and start over. Practice doing the down in different areas of the house, in public, and on different surfaces: the floor, grass, asphalt. Use it when you're on the phone, working at the computer, or having dinner with the family. Avoid using the down command when you want your pug to get off something. If he's jumping up on someone or you want him off the furniture, say "Off," not "Down."

Stay

When your pug has mastered the sit and down commands, you can start working on the stay command. Give the sit or down command. Standing next to or in front of your dog, place your hand palm up, toward his face, and say "Stay," using a firm, low tone of voice. Back up a few inches. Wait a couple of seconds and say "Good stay!" and give him a treat. Then give a release word, such as "Okay," meaning that it's all right for him to move. If he moves before you release him, put him back in place and start over.

Practicing the Stay Command

Schedule a training session for the stay command a few times each day. It's a good idea to practice this command when your pug is already tired or calm. Try it after a meal, walk, or playtime.

 **Fact**

Pug people joke about how untrainable their dogs are, but in reality your pug is smart and wants to please or at least entertain you. If you base your training techniques on his love of attention and food, you're sure to be successful in teaching him almost anything you want.

Gradually increase the length of time you ask your dog to stay by just a few seconds. Work up to ten seconds, fifteen seconds, thirty seconds, and so on. Start increasing the distance you move away from him as well. Remember, if he breaks the stay, put him back where he was and start over. There's no need to scold him.

Strengthening the Stay Command

When your pug appears to have a good understanding of the stay command, add some distractions to test his mastery of it. Drop your keys, clap your hands, ask someone else to walk by him. Praise him ("Good stay!") and give a treat whenever he ignores a distraction and remains in place. If he breaks the stay, put him back and start over.

Gradually increase the level of distractions by having someone ring the doorbell or walk another dog nearby. Jump up and down and meow like a cat. Practice indoors and outdoors so he'll encounter different types of distractions that you didn't set up (cars driving by, kids playing next door). Eventually, your pug should remain in position until you release him.

 Alert!

Whatever command you're working on, pay attention to how your dog is progressing. If he doesn't respond or frequently breaks the command, go back a few steps in training to a point where he was successful. Work from there to improve his mastery of the command.

Once you're sure he has a solid stay, see if you can teach him to stay even if you're not in the room. Start leaving the room after giving the command. This works best if you have someone else in the room who can put him back in place if he tries to follow you. Assuming he stays, wait thirty seconds and then go back and praise him. Gradually increase the length of time you're out of the room.

Come

Besides being generally useful in retrieving your pug from wherever he might be nosing around, the come command can save your pug's life if he's ever in danger. Use it to call him for dinner, to get him ready to go somewhere, or to get him out of the path of a speeding car or lowering garage door. The come command is easy to teach. The trick is making sure your pug responds to it instantly, every time. This takes time, consistency, and plenty of praise and other rewards.

 fact

The obedience trial term for the come command is "recall." You want your pug to have a perfect recall.

Start teaching the come command as soon as you bring your puppy or dog home. Puppies, especially, will follow you instinctively. Use this behavior to your advantage by saying, "[Dog's name], come!" every time your pup is headed toward you anyway. Use your most excited tone of voice, and reinforce the verbal command with body language by kneeling down and spreading your arms wide in a welcoming gesture. When Pugsley reaches you, give him lots of praise and petting. This is one command your dog just can't get wrong—except by not coming.

Using a Clicker to Teach the Come Command

Start at short distances of two or three feet. Click every time you see your pug walking toward you, and reward him when he reaches you. Add the verbal command "[Dog's name], come!" as he heads in your direction.

Practicing the Come Command

Gradually start calling your pug from a greater distance. Vary the rewards he gets for coming so that he'll always want to see what's going to happen when he reaches you. In addition to praise and hugs, good rewards might be an extra-special treat or the offer of a favorite toy that's not always available. Practice this command several times a day, every day, throughout your pug's life.

Reinforcing the Come Command

One way to make the come command fun for your pug is to play chase games. Encourage your puppy to chase you as you run around the yard or through the house. You want him to think that following you is a great game. On the other hand, avoid playing the game where you chase the dog. That only teaches him that running away is fun. If your puppy is running away from you, turn the tables by running in the opposite direction and encouraging him to follow you. When he does, give him lots of praise and petting.

To further reinforce that coming to you is a good thing, use the come command every time you feed your pug, take him for a walk, or initiate a play session. "[Dog's name], come! Dinner!" "[Dog's name], come! Let's go for a walk!" If he's playing, call him, give him a treat, and let him go back to what he was doing.

Testing the Come Command

When you're sure your pug understands the come command, start testing him in controlled situations. Practice in a confined area or make sure he has a fifteen- to thirty-foot clothesline attached to his collar or harness. Let him wander off. When he's not paying attention to you, call him, using a happy tone of voice. He should respond right away. If he doesn't, wiggle the line to encourage him to come toward you (don't drag or jerk him). Give lots of praise when he reaches you.

 Essential

Never call your pug and then scold him because he was doing something wrong (such as knocking over the bathroom trash can). That's the quickest way to teach him not to come. Instead, praise him every time he comes to your call. It's also a good idea not to call him for something he dislikes, such as getting his nails trimmed. Go get him instead.

If he's not wearing a leash, go get him and walk him to the place where you gave the command, saying "Come" as you walk. When you reach the spot, say "Good come!" Practice until he comes reliably, no matter how far away he is or how interesting his other activity. As his recalls improve, start teaching him to sit in front of you or at your side when he reaches you. When he's mastered that, reward him only for straight sits or only for very fast responses.

Walk Nicely on a Leash

Dogs love to sniff, even short-nosed dogs such as pugs. And as low to the ground as a pug is, his nose is always alerting him to interesting things to smell. Then there are other dogs to meet and new people to greet. All of these distractions can make for an unpleasant walk if your pug is always pulling on his leash in search of the next best thing.

 **Fact**

Use your pug's name as part of the command any time you want him to move; for instance, with "Come" or "Let's go." Any time he needs to stay in place ("Sit" or "Down"), use only the command word, without his name.

You can, however, teach your pug to walk nicely without pulling. He doesn't have to walk sedately at your side in a formal heel position (except in the obedience ring), but not pulling is a must. You always want some slack in the leash.

Teaching Your Pug to Walk Nicely

Attach the leash to his collar or harness. Hold it in your left hand with your pug standing on your left. Encourage him to walk forward by saying, "[Dog's name], let's go" (or whatever phrase you choose). Praise him or click and treat (or praise, then click and treat) when he starts to walk with you. He'll probably stop to eat the treat. When he's finished, begin again, this time clicking after more steps forward. Click only when he's moving.

As you walk, reward your pug with praise or a click and treat any time he is paying attention to you and not pulling. Keep his attention on you by smiling and saying, "Watch me!" Gradually increase the length of time he walks before you give a reward. Vary the rate at which you give rewards so he's motivated to walk nicely all the time.

Any time your pug starts pulling, stop walking, but be careful not to jerk him to a stop. When he looks at you and there's slack in the leash, start up again, reminding him to focus on you ("Watch me!") and rewarding him periodically for walking nicely without pulling. Stop and start again as necessary.

Practice Walking Nicely

Practice inside your home, in the yard, and around your neighborhood. Introduce distractions such as other people or dogs walking by to help your pug learn to stay focused on you. Schedule walks after playtime so your pug is less likely to have energy to pull. Here's one trainer's test for mastery of the art of walking nicely: when you can walk your dog while holding an open cup of liquid without spilling it (don't try this with something hot!).

Teaching Manners

MANNERS ARE MUCH MORE than knowing a few basic commands. They include understanding the boundaries of behavior that exist in a human environment. Without them, your pug will be most unpleasant to live with. To ensure a happy relationship, let him know who's the boss and teach him the household rules he needs to know.

Laying Down the Law

Among themselves, dogs abide by a strict set of rules of behavior, so don't let your pug get away with being a free spirit. It's his nature to follow a leader—or to be a leader himself if no one else steps in to take the role. Your pug will happily run the household if you let him, so prevent this by establishing yourself as the one in charge. You do this by setting boundaries and establishing rules. If he knows what the rules are, and that you expect him to follow them, he'll be much less likely to get into trouble. Here are some ways to show that you're the leader of the pug pack:

- Show your pug what he can and can't do.
- Expect your pug to behave toward you in certain ways, such as not grabbing treats out of your hand or stampeding you at mealtime.

- Train your pug so he learns to respond to your commands the first time you give them.

These are kind but effective ways to teach your pug that you're in charge.

Another way to establish leadership is by requiring your pug to perform a command before you do something for him. This is the canine version of the magic word "please." For instance, ask your pug to sit before you feed him. Then put down his food, releasing him with an "Okay!" or "Chow!"

 **Essential**

Pugs have a relatively short attention span and lose interest if asked to do the same thing over and over. Give your pug a break after about fifteen minutes to do something he wants to do.

Other ways your pug can show respect are by moving out of your way or waiting for you to go first out the door. Teach him to wait before you go out the door, until you start walking, or until you tell him it's okay to jump in the car. Practice waiting at curbs before you cross the street. Wait is a variation on the stay command and is taught in much the same way (as described on page 214). You're simply using it in specific circumstances and giving it a different name. Or you can just use the stay command.

Regular training sessions also help your pug understand his place in the family pack. They don't have to take long. Spending five minutes in the morning and five minutes in the evening working on obedience commands will do wonders for your pug's attitude. Don't forget to praise him for a good performance. Being a leader means letting your dog know when he's done a good job, as well as when he's made a mistake.

Working for Attention

Pugs love attention, and they'll demand it all the time if you let them. Most of us would like nothing better than to spend all day playing with Pugsley, but it's just not possible. The sooner your pug learns that, the better. Teach him that he gets attention on your schedule, not his.

 Question?

What's the best way to help my pug enjoy our training sessions? Try to make training seem like a game rather than work. Keep things upbeat, offer lots of praise for even small achievements, and work toys and treats into the training routine.

If he constantly demands attention, petting, or playtime from you by jumping up, nudging you with his nose, or pawing at you, respond in one of two ways. First, you can ignore him. It's your prerogative to initiate attention-giving. Your other option is to require him to perform a command such as sit or down before you grant his request for attention.

Finally, as much as you love your pug, there will be times when you need to get things done around the house. If he's underfoot, don't be reluctant to crate him for an hour or two. Being in the crate gives him a chance to relax on his own and keeps him out of trouble.

Pretty Is As Pretty Does

Just a few simple commands will help your pug become a pleasure to live with. They are off, place, leave it, drop it, and wait. You'll be amazed at how useful they are around the house and out in public. They will keep your pug polite and safe.

Off

There's nothing cuter than a pug puppy jumping up for attention. A pug adult jumping up for attention is almost as cute. Nevertheless, this can be an annoying behavior, especially when the dog's toenails scratch your bare legs. Teaching your pug to sit for attention is a much better option.

The main difficulty you'll find in teaching off is that lots of people think jumping up is cute, so it's hard to persuade them to participate in the training process. Don't let them undermine your training by saying "Oh, it's okay" when your pug jumps on them. Explain that you're teaching him not to behave that way, and ask for their cooperation.

When to Use "Off"

Use the off command when your pug is jumping up on people or to move him off a piece of furniture. Don't use it interchangeably with the down command. The two words mean different things, and you want to avoid confusing your dog.

Teaching "Off"

Any time you see that your pug is about to body-slam you, say "Off," turn aside, and walk away so he misses his target (you'll have to move fast). Before he recoups, tell him to sit, and praise or pet him for doing so. This shows your pug that he gets attention when he sits, not when he jumps up. Another way to respond to jumping up is to ignore the dog (fold your arms, turn your head away from him, and stand like a tree) until he sits on his own. The second he does, click and treat him, saying "Good off!" Whichever method you use, your pug needs to learn that "Off" means four feet on the floor.

Your pug probably greets guests by jumping on them as they come through the door. Put a stop to this by practicing sits and downs at the door. Ask family members or neighbors to help. Have them knock or ring the doorbell. Put the dog in a sit/stay or down/stay and open the door. Praise or click and treat if your pug stays where he is. If he jumps up, use your "try again" word or sound and start over. Don't let anyone pet or talk to him until he performs correctly.

Off the Furniture

Once your pug understands that "Off" means all feet on the floor, you can also use the command to tell him to get off the furniture. If you need to make up the bed or change the sheet on the sofa that protects it from pug hair, firmly say "Off" and point to the floor. If he complies, praise him ("Good off!") or click and treat the behavior. Also say "Off" any time you see him getting off anything so that he learns to make the connection between his action and the command.

 **Essential**

Be sure everyone in the family knows how to respond to jumping up. If you're not all consistent, your pug will take advantage of the chaos and go his own way. Never use unnecessary and painful physical corrections such as stepping on the dog's toes or kneeing him in the chest.

If he doesn't make the connection, help him off the furniture by luring him with a treat or toy or gently guiding him with your hands or the leash, saying "Off" as you do so. Then praise him or click and treat once he's on the floor. Use the treat lure only two or three times in the beginning or your pug will start to demand a treat in exchange for getting off the sofa or bed. In this case, the treat's only purpose is as a lure to get the training process started.

To practice some more, encourage your dog back on the forbidden furniture by patting it and saying "Up!" This serves two purposes. It allows you to repeat the off command sequence, and it starts the process of teaching your pug that it's only okay to get on the furniture when you invite him. As he improves, you can pair the verbal command with a hand signal, such as a sweeping motion of your forearm.

If you want, you can teach your pug that he's allowed on the furniture only when you invite him up. And before you invite him up, require him to perform a sit or down command. Any other time you spot him on the sofa or bed, use the off command. You can also designate certain pieces of furniture as "his." Invite him up only on the designated furniture, and consistently use the off command for everything else.

Essential

There's no point at which you can rest on your laurels and say that your pug is trained. He's always learning, both good things and bad. Continue training your pug throughout his life.

Go to Your Bed/Place

This is an easy command to teach. It comes in handy when you need to put your pug in his safe place before you go out somewhere or at bedtime. Use this command any time you want your pug in his crate, on his bed, or in his safe room.

Every time you put your pug in his crate, say "Crate" or "Bed" in a happy tone of voice and give him a treat. It doesn't have to be a large biscuit; a training-size treat will do just fine. You can also click and treat and say "Crate" every time you see him go into his crate on his own. Your pug will quickly learn that the word "Crate" means good things. With this very food-oriented breed, it won't take long before all you have to do is say the magic word and he'll go running for the crate.

To transfer this command to a dog bed or safe room, use the same technique. Say "Bed!" or "Place!" every time you see him there and praise him ("Good bed!") or click and treat him for being there. Then practice giving the command, rewarding him when he responds correctly and taking him to the designated area and repeating the command if he doesn't.

Leave It/Drop It

Dogs are highly oral, meaning they like to pick things up in their mouths. Pugs, especially, will taste anything in the hope that it's food—and what they consider food can range from decaying animal carcasses or old bones they've found on the ground to your favorite pair of shoes. To ensure that your pug doesn't eat or chew on anything he shouldn't, teach the commands "Leave it" and "Drop it."

Leave It

Practice the leave-it command on walks. Any time your pug shows interest in something you don't want him to have, say "Leave it" in a happy tone of voice. If he turns to look at you, click and treat him for paying attention to you and walk away from the object.

 **Question?**

I'm firm, so why does my pug still ignore commands? Like most of us, pugs hate being ordered around. Firmness and consistency have their place in training pugs, but your pug needs to feel as if there's something in it for him before he'll comply with your desires. Try different rewards to see what motivates him.

Another way to teach "Leave it" is to have some extra-special treats on hand as you walk. If your pug stops to nose or chew on something unsavory, show him the treat and then move it in the direction you want to go. When he follows the treat, say "Leave it" as you walk away. Give the treat when you're several feet away from the item he was interested in. Your pug will learn that "Leave it" means to move away from something.

When your pug starts making the connection between "Leave it" and moving on, practice the command without the treat. Test your dog's willingness to obey by mining the walkway with really enticing items. Give lots of praise every time he responds correctly to the words "Leave it."

If you want to practice "Leave it" another way, hold a good-smelling treat in a closed hand. Hold out the hand so your pug knows you have a treat. If he starts to sniff, jump on you, paw at your hand, or nudge you in an attempt to get the treat, say "Leave it." Don't repeat the command and don't open your hand. As soon as he stops trying to get the treat, say "Good leave it!" and give him the treat. Practice until your dog ignores the hand with the treat as soon as you say "Leave it."

You can also teach leave it using the tree method. Set up distractions with items your pug will want to get, such as treats, bones, or an empty food carton or fast-food wrapper. Stand just out of range of the object with your dog on a leash, and let your dog make all the attempts he wants to get it. While he does, simply stand silently—like a tree. As soon as he stops trying to reach the item and either sits or looks toward you, click and treat, saying "Good leave it" as you do so.

Essential

Your pug is never too old to learn good manners. An older pug may even learn more quickly because he has a longer attention span than a puppy. Be consistent, and use positive reinforcement to teach him what you want him to know.

Continue this scenario until your pug learns that he gets rewarded for staying with you. Then you can increase the difficulty of the exercise by requiring him to walk by the item before you click and treat. Any time he tries to go for the item, ignore him until he returns his attention to you. It helps to have an assistant who can whisk the item out of the dog's reach so you don't have to pull the dog away from it. In advanced "leave it" training, walk your pug closer to the object, add objects that are even more desirable, or have a helper offer the dog some type of food. This helps ensure that your pug will leave anything you tell him to.

Drop It

To teach the drop-it command, first give your pug something he likes, such as a soft toy. Don't give him anything he shouldn't be chewing on in the first place. When he has the item in his mouth, take it in your hand and say "Drop it." If he lets go, give him lots of praise; then return the item to him. Let him have it again for a minute; then repeat the command. Practice with different types of items so he learns to drop anything you tell him to.

If he doesn't drop it, gently remove the item from his mouth, saying "Drop it" as you do so. When it's out of his mouth, say "Good drop it!" Then return it to him and start over again.

The other way to approach a refusal is with an offer of a trade. If your pug doesn't want to give something up, show him another favorite treat or toy. If he drops the item in his mouth to get the new object, say "Drop it" as he does so, then praise him and give him the treat. Then give back the original item, assuming it's not something harmful. This teaches your pug that he gets rewarded for obeying drop it, both by a treat and by getting the first item back.

 **Fact**

If your pug flat out refuses to drop something, try picking him up. Most dogs become distracted by this and lose their grip on the object. Grab it up and say "Good drop it," then put him back down.

Practice frequently until you're sure your pug associates the action of dropping something with the words "Drop it." Then you can start using it as a command. Gradually reduce the number of times you reward him for responding until finally you're giving only praise.

Wait

Start teaching this command at doorways, either in your home or outside at the car. Take your pug to the door, and tell him to sit. Palm up in front of his face, say "Wait." Then start to open the door. If he moves, close the door and start over. Repeat until he remains in the sit position as you open the door. Click and treat every time he waits without moving. When you're ready, say "Okay" and let him follow you out the door or get into the car. Practice this command every day until your pug stays steady as a rock until you give the okay to move out.

▲ This pug is performing a recall. After staying on command, the dog goes to the handler once called.

CHAPTER 18

Socializing Your Pug

YOUR PUG IS A NATURAL PARTY ANIMAL. He's born to be friendly toward people and other animals. Nonetheless, he still needs to learn about the world around him so he can experience new situations with confidence. The act of introducing your pug to new people, places, sights, and sounds is called socialization, and it's a key factor in your pug's healthy development. A well-socialized pug can go anywhere with you, from park to palace, and do you proud.

In the Home

You can start socializing your pug at home right away. Encourage everyone in the family to give him lots of attention and affection. Pet him, and call him by name to accustom him to your presence and voice. Introduce him to the neighbors and to delivery people who regularly visit your home. Invite neighborhood kids to come play with him, and show them how to hold and pet him. Let him meet other dogs as long as you know they are vaccinated.

Your pug begins learning about his environment the minute he walks into your house. Some of the things he'll learn about (if he hasn't already encountered them at the breeder's home) are vacuum cleaners, blenders, doorbells, fireworks, and thunderstorms. Be careful how you react the first time your pug pup encounters these things. He'll take his cue for future behavior from your response.

Be matter-of-fact, whether he reacts with surprise or fear or curiosity. "That's just the dishwasher/vacuum cleaner/blender." Don't comfort him if he seems frightened by the noise. Your reassurance will make him think that there really must be something to be afraid of. It's a sure way to create a dog that's afraid of loud noises.

 **Essential**

Introduce your puppy to different surfaces around the home and in public. He should be comfortable walking on or through grass, concrete, gravel, asphalt, grates, slippery floors, stairs, sand or dirt, rocks, snow, and puddles.

Among the noises your pug should take in stride are the television and stereo, clattering pots and pans, dropped books or other items, whistles and sirens, balloons popping, party noisemakers, popcorn popping, and electric saws and drills. Reward your pug any time he shows curiosity about a sound—if he cocks his head or approaches the vacuum cleaner, for instance. Calm behavior in the presence of loud noise warrants a treat and praise.

Out and About

Walking your pug is important for his physical health, but did you know that it provides emotional benefits as well? Your daily walk is a great way to introduce your pug to everything he'll encounter in your neighborhood: other animals, birds at a nearby lake or park, children on bicycles and skateboards, and more. During walks, your pug can sniff out where other dogs lift their legs, what paths the local cats take, and whether a strange dog has entered the area. You might not be able to tell any of these things, but your pug's nose, flat as it is, smells all and knows all. A walk is also a good opportunity to practice obedience skills and manners, such as sitting, waiting at curbs before crossing the street, not pulling on the leash, and not jumping up on people.

Meeting People and Dogs

As you meet people along the way, give your pug an opportunity to greet them. This is a great way to practice walking up to people and greeting them politely by sitting instead of jumping up. If a person you encounter also has a dog, that's another opportunity for socialization. Keep leashes slack so the two dogs can sniff each other without feeling tension at the end of the lead. When owners pull leads tight, it transmits their own anxiety to the dog at the other end. Your pug should look forward to meeting other people and dogs.

 Essential

Be patient and persistent, and give lots of praise when your pug greets people happily, shows curiosity, or remains calm in a new situation. Don't expose him to a bunch of different things all at once. Any dog would be overwhelmed if confronted by a vacuum cleaner, blender, popcorn popper, and electric saw all going at once!

Urban Dog

City-dwelling pugs will experience traffic noise and crowds of people on a daily basis. Accustom them to these sounds early on. A dog that's startled by sudden noises or the approach of a stranger might bolt and be lost or hit by a car. As soon as your veterinarian says it's okay for your pup to go out in public, start taking him on walks that will expose him to the sights and sounds of the city. You can do this as early as eight to ten weeks of age as long as he doesn't come in contact with other dogs and his paws don't touch the ground: carry him in your arms or in one of the many designer bags, backpacks, or front packs made for carrying small dogs. One way to carry your pug pup is in a large straw shoulder bag. He can ride anywhere in comfort and can pop his head out to say hello or see what's going on. Carrying your pug this way is a great bonding and socialization opportunity.

Different Folks, Different Strokes

Introduce your pug to people of different ethnicities. Let him see people doing different activities, such as walking, running, bicycling, skateboarding, hopping, crawling, or swimming in a pool. He should see people using walkers, wheelchairs, or crutches, and people carrying packages or pulling suitcases or wagons. Take him to outdoor shopping centers, pet supply stores, parks, and beaches.

Preventing Separation Anxiety

Socialization doesn't always have a social component. Learning to be alone is another facet of teaching your pug about life. This is especially important if your pug will be by himself during the day. Dogs that don't learn to stay alone comfortably can develop separation anxiety, which often results in destructive behavior and emotional problems.

Gradually accustom your pug to being left alone. Start by leaving him in a room for just a few minutes. If he has a habit of following you from room to room, put him in his crate or close the door. Gradually increase the time you're out of the room. Graduate to leaving the house to go into the yard or get something out of the car. Put your puppy in his crate or safe area where he can't do any damage.

 Essential

Dogs are social animals. Give your pug plenty of attention and playtime when you are at home. He's not the kind of dog that will be happy left to his own devices.

When you're away, leave a favorite soft chewie or other toy to help prevent boredom. Rotate toys on a regular basis so your pug doesn't get bored with his entertainment options. Turn on a radio or television so he has something to listen to. If you're going to be gone for more than four hours, take him for a walk just before you leave so he has a chance to potty and get a little exercise.

When you leave, don't make a big production of saying goodbye. You want your pug to view your comings and goings as normal occurrences. If you act anxious and give him lots of hugs and kisses before you leave, he'll be disappointed when you leave. Instead, put him in his crate or safe place, give him a treat and toy, and say goodbye in a matter-of-fact tone of voice. Behave the same way when you come home. Greet him calmly, and after you get settled, take him outside for a play session.

Is Your Pug a Shrinking Violet?

It's unusual for a pug not to be a bold and confident people-greeter, but it can happen if a pup isn't well socialized by the breeder. If your pug hides behind your legs when other people or dogs come around, you'll need to help him develop more confidence and trust. Gradually introduce him to new people or animals in carefully controlled situations.

Before you introduce anyone to your wallflower puglet, lay down the following guidelines:

- Ask the person to remain still and quiet, not petting the dog or making eye contact.
- Let the pup approach on his own terms, even if it takes a few minutes.
- Give him plenty of time to sniff and circle the person.
- When the puppy seems comfortable, the new person can slowly crouch down so she's at dog level.
- Give her a treat to offer the puppy.

If your pug seems more confident after this introductory dance, the new person can slowly reach out to scratch the dog beneath the chin. She should avoid patting the dog on the head; lots of dogs view this as an aggressive move. Have the person continue giving small treats, so your dog learns that meeting people is fun and rewarding. Repeat this pattern every time your pug meets someone new.

Praise your shy pug any time he's willing to approach someone, be petted, or take a treat. Ignore any fearful behavior. Whatever you do, don't make soothing, reassuring noises when he shows fear. This only encourages him to believe that there's something to be afraid of.

Alert!

Never force your dog to go up to someone he's afraid of. Fearful dogs that feel trapped may bite. Just as bad, your pug will no longer trust you as the person who protects him from scary things.

If your pug is anxious around other dogs, start by introducing him—one at a time—to dogs that you know are very friendly and easygoing. It helps if the other dog is smaller than your dog, so he'll feel less threatened, but that's not always possible with a pug. As his confidence grows, gradually introduce him to bigger dogs, rowdier dogs, and dogs of different breeds.

Play Dates

Even well-socialized pugs can benefit from regular play dates with other dogs, ideally other pugs. This is especially true if your pug is an only dog. And playing with other dogs isn't just fun and games. It's also a great way for your pug to learn proper dog etiquette from older, more experienced dogs. A play group is a good place for you to meet and talk to other dog owners and share information about behavior, health, and nutrition. It's nice to have a support group you can count on when you have questions about or problems with your dog.

Play Group Ideas

To find or set up a pug play group, talk to people in your neighborhood or training class who might be interested in getting together on a weekly or monthly basis. You can also find like-minded pug owners in your area by posting a suggestion for a dog play group on a pug e-mail list or asking the local pug club to print your request in its newsletter or on the Web site. Pick a date, time, and place that's convenient for most of the people interested, and send out an e-mail reminder a week beforehand. Some play groups even arrange an occasional speaker, such as a veterinarian, to speak on such topics as new vaccination protocols or raw diets. Play groups can also form spontaneously at dog parks or when a couple of pug lovers decide to get together on the spur of the moment with their dogs.

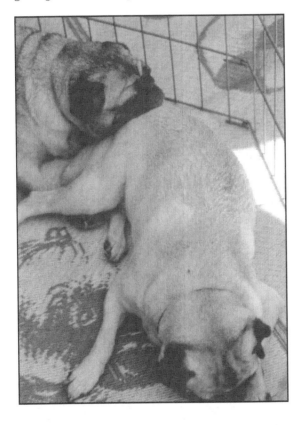

◀ These socialized dogs are able to lie comfortably with each other.

Dog Park Etiquette

Rules and manners make life better for everyone, dogs and humans. Here are some guidelines to keeping things civil and healthy on play dates or at dog parks:

- Dogs should be friendly and well trained.
- Keep your dog on leash until you're sure of his behavior.
- Pick up your dog's waste and dispose of it appropriately.
- Don't let rough play get out of hand.
- Make your apologies and take your dog home if he behaves aggressively or starts a fight.
- If your female pug isn't spayed, leave her at home when she's in heat.
- Bring water for your dog.
- Be sure your pug is fully vaccinated before taking him to a dog park.

Visits to the Veterinarian

Besides being necessary for good health, a visit to the veterinarian is a great way to socialize your pug. He'll meet new people, sniff strange smells, and hear yowling cats and barking dogs. Strangers will handle him, which can be stressful for some dogs, but it is a good learning experience. There are plenty of ways you can help prepare your pug for the veterinary visit so that it's a happy one for him (except, of course, for the indignity of having his temperature taken or the momentary pain of a vaccination). First, stay calm yourself. If your pug senses that you're nervous about the visit, he'll pick up on your anxiety and reflect it himself. Project a calm, happy demeanor.

How to Behave at the Veterinarian's Office

If you've been examining your pug at home by looking in his ears, examining his teeth and eyes, playing with his paws, and touching his tail and other parts of his body, he'll be more prepared for a veterinary exam. Have other members of the family examine him too, so that he's used to being touched by different people. Your veterinarian will be grateful that your dog is so easy to handle.

A well-socialized pug walks into the veterinary office with a smile on his face and a wagging tail. To help ensure that your pug enjoys visiting the veterinarian, take him there early and often. Schedule a first visit just on a "getting-to-know-you" basis. The veterinarian can examine your dog, but schedule shots for another time, so there's no painful association with that first office visit. Let staff members give your pug a treat or two to seal the new friendship.

Riding in the Car with Dogs

Going for a ride is a favorite canine activity. Teach your pug car manners so trips will be fun and safe. Car manners include waiting to get in the car until you give the okay, sitting politely in the seat, restrained by a doggie seat belt; riding in a crate without complaint; and not hanging the head out the window and barking at other dogs.

Teach your dog to wait at the car door until you give him the signal to jump in. This gives you time to get his crate arranged or set up his seat belt if necessary. Use the wait command that you learned in Chapter 17.

Yes, it's fun for dogs to hang their head out the window, tongue lolling, but they can be injured by flying debris. Your pug can still enjoy the breeze from a rolled-down window while he's seat-belted or crated.

 Essential

Your dog should always be restrained in some manner in the car. A loose dog can distract you or be thrown through the windshield in the event of a sudden stop or accident. You can get him a doggie seat belt or confine him to his crate.

Have a leash available when you arrive at your destination. Tell your pug to wait, and snap on the leash before you let him out of the car.

To accustom your pug to riding in the car, take him on brief errands. Picking up the dry cleaning, going to the drive-through teller, and visiting the drive-through window at a fast-food restaurant are all great practice rides for your dog. (Don't let those big brown eyes talk you into sharing your burger with him.)

Dealing with Carsickness

Sometimes dogs get motion sickness, just as people do. Signs of carsickness are yawning, whining, drooling, and vomiting. To help your dog recover from a bout of carsickness, roll the window down to let in some fresh air. It can also help if the dog is able to see out the window. If your pug gets carsick in the crate, try restraining him with a doggie seat belt so he can sit up and see the view.

With behavioral modification, you can help your pug overcome carsickness and learn to love car rides. This can take several weeks and—like all dog training—requires patience and practice. Start by just sitting in the car with your dog. If he doesn't show any signs of carsickness just sitting in the car, praise him and give him a treat. Do this for several days.

 Essential

If you try everything and your pug still gets carsick, your veterinarian can prescribe medication to help him ride comfortably. Give it about an hour before you leave the house, or as directed.

After your dog has gone for at least three days without being carsick in a motionless car, get in the car with him and start the engine. Don't go anywhere, just sit in the driveway for a few minutes. Again, praise and treat your dog if he's able to sit in the car without getting sick. Practice this for several days.

If he's doing well with the practice sessions, start the car and back down the driveway. Then drive back in. Continue praising and treating your dog for riding calmly without getting sick. Gradually increase the length of the rides until your pug no longer gets sick in the car.

Becoming Accustomed to New Situations

Dogs are pretty adaptable creatures. They've had to be to live successfully with us for so many millennia. Nonetheless, it helps for them to have some guidance when they encounter new situations. Welcoming a new baby into the home and moving to a new house are two examples of changing circumstances that call for your guidance in helping your pug adapt.

A Baby in the House

Dogs in the wild live in packs structured hierarchically, like families. Every pack member helps to care for pups. Like their wild cousins, pugs love the family "pups," and they can accept babies willingly, if they're prepared for the new arrival. Begin introducing your pug to the idea of a baby months before Junior arrives.

Practice your commands while holding a doll or walking back and forth with it. Wrap the doll in a baby blanket and let the dog sniff it. Praise or reward your pug with treats for behaving calmly toward the "baby." Record the sounds of a baby crying or making other noises and play them frequently so your pug learns to recognize and accept them.

 Alert!

If you haven't obedience-trained your pug, do it before the baby arrives. A dog can accidentally injure mother or baby by jumping up on or running into Mom while she's carrying Junior. Teach your pug to respond faithfully to the commands sit, down, off, stay, and come.

If it's possible, arrange for your pug to meet other babies so he can become accustomed to their scent, sound, and appearance. This helps him learn to recognize them as humans, not toys. With the consent of the parent, let the dog sniff the baby, so he can add "infant smell" to all the other scents stored in his brain. Don't hold the baby out to the dog, or he may mistake it for prey or a toy and try to grab at it. Sit, cuddling the baby in your arms, and have the dog sit in front of you as he sniffs. This is best done only with a pug that is well trained.

First Introductions

Send a blanket impregnated with Junior's scent home before the baby arrives. Let your pug sniff it to his heart's content so he'll recognize the baby's scent. When mother and baby arrive home from the hospital, let your pug greet Mom first, without baby. Introduce baby and dog later, after your pug has had some time to get used to the presence of the new family member.

Alert!

Keep diaper pails tightly sealed so your pug doesn't raid them. He's not being disgusting; he's just helping you hide evidence of the baby from any predators that might be lurking around.

Keep dog-baby introductions gradual and controlled. To make introductions, attach your pug's leash and tell him to sit or down and stay. If you're concerned that the dog might try to lunge at the baby, put a halter or muzzle on him first. (Practice having him wear it before the baby comes home so he's used to it.)

From a distance of ten or fifteen feet, show the dog the baby. If your pug remains calm, the person handling him can gradually walk him closer to the baby. He must remain calm before he's allowed to get within sniffing distance. Again, don't hold the baby out to the dog, but cuddle it close.

Keep your pug on leash for his first few interactions with the baby. Reward him for behaving nicely and calmly around the baby. You want him to associate the baby with good things. Once you're satisfied with his behavior in Junior's presence, you can let him in the room off leash. Put him in a sit/stay or down/stay so he doesn't get underfoot.

Keep Your Pug Happy!

Continue giving your dog attention after the baby arrives. Your pug is used to being an important member of the family. Don't ignore him because you don't have time for him. Involve him in the baby's daily routine by taking the two of them for walks or letting him stay in the room in a down/stay or sit/stay while you perform baby-care chores. With your help, your pug should adjust well to Junior's presence. He'll settle happily by your side as you hold the baby—just waiting for a chance to hop in your lap if you lift Junior up just the slightest bit and give him room.

Moving to a New Home

"Whither thou goest, I go" may well be the canine motto. Dogs are territorial animals, to be sure, but they associate home with their people, not with a specific place. As long as you're there, your pug will be satisfied with any place you choose to live. Nonetheless, there are steps you can take to help him become comfortable in a new home.

 Essential

If you don't have a fenced yard, keep your pug indoors when you aren't around to supervise activity in the yard.

Relocating to a different city or state? Visit the veterinarian to make sure your pug is up-to-date on vaccinations and in good physical health. If he's prone to carsickness, stock up on his prescription medication so he'll have a comfortable car ride or flight to the new location. Ask your veterinarian if he can refer you to a veterinarian in your new area.

For a long car trip, bring a supply of drinking water from your old home. Some dogs get an upset stomach when their water supply changes. Gradually mix in the old water with the new water so your dog can adjust more easily to the change.

If the previous owners had a dog, your pug may feel compelled to mark his new territory. Before you move in, have the carpets cleaned to eliminate or reduce the scent of the other dog. This can also help get rid of any fleas that might be lurking, just waiting to pounce on your pug.

If possible, move your furniture in before you bring your pug to the new house. He'll recognize the smell of your furnishings and feel more comfortable in the new place. When you bring him into the new house, take him first to his food and water dishes and show him his bed or doghouse. Then let him explore his new yard. Maintain his familiar routine as much as possible during the move and the subsequent unpacking.

CHAPTER 19

Behavior Problems

I N GENERAL, pugs are pretty well-behaved dogs. It's rare for them to present their people with serious behavior problems. Most behavior problems occur during adolescence, at six months to eighteen months of age, but they can also develop in response to being left alone too frequently or changes in the family, such as the birth of a baby. There are many positive, successful techniques you can use to solve behavior problems.

Stopping a Problem Before It Starts

It can't be stressed enough: You can't overdo socialization and training when your pug is a puppy. Many behavior problems will never develop—or can be easily solved—if your pug learns early in life that you are in charge, that there are all kinds of interesting sights, sounds, and people in the world, and that doing what you ask always leads to good things. Take your pug to puppy kindergarten, let him run errands with you (as long as you *never* have to leave him in a hot car), sign him up for basic obedience training after puppy kindergarten, and make friends with other pug owners so you can set up regular play dates. Your pug is happy when you're happy, but he needs your guidance to show him how to make that happen.

Problems and What to Do

Like any dog, your pug may bark too much, beg at the table, chew, scavenge through the trash, whine, or become mouthy or nippy. Real aggression is next to nonexistent in pugs, but you should be able to recognize it and know how to handle it if it occurs. Other potential problems include fearful behaviors such as noise shyness and separation anxiety.

Remain patient if your pug develops a behavior problem. Behavior modification isn't accomplished in a day, or even a week. Sometimes it takes months. Continue to show him what you want, and consistently provide firm, fair discipline when he breaks the rules. The following sections describe ways to manage or retrain your pug if he develops one of these common behavior problems.

Barking

Pugs can't talk, but boy do they let you know what they're thinking through the noises they make. They snuffle, snort, bark, and bap. Each of these vocalizations can have a variety of meanings, depending on the situation. Your pug may be greeting you or guests, alerting you that someone's at the door, demanding a meal, or just letting the world know he's bored. It's okay for your pug to bark or whine—everyone needs an outlet for thoughts and emotions—but like all of us, he needs to learn when it's okay to verbalize and when he should keep his mouth shut. With training, your pug can learn the answer to that age-old canine question: to bark or not to bark.

Start training the first day he comes home with you. If he barks when someone comes to the door (either before or after they knock or ring the doorbell), praise him for being alert. If he doesn't bark, help him get into the spirit of things by saying "Who's there? Who is it?" Do the same thing for any other situations in which you want your pug to bark. Obviously you don't want to create a house fire to teach your dog to bark in an emergency; you'll just have to rely on his native intelligence and sense of self-preservation for that.

How to Stop Barking

When your pug has learned to alert you to people approaching the house, teach him how to be quiet. Let him bark once or twice, then say, "Enough" or "Quiet." Your voice should distract him enough that he stops barking. If he does, say "Good quiet" and give him a treat. Gradually extend the length of time between his silence and giving him the treat. Use the same technique to stop whining.

If your pug won't stop barking, change the subject, so to speak. Call him to come to you. Most likely, he'll stop barking and run to see what you want. Then you can praise him for coming instead of yelling at him for barking. It can also help to make a loud noise by clapping your hands or tossing a shake can (a clean, empty soda can with a few pennies or rocks inside it). The sound startles him, he stops barking, and you instantly praise him: "Good quiet!"

 Essential

Never aim the shake can at your pug. You don't want to hit him with it. And it's best if he doesn't see you clap your hands or jiggle the shake can. It should seem as if the noise came out of nowhere.

Why Does He Bark So Much?

What if your pug barks too much for no reason? The first thing to understand is that there's always a reason. It's your job to discover why he's barking excessively. Is he bored because he's alone all day? Are the squirrels in the yard taunting him? Is he warning off all the delivery people who come down the street during the day?

If your pug is barking because he's bored, punishment is not the way to go. You need to find a way to resolve his boredom. After all, you'd start barking at falling leaves too if you had to sit home all day with nothing to read, no television to watch, and no one to talk to. Rotate his toys so he always has something new. Prepare a goodie bag full of treats that he has to work at to get into: use a paper bag, fill it with toys and treats, and tape it closed. Give it to your dog before you leave for work. He'll be so busy getting into it, eating the treats, and playing with the toys that he won't have time to bark.

Begging

The easiest way to deal with begging is not to let it start in the first place. Never feed your pug from the table or offer him scraps while you're cooking. As it is, your pug will already be constantly underfoot in the kitchen, hoping for a dropped tidbit. Don't permit it. It's not only annoying, it's dangerous. You could trip over the dog while you're moving around in the kitchen, injuring one or both of you. Teach him to stay in an out-of-the-way place or put his crate in the kitchen so he can watch but not participate in meal preparation.

Training classes won't magically solve all your pug's behavior problems, but they can increase the bond between the two of you, as well as increase your dog's confidence, making him more willing to work with you and less likely to behave fearfully.

If you can't resist giving your pug a treat while you're preparing a meal, make him sit or do a down first. Then send him back to his place. No hanging around hoping for more. Only give him treats when you've called him to come and then required a sit or down.

Feed your pug before the rest of the family eats. He won't be quite as hungry (though pugs are always hungry, or at least willing to eat), and he'll be less likely to bother you at the dinner table. If he's allowed in the room while the family is eating, put him in a down/stay. And, of course, there's nothing wrong with putting him in his crate during mealtimes.

▲ Pugs are playful by nature, but behavior problems
must be corrected before they turn into bigger issues.

Chewing

Most dogs like to chew. Young pugs have a physiological need to
chew; it's simply part of their development. It's also a way for them
to explore their surroundings. Older pugs may continue the chewing habit simply because it's enjoyable. Chewing is a way to pass the
time when there's nothing else to do. To keep chewing constructive
and not destructive, provide your pug with lots of different chew toys
and teach him what not to chew.

Good Chewing

Praise your pug every time you see him gnawing on a toy to
teach good chewing habits. Help make toys even more appealing by
handling them frequently so they bear your scent. This works especially well with the soft chew toys favored by pugs. Your pug wants
to be close to you, even when you're not home, so chewing on something that smells like you is the next best thing. That's often why dogs

chew up their owners' favorite shoes or other items of clothing. It's not spite; it's admiration. Take it for the compliment it is, and put your things away next time.

You can also make some chew toys more attractive by mining them with treats. A Kong toy or hollow rubber bone is great for this purpose. Fill it with peanut butter and stud the peanut butter with small biscuits or baby carrots. Your pug will spend hours trying get at all the sticky, crunchy goodness.

How to Prevent Chewing

The two best ways to stop inappropriate chewing before it starts are to put your things out of reach and to crate your pug or put him in his safe room when you can't be there to supervise. That way, your possessions don't get destroyed, and your dog doesn't get scolded for misbehaving. It's a win-win situation. Make sure he has something nice to chew on when he's confined.

 Essential

> To help your pug understand that he must obey the rules of the house, be consistent with corrections. Look him in the eye and say "Wrong" or "No" to deter an undesirable activity.

When you find your pug chewing on something he shouldn't, give an immediate verbal correction, like "Aaaght" or "No!" If he's chewing on something life-threatening, such as an electrical cord, instantly follow the verbal correction with a squirt from a spray bottle or the toss of a small throw pillow. Your pug needs to learn that there are serious consequences to chewing on cords—before he gets electrocuted.

If he's chewing on something not so dangerous—but still forbidden—give the same verbal correction. That should be enough to distract him. When he stops chewing to look at you, give him a toy to chew on instead. Don't forget to praise him every time you see him chewing on something appropriate.

Preventing inappropriate chewing can save your dog's life. Chewing on the wrong things can lead to electrocution (electrical cords) or intestinal blockages (chewing and swallowing socks or dishtowels). Protect your furniture and your clothing, as well as your dog's life.

Mouthing and Nipping

Dogs use their mouths as surrogate hands. Mouths are great for picking up, carrying, and tasting things. Dogs also use their mouths to defend themselves or objects they perceive as theirs. While this is all perfectly natural and understandable, your pug must learn that he can never use his teeth on people. In some locales, a single dog bite is enough to require a dog to be euthanized, so teaching your pug not to mouth or bite people is a must.

A pug puppy's lessons in how to use his mouth and teeth begin with his littermates and mother. They yelp loudly or cuff him with their paws if he bites too hard. You can continue that lesson by screeching loudly and then walking away any time your pup bites down too hard on your hand. Remember, dogs—especially pugs—hate being ignored.

Help your pug develop nice mouth manners by offering tiny treats held in your fingers. Again, if you feel his teeth bite down, yell "Ouch" and walk away with the treat. Try again in a couple of minutes and repeat until he learns how to take food gently. (Kids should not try this at home—parents only.)

Scavenging

All dogs love to raid the trash, and pugs are no exception. They might not be able to get into large trash cans, but they're masters at tipping over small office, bedroom, or bathroom trash cans and rummaging through or eating the contents. Your pug is probably not hungry, though he will look for food and eat it, even on a relatively full stomach.

How to Prevent Scavenging

With this behavior problem, deterrence is usually the best solution. Keep the trash behind closed doors (store it beneath the kitchen or bathroom sink and put child locks on the cabinet doors), place it up high, or use a can with a tightly fitting lid that your pug can't remove.

If that doesn't work for you, make getting into the trash counterproductive. If your pug enjoys playing with empty toilet paper rolls—which can make great toys for small dogs—and pulls one out of the trash, take it away. Later, you can give him a different roll to play with. Eventually he'll learn that paper towel rolls that come from you are fair game; those raided from the trash get taken away.

Catch your pug with his head in the trash? Clap your hands or give the game-show-buzzer sound: Aaaaght! The noise should startle your dog into pulling his head out. Then you can praise him for not being in the trash—"Good no trash"—and put the can away.

Whining

Dogs whine when they want something, when they're frustrated, or when they're excited. If your pug's whining gets out of hand, just ignore it. Try to distract him with some other activity, such as practicing obedience commands. As with barking, never reward whining by giving the dog what he wants. If he's whining to get out of his crate or because he wants some of the chicken you're cutting up for dinner, turn your back on him. He doesn't get anything until he's quiet.

Aggression

Aggressive behaviors in dogs include biting, growling, curling the lip, and other threatening behaviors. Aggressive tendencies are rare in pugs, but any dog can become aggressive given the right circumstances or a poor temperament inherited from parents. Aggression is one of the many ways in which dogs communicate, but that doesn't mean it's okay for your pug to ever behave aggressively. Because he lives in a human family, he needs to learn to temper his behavior to human standards.

 **Fact**

You can tell your pug is smiling by studying his body language. A smile is expressed with the lips pulled to the side and a tail that's wagging. This is typical friendly pug demeanor.

Dogs can show aggression toward their owners, toward strangers, or toward other animals. Although it doesn't seem that way to us, most forms of aggression are motivated by fear. Some fears that can cause aggression in dogs include an invasion of territory by a stranger, another dog, or a new baby in the home; the fear of a mother dog that her pups will be harmed by an approaching stranger; or the fear of being hurt physically in some way.

How to Prevent Aggression

You can prevent fear and possessive aggression with plenty of socialization in puppyhood. Puppy kindergarten, obedience class, and play dates at parks with other dogs and people are also good ways to deter aggression. Training helps your pug learn to defer to you as the family leader and protector of territory. Neutering at adolescence can also help reduce the incidence of aggression.

How to Deal with Aggression

If your pug behaves aggressively for no apparent reason, take him to the veterinarian to rule out a physical problem that could be causing pain. If that's not the issue, seek the help of a qualified behaviorist who can advise you on behavior modification techniques.

Noise Shyness

Some dogs can develop a debilitating fear of thunder, fireworks, gunshots, and other loud noises. A noise-shy dog can get lost or hurt. He will be easily startled by loud noises, which will cause him to hide or run away. If your pug exhibits noise-shyness, here are some ways to help him overcome his fear.

How to Avoid Noise Shyness

Don't cuddle or talk soothingly to your pug while he's displaying fearful behavior or you'll reinforce the idea that there's something to be afraid of. Behave normally, and ignore his behavior. Make sure he has access to a safe place such as his crate or safe room, but don't confine him to a particular spot. He should feel free to move around. Distract him with a favorite toy or a training session, ideally before he starts showing fearful behavior.

Separation Anxiety

This condition is a panic response that occurs when a dog's people leave the home. Dogs with separation anxiety become highly distressed, usually within an hour of the person's departure. They may dig, chew, or scratch at doors or windows in an attempt to get out and find their owners; howl, bark, or whine; or potty in the house. Behaviorists aren't sure why some dogs develop separation anxiety while others don't, but it sometimes develops when the dog is not used to being left alone; after the dog has been boarded at a kennel; or after a change in the family routine, such as moving to a new home, the addition of a baby or new pet, or the departure of a teenager for college. Dogs with separation anxiety often follow their people from room to room, greet them frantically when they return home, and act depressed or anxious when they see their people preparing to leave.

How to Prevent Separation Anxiety

Practicing sit/stays and down/stays can help your pug learn to tolerate your absence. Give the command, and move away from the dog. Eventually, move into another room, one where he can still see you. When he's comfortable with that, try going to a room where he can't see you. Give lots of praise and treats when he remains in place while you're gone. Work these sessions into your daily routine, telling your pug to stay whenever you need to go into another room for something.

Patience Is a Virtue

If your pug has a severe case of separation anxiety, behavior modification and—in some cases—antianxiety drugs can help solve the problem. Patience, not punishment, is a must. In fact, punishing your pug for behaviors related to separation anxiety can make the situation worse by increasing his anxiety.

Behavior modification takes time. To deal with your pug's anxieties in the meantime, consider having a pet sitter or a neighbor come in while you're gone; making use of dog day-care centers; or taking your pug with you whenever possible. For severe cases, talk to your veterinarian about prescribing an antianxiety drug to help your pug cope in the short term. This isn't a cure in and of itself, but it can be used successfully in conjunction with behavior modification. As your dog improves, you can taper off the medication as your veterinarian directs. Other techniques for preventing separation anxiety can be found in Chapter 18.

CHAPTER 20

Pugs At Work and Play

T HE PUG DOESN'T HAVE the precision of a Border collie, or the speed of a Shetland sheepdog, or the perfect obedience of a golden retriever, or the nose of a bloodhound, or the power of a Doberman pinscher, or indeed very many qualities at all that would mark him as a canine athlete. What he does have going for him is a sense of humor, a love of showing off, the heart of a mastiff, and an abundance of charisma.

Conformation

A dog show, or conformation show, is an event where dogs are judged on how well they measure up to the breed standard and to the other dogs in the ring on that day. It's much more than a beauty contest, though. The conformation ring brings together breeders and their dogs to evaluate those pugs that are best suited for breeding. Each pug's structure (conformation), movement, and attitude are judged against the breed standard. The dogs that most closely meet the breed standard earn championships and are considered good breeding prospects.

Pugs earn points toward championships at all-breed dog shows. Each win brings one to five points, depending on the number of dogs defeated. A three-, four-, or five-point win is called a major. A pug must earn a total of fifteen points under three different judges to earn a championship. Two of the wins must be majors, each received from a different judge.

In addition to meeting the standard physically, a good show pug has character and expression, qualities defined as showmanship. The best show dogs have a style and attitude that draws all eyes to them. Showmanship can make a great pug stand out even more and can even bring a lesser pug to the judge's attention. Some pugs just seem to "ask" for the win, and they often get it, even if they aren't necessarily the best in the ring that day.

 **Fact**

In the best of all worlds, only the most deserving pugs would earn championships, but a top handler can "finish" almost any dog as long as the owner is willing and able to spend unlimited amounts of money. That doesn't make for a very good champion, though. A pug should be able to earn a championship on his own merits.

Most conformation shows are run under the auspices of the AKC. The United Kennel Club (UKC) also offers conformation titles and hosts shows. AKC shows are more numerous, but UKC shows are more family-oriented, prohibiting the use of professional handlers. Top-winning pugs can make it all the way to the best-known and oldest American dog show of them all: Westminster. The pug that took Best of Breed at the 2004 Westminster Kennel Club show was Ch. Kendoric's Riversong Mulroney.

Specialty Shows

Specialty shows are limited to dogs of a single breed, which in this case is pugs. They are usually judged by breeders who are experts in every facet of pug conformation. You can see some of the best pugs in the country at a specialty show. Specialty shows can be local, regional, or national. Attending a national specialty show allows you to see a variety of pugs from around the country. The climax of a national specialty is the Best of Breed competition, where pugs compete for the honor of being the best pug in the country.

Some of the classes at specialties that aren't normally found at the average all-breed dog show are the Veteran, Brood Bitch, and Stud Dog classes. The Veteran classes showcase dogs that are still sound, even at seven or more years of age. They represent the lines that smart breeders want to use. Brood Bitch and Stud Dog classes showcase the offspring of the dog entered. Sometimes you can see three generations shown together. Another class unique to a specialty show is the Sweepstakes. The Puppy Sweepstakes put on display the younger generation of pugs.

Conformation Training and Handling Tips

If you've never shown a dog before, consider attending a handling class offered by your local dog club. You can sign up for it when your pug is about three months old (he can't be entered in a show until he's six months old). In class, you'll learn how to display your dog's outline in the show ring (called stacking), gait (move) him properly, and groom him appropriately (see Chapter 13 for grooming tips). Your pug will learn how to stand for examination on the table and gait around the ring at the appropriate speed. The two of you can practice your newfound skills at matches (practice shows).

Pacing is important. Pugs are shown at a walk on a loose lead. Pugs tend to want to charge forward, so you need to teach your dog to stay with you. Most judges don't like seeing dogs on tight leashes.

One of the best things you can teach your pug when he's young is to permit himself to be hand-stacked. Lots of pugs learn to free-stack—meaning they set themselves up in the proper position—but in a crowded ring there's not always room to do that. That's where hand-stacking comes in. Teach your pug to let you put his feet in position—foursquare—and to hold that position. As you did with the stay command, start by asking him to hold the position for only a few seconds and gradually increase the length of time he must stay stacked. Start teaching this at an early age. If you wait too long, it will be difficult if not impossible to teach.

Make showing fun for your pug. He should enjoy himself in the ring rather than being on edge because he senses your anxiety or bored because he'd rather be doing something else. Use liver or a favorite fleece toy as bait to keep his attention and bring out his natural charisma. A pug that's having a good time is already a winner.

 **Essential**

If you want to be successful in the ring, watch and talk to and learn from other handlers. Don't be afraid to ask for help. Pug people are pretty friendly, and more than likely they'll be happy to show you the ropes.

Show a little style yourself. Dress professionally but comfortably so you can move with ease. Wear a nice skirt or slacks and a neat shirt. It's a good idea to wear a color that contrasts with your pug. You don't want your dog's outline to disappear against your clothes. Wear light-colored clothing if you're showing a black pug and colored or dark clothing if you're showing a fawn pug.

Professional Handlers

If you have a nice pug—one with good conformation and the appropriate temperament—you shouldn't have any problem showing him to his championship. Handling your own dog to a championship is a great achievement that you can always cherish. Nonetheless, you may prefer to hire a professional handler for perfectly valid reasons. You may not enjoy being in the spotlight, even though your pug is the one being judged; you may not have the skill and coordination to handle a dog well; or you may simply not have enough time.

Professional handlers show ten to twenty dogs a show at as many as 120 shows a year. Not surprisingly, they understand the physical and mental conditioning show dogs need. Not just any handler will do, though. You want someone who knows how to care for, condition, and motivate your pug. Some handlers specialize in toy breeds and have a deep understanding of the particular conditioning and personality issues involved in showing a pug.

The handler should have a rate card or rate sheet that explains exactly what expenses you're paying for (travel, food, advertising, and so on). A contract should spell out the yearly budget, travel plans, who gets the trophies, and any other important details. To avoid surprises or disappointments, you and the handler must be honest with each other from the beginning.

With that in mind, understand where your pug falls on the handler's priority list. If you simply want your pug to finish his championship, it won't be a big deal if an assistant handles him from time to time. Your handler may have several dogs to show at the same time, and he can't be in three rings at once. Be clear on how the system works, and accept that your pug isn't always going to be at the top of the heap.

Obedience Trials

Obedience training has more benefits than simply teaching your pug a few nice manners. If you're the competitive type, you and your pug can get involved in competitive obedience trials, testing your skills against other dogs and their owners. Pugs aren't the most common breed seen in obedience trials, and they don't usually earn the highest scores, but they are out there, and a number of them have earned advanced obedience titles. Competing in obedience with a pug can sometimes be frustrating, but it's a real thrill when he succeeds.

About Obedience Trials

Obedience trials were originally developed to demonstrate a dog's usefulness as a companion for people and to showcase dogs that had been trained to behave properly in the home, in public, and around other dogs. An obedience trial tests a dog's ability to perform a given set of exercises. A dog must receive three qualifying scores, known as legs, under three different judges to earn a title. A qualifying score is 170 out of 200 possible points. Points are deducted for faults such as dropping out of heel position, sitting too slowly or refusing to sit, or breaking the sit or down commands. Handler errors include tugging on the leash and repeating commands. Competition is divided into three levels: novice, open, and utility. Dogs that make it through all three levels can earn points toward an obedience trial championship (OTCh). At least one pug has earned a Utility Dog Excellent (UDX) title, but so far none has achieved an OTCh.

▲ These pugs show off their obedience ribbons.
Any pug can be a star performer with time.

Any pug may compete in obedience trials, even if he doesn't have official AKC registration papers. All that's needed is an indefinite listing privilege (ILP) number indicating that the dog has been recognized as a pug. Unlike conformation shows, spayed or neutered pugs are eligible for obedience competition.

Obedience trial competition requires rapid response and more precision than regular household manners. The goal is for dog and handler to perform as a smoothly functioning team. Your pug must obey you flawlessly (or at least well enough to get the minimum number of points), and you may use only verbal commands or hand signals to direct him. You can use treats, lures, and clickers during training but not in competition. Your trainer can teach you competition obedience skills, or you can benefit from one of the many books and videos available on the subject. The advantage of working with a trainer is that she can watch you and help you correct your timing or any other mistakes you might be making before they become habits. A trainer can also offer tips on the best ways to motivate your pug. Again, choose someone who uses positive motivational techniques.

Both the AKC and the UKC hold obedience trials. They often take place in conjunction with conformation shows and can be found across the country almost every weekend of the year. Contact the AKC or the UKC (see Appendix A) for copies of obedience rules and regulations.

Skills for Novice Competition

If your pug has been to puppy kindergarten or basic obedience class, he already knows many of the commands he'll need for obedience competition at the Novice level. In addition to sit, down, stay, and come, he must also be able to heel on and off leash at different speeds, move in a figure-eight, and stand still for the judge's examination. Before entering a real competition, you and your pug can practice your skills at obedience matches.

 **fact**

Food will always motivate your pug, but so will happy praise, petting, and play. Your goal is to build and maintain trust and confidence, the foundations of a good relationship. You are most likely to succeed if you train in small steps, set up every learning situation to help your pug perform correctly, and practice frequently over a period of weeks and months.

Novice competition has two classes: Novice A and Novice B. Novice A is for obedience teams that are just starting out. This means the handler hasn't yet put an obedience title on a dog. Novice B is for handlers who have previously titled a dog in obedience. Professional handlers and trainers can compete in Novice B. Dogs must perform the same exercises whether they're competing in Novice A or Novice B. When your pug earns three legs in Novice competition, he receives the title Companion Dog (CD).

Skills for Advanced Obedience Competition

In Open obedience classes, your pug must perform off-leash and for longer periods. He must also perform jumping and retrieving tasks. Pugs that earn three legs in Open competition receive a Companion Dog Excellent (CDX) title. Utility classes are still more difficult and add scent discrimination exercises. In Utility competition, dogs can earn Utility Dog (UD) and Utility Dog Excellent (UDX) titles. The best of the best can earn the title of Obedience Trial Champion, something no pug has yet achieved. It's something to work toward!

Canine Good Citizen

If obedience competition sounds like way more work than you're interested in, don't give up. Your pug can still earn a title. The Canine Good Citizen title, or CGC for short, is offered by the AKC to any dog that can pass a simple series of tests—simple, that is, for any well-mannered pug that knows the basics of civilized interactions. The CGC test, implemented in 1989, is a certification program for dogs that have good manners at home and in public. The program stresses responsible dog ownership and basic good manners for dogs. Dogs that pass the CGC test receive a certificate from the AKC and are recorded in the AKC's CGC Archive.

Since its development, the CGC program has become popular in many communities. Police and animal control agencies often recommend the CGC program when they encounter owners with problem dogs, and some therapy dog groups make the CGC test part of their screening process. Some 4-H groups use the CGC program to teach children how to train dogs. At last count, fourteen states had recognized the CGC program as a good way to promote responsible dog ownership.

The CGC Test

The CGC test calls for a dog to be in healthy, well-groomed condition and to demonstrate certain behaviors. All in all, there are ten items on the test. It can be administered by local dog clubs, private trainers, and 4-H clubs. Unlike an obedience trial, you can praise your dog during the test and pet him between exercises. On the other hand, you're not allowed to use treats and toys to lure your pug into performing. The following elements make up the CGC test:

- Accepting a friendly stranger
- Sitting politely for petting
- Appearance and grooming
- Walking on a loose lead
- Walking through a crowd
- Sit/stay and down/stay on command
- Coming when called
- Reaction to another dog
- Reaction to distraction
- Supervised separation

The only equipment you need is a leash and a buckle or slip (choke) collar made of leather, fabric, or chain. Special training collars such as pinch collars and head halters are not permitted in the CGC test. Bring written proof that your pug is vaccinated against rabies, plus his brush or comb for the judge to use on him during the test. The evaluator will supply the twenty-foot line needed for the sit/stay and down/stay exercises.

CGC Exercises

The first exercise is accepting a friendly stranger, second nature to the average pug. The stranger (the evaluator) will approach you and your dog and speak to you in a normal tone of voice, ignoring the dog. Your pug should stay by your side, not showing resentment or shyness, and should not try to approach the evaluator.

The second item, sitting politely for petting, demonstrates that your pug will allow a friendly stranger to touch him while he's out with you. With your pug at your side, the evaluator will pet him on the head and body and may speak to him. Your pug should accept the attention without shyness or resentment.

The appearance and grooming portion of the test demonstrates that your pug will allow someone other than yourself to groom and examine him. It also demonstrates your own care, concern, and sense of responsibility for your dog. The evaluator will check your dog to see that he looks clean, healthy, and alert, and isn't overweight or underweight. Using the comb or brush you provide, the evaluator will gently groom the dog, examine his ears, and pick up each front foot. You can talk to and praise your pug during this part of the test.

The fourth exercise, walking on a loose lead, demonstrates that you can control your pug. He can walk on either side of you (unlike an obedience trial, where he must be on your left side). The evaluator will direct you to take a certain course, which will include a right turn, a left turn, an about turn, and at least one stop in between and another at the end of the exercise. Your pug should pay attention to you and respond to your movements and changes of direction, but a perfect heel position isn't necessary, and he doesn't have to sit when you stop. You can talk to or praise your dog during the exercise.

 Alert!

You should never yell at your dog during the CGC test—it's frowned upon. Be sure that you always give commands in an even, calm tone of voice.

The next test, walking through a crowd, demonstrates that your pug is calm and under control in public places with foot traffic. During this exercise, you'll walk around and pass close to at least three people. Your dog can show interest in the people but should continue to walk with you instead of trying to go to them or jump on them. You can talk to and praise your pug during the test.

In the sit/stay and down/stay exercises, your pug must respond to your commands and then stay until he's released. Before these exercises begin, the evaluator will replace your pug's leash with a twenty-foot line. You can take a reasonable amount of time to get your dog into position and give commands more than once, but you can't physically force him into position. A gentle touch to offer guidance is permitted. When the instructor directs you, tell your dog to stay, walk to the end of the line, turn, and go back to the dog, and release him at the evaluator's direction.

Next, your pug must come when called. The exercise calls for you to walk ten feet from the dog, turn to face him, and call him. It's okay to encourage him to come. You're permitted to tell your dog to "Stay" or "Wait" before you walk away.

The "reaction to another dog" portion of the test demonstrates that your pug behaves politely around other dogs. You and your pug will approach another handler and her dog from a distance of twenty to thirty feet. When you meet, the two of you will shake hands and speak for a few moments. Your dogs should show only casual interest in each other, and neither dog should approach the other dog or person.

In the "reaction to distraction" test, your pug must demonstrate that he's confident in the face of distracting situations, such as a jogger running by or a person dropping a crutch or cane. It's okay for your pug to express interest or curiosity, or even to appear slightly startled, but he shouldn't panic, try to run away, show aggression, or bark. You can talk to him or praise him during the exercise.

Finally, in the "supervised separation" portion of the test, your pug must maintain his training and good manners even when you're out of sight. The evaluator will say something like "Would you like me to watch your dog?" which is the cue for you to hand her the leash. You then go out of sight for three minutes. Your dog doesn't have to stay in a certain position, but he shouldn't continually bark, whine, or pace.

Growling, snapping, biting, attacking, or attempting to attack a person or another dog are all immediate grounds for dismissal. Dogs also fail the CGC test if they eliminate at any time during testing. The only exception is during the last exercise and only if that exercise takes place outdoors.

Agility

This fun, fast-paced sport requires the dog—directed by his handler—to navigate a series of obstacles such as A-frames, balance beams, tunnels, and weave poles and to go over or through different types of jumps. Dogs earn—or lose—points based on their speed and accuracy. A pug might not be the fastest breed on the agility course, but he can certainly make up for it with accuracy. Agility always draws an appreciative crowd and this too appeals to the pug's hammy side. It's an especially good sport for highly active, verging on out-of-control pugs—yes, they do exist!

Because competitive agility is done off-leash, you do need to have a certain amount of control over your pug. Before starting agility training, your pug should respond readily to basic obedience commands, in particular sit, down, stay, and come. Even before they begin formal agility training, young puppies can practice some of the elements of agility, such as going through tunnels, balancing on the teeter-totter, weaving through poles, and going over the A-frame. Here are two important tips: keep things fun, and don't practice in the heat.

 Fact

Organizations that sponsor agility competitions are the AKC, the UKC, the United States Dog Agility Association (USDAA), and the North American Dog Agility Council (NADAC). See Appendix A for contact information. Agility titles your pug can earn vary from organization to organization.

Take your pug in for a veterinary exam before you begin training. Any pug with brachycephalic syndrome, luxating patellas, or hip dysplasia probably should take a pass on agility competition. Be aware, too, that your pug's skeletal development should be complete before he does much repetitive jumping. The growth plates close at twelve to fourteen months of age. Before then, limit any jumping he does (including on and off the furniture).

Freestyle

Nicknamed the tail-wagging sport, freestyle involves developing a routine set to music that shows dog and handler working together, expressing their creativity through movement and costume. You can base a freestyle routine on obedience exercises, tricks, or any other behaviors your pug knows and enjoys performing. It's a perfect activity for the fashionable, attention-loving pug.

Freestyle takes two forms. Heelwork to music involves heeling on all sides of the handler, with the dog no farther away than four feet. Musical freestyle is an anything-goes routine that often encompasses jumping and fancy tricks. Handlers choose the beat that goes with the dog and choreograph moves based on their dogs' abilities. Pugs can start training for freestyle at any age, and even dogs with health issues can participate. Simply adapt your choreography and music to your pug's speed and ability level.

Freestyle is a growing sport, and competitions take place across the United States. Freestyle titles your pug can earn are W-FD, W-FDX, W-FDM, and W-Ch.FD. For more information about freestyle, contact the World Canine Freestyle Organization, listed in Appendix A.

Tracking

Despite his short nose, the pug is just as capable of learning to follow a scent as other dogs. By teaching your pug to track, you'll have a dog with a useful skill as well as a fun way to enjoy the outdoors with him. Your pug can earn an AKC tracking title by completing a single successful track. A bonus is that tracking practice and tests usually take place early in the morning, so your pug won't have to suffer the heat.

A tracking trial tests whether a dog can follow a trail by scent. Titles that can be earned by following a human scent trail are Tracking Dog (TD), Tracking Dog Excellent (TDX), and Variable Surface Tracking (VST). For the TD test, the track is 440 to 500 yards long, with a minimum of two right-angle turns, and must be half an hour to two hours old. The person laying the track must be unfamiliar to the dog. At the end of the track, the person laying the track drops a scent article, which the dog must locate. The TDX track is longer, older (three to five hours), and more complicated, and it takes in varied terrain such as ditches, streambeds, and tall grass. Its length is 800 to 1,000 yards, and it has several turns and two cross tracks. Along the way are dummy scent articles meant to lure your dog off the trail.

 Fact

Scent is a combination of an individual's body odors, personal chemical makeup, and fabric and texture of clothing and footwear. The length of time scent stays present in the environment is affected by weather conditions and type of ground cover.

Tracking Dog and Tracking Dog Excellent tests usually take place in rural areas, but the VST tests a dog's tracking ability in more developed locales such as suburban neighborhoods or city streets. The length of a VST track is 600 to 800 yards, and it goes over at least three types of surfaces, such as asphalt, concrete, grass, gravel, or sand. To add to the difficulty, a portion of the track must lack vegetation, which helps hold scent. The track must be three to five hours old with four to eight turns. A dog that passes all three tests earns the title Champion Tracker (CT).

The most difficult aspect of teaching any dog to track is learning to trust the dog. You don't know where the scent trail is because your puny nose isn't capable of even finding it, let alone following it. This is one form of training where your dog teaches you. You'll learn to read his body language to determine whether he's on or off the track. Clickers, toys, food, and praise are all useful in teaching your pug to follow a scent trail. Ask your trainer if she teaches tracking or if she can refer you to someone who does.

Therapy Work

For more than twenty years now, researchers have known that petting a dog can lower blood pressure, increase happiness, and ease loneliness. Programs to bring dogs into nursing homes and children's hospitals have been wildly successful, thanks to certification programs that help prepare dog and handler to meet and greet patients. Animal-assisted therapy, as it's known, is a pug-perfect occupation. It calls for dogs that enjoy meeting people, want more than anything else to sit in a lap or get petted, take new experiences in stride, and—bonus points—can perform entertaining tricks. That's a pug in a nutshell.

Therapy Dog Requirements

Therapy dogs are a lot like Boy Scouts. They must be clean, neat, well mannered, friendly, courteous, kind, cheerful—you get the picture. That means well groomed, no fleas or other parasites, no snatching food, and no potty accidents. In addition, dogs must become certified to do therapy work. You can't just walk into a nursing home with your pug and say, "I'm here to visit!" Both of you must be trained to certain standards. Your pug must pass a temperament test and become accustomed to wheelchairs, walkers, crutches, and so on.

Becoming Certified

Nationwide therapy-dog certification organizations include the Delta Society, Therapy Dogs International, and Love on a Leash. You can find out how to contact these organizations by looking in Appendix A. Many trainers offer therapy-dog certification classes. If you can't find such a class in your area, though, the Delta Society's Pet Partners program offers a home study option.

The Senior Pug

PUG OWNERS ARE FORTUNATE because the breed generally enjoys a long life span. In the absence of disease or trauma, you can expect your pug to live for at least ten years and often well into his teens. Pugs that are kept healthy usually live twelve to fifteen years and some have been known to carry on until they are eighteen or nineteen years old.

When Is a Pug Old?

A dog is considered to be old at seven years of age. At this age, however, many pugs still look and act young. The time when old age really sets in depends on the individual pug. Some pugs are still spry at ten or fifteen years of age, while others appear to be little old ladies or men by the age of eight. Physical changes that indicate the onset of old age include the following:

- Graying muzzle
- Thinner coat
- Less energy
- Poor dental health
- Haziness of the eye lens
- Cataracts
- Decreased sense of smell

- Stiff or painful joints
- Less tolerance of temperature extremes

Other signs of aging include weight gain or weight loss, changes in appetite, more frequent urination caused by excessive thirst, and poor skin condition. Some geriatric pugs sleep more or pay less attention to what's going on around them. Others develop behavioral or mental changes such as becoming fearful of storms or strangers. If your pug begins to act or look old, it's time to schedule a geriatric exam for him. Pugs are a young-at-heart breed, and they often act like puppies their entire lives. If your pug stops acting young, he may have a health problem that needs to be dealt with. Fortunately, many new diets, medications, and procedures can help ease your pug's transition to this new period of his life.

 **Essential**

The best ways to ensure that your pug has a long and healthy life are to give him plenty of exercise to prevent obesity, feed him a high-quality diet, provide regular veterinary care, and last but not least, give lots of love and attention.

Your pug's nutritional needs may change, and it's a good idea for him to see the veterinarian more often to ensure that problems are caught early. Fortunately, these are good times for older dogs. Veterinary advances can help your pug stay healthy and comfortable in his golden years.

A Golden-Age Health Exam

By starting to screen your pug at age seven for diseases associated with aging, you and your veterinarian are more likely to catch problems while they can still be dealt with easily. Even if your pug still acts like a pup, a geriatric screening exam establishes a basis for comparison as he grows older. An annual exam should include a thorough physical to check for stiffness, heart murmurs, bad breath, skin lesions, and other typical signs of aging, as well as blood work to assess liver and kidney function and check for anemia or hidden infections. Regular blood testing can help identify diseases in their earliest and most treatable stages.

▲ This pug demonstrates that even old pugs can learn new tricks.

What if your pug does develop a health problem? Remember that dogs age at a more rapid pace than humans—the equivalent of five to seven years for every chronological year that passes. Changes can occur rapidly, so it's a good idea to monitor health problems with exams every six months instead of annually.

Good parasite control is also essential in older dogs. It's a must, of course, for pugs of any age, but older dogs are physiologically less able to deal with the consequences of parasite infestation, such as blood loss and nutrient deficits. An effective flea, tick, and intestinal parasite prevention program will do your senior pug a world of good.

Senior Nutrition

Your pug's nutritional needs will likely change as he ages. Older dogs are less active than they were in their prime, so they need fewer calories to maintain an appropriate weight. Because their digestive system is less able to efficiently metabolize protein, they need a high-protein food to ensure that their nutritional needs are met.

 **fact**

You may have heard that older dogs shouldn't eat a high-protein food because the amount of protein is difficult for the kidneys to process. Although a low-protein diet may be prescribed for dogs with kidney disease, it's not necessary to restrict protein for normal, healthy dogs, no matter how old they are.

You can find any number of foods formulated for the needs of older dogs. As always, look for a food that contains high-quality ingredients. The ideal food for an older dog has about 25 percent protein and is low in fat and calories. Some diets for senior dogs have higher levels of fiber to help decrease caloric density. Your pug will feel full, even though he's taking in fewer calories. You can do the same thing by slightly reducing the amount of dog food you give and adding plain canned pumpkin (not the sweetened kind) to your pug's meals.

Supplements

A healthy pug that's eating a balanced diet usually doesn't need vitamin or mineral supplements. Sometimes, however, supplements can help improve certain conditions related to aging. For example, in the event of reduced kidney function, your veterinarian might advise supplementing your pug with a B-vitamin. Dogs with dry, itchy skin can benefit from essential fatty acids, vitamin E, and zinc supplements. Before you start adding supplements to your pug's diet, ask your veterinarian for advice.

Lack of Appetite

If your pug doesn't go after his food the way he used to, his lack of appetite might be related to a decreased sense of smell. An older dog's senses, including smell, aren't always as sharp as they used to be. When dogs can't smell food, they're not so interested in tasting it. Help him out by warming his food in the microwave to increase the scent. This works with dry food as well as canned food. Be sure to test the temperature with your finger before giving it to him. You can also tempt his taste buds by adding a little canned food or low-sodium beef or chicken broth to his meal.

Weight Gain or Loss

The gain or loss of a pound or two might not seem like much to you, but for a pug it can be as much as 10 percent of his body weight. Both weight gain and weight loss can have serious consequences. Sometimes they're symptoms of underlying health problems.

Weight control is always a must for pugs, and even more so the older they get. Fat, old pugs are more prone to disease, especially arthritis, congestive heart failure, and diabetes. Continue to exercise strict portion control, and don't slack off on the daily walks. If your pug is still putting on the pounds, try switching him to a lower calorie diet or feeding him several small meals each day so he doesn't feel deprived.

Unexplained weight loss is often a sign of disease. Pugs that eat ravenously but still lose weight may have developed diabetes. If weight loss occurs because your pug has developed a picky appetite, his teeth might be hurting him. Weight loss can also be an early, subtle warning sign of cancer. In any event, your pug needs to visit the veterinarian for a definite diagnosis—fast! Don't take a wait-and-see attitude.

Even with the best care and diet in the world, your pug will eventually develop some sort of health problem related to the aging process. It's just a fact of life. Happily, when these problems are caught early, veterinary medicine has many ways of treating them, ensuring your pug a long and comfortable life.

Arthritis

This painful degenerative joint disease is commonly seen in older dogs. Pugs as a breed don't seem to have a high incidence of arthritis, but it can occur. Signs of arthritis, which may be subtle or obvious, include a decreased activity level; reluctance to walk very far or very fast; avoidance of running, jumping, or climbing stairs; stiffness when getting up or lying down; flinching when touched; and swollen joints that seem hot or painful. In severe cases, dogs may exhibit entirely un-puglike behavior, such as snarling or snapping when touched.

 Alert!

While aspirin and other analgesics work wonders for arthritis pain in humans, never give them to a dog without a veterinarian's okay. A single tablet of ibuprofen, for instance, can kill a dog the size of a pug. Aspirin in small doses can relieve arthritis pain, but don't give it without first asking your veterinarian what amount is safe.

What can you do for arthritis? There's no cure, but you can take steps to ensure that your pug stays comfortable. If you're reading this while he's still a puppy, teach him now to wait to be lifted on and off furniture and in and out of the car. This creates less risk of hurting his back and joints. Keep his weight at a healthy level. Excess pounds can stress joints. If your arthritic pug is overweight, help him shed pounds by decreasing the amount of food you give or switching him to a lower calorie food. Medications are available to relieve pain and inflammation. These canine nonsteroidal anti-inflammatory drugs (NSAIDs) are generally safe for long-term use, but regular blood testing is a must to make sure they aren't affecting liver, kidney, or digestive functions. If your pug develops side effects such as vomiting or diarrhea after taking a canine NSAID, the veterinarian may need to adjust the dose or try a different medication.

For mild cases of arthritis, supplements called nutraceuticals can help ease aches and pains. Nutraceuticals that contain naturally occurring compounds such as glycosaminoglycans (GAGs), glucosamine, chondroitin, and ester C are believed to help rebuild cartilage and promote joint flexibility and mobility. While the benefit of nutraceuticals in dogs hasn't been scientifically proven, they have an edge over canine NSAIDs because they rarely cause side effects, although it can take up to two months before you see an improvement.

Brachycephalic Syndrome

Brachycephalic syndrome comprises stenotic nares and soft elongated palate (discussed earlier in Chapter 3) as well as everted sacules and hypoplastic trachea. Sacules are two small pouches on either side of the larynx (voice box). The purpose of the sacules isn't clear, but they become a problem when a pug with brachycephalic syndrome has a large velocity of air through the crowded air space in the throat. The sacules turn inside out, or evert, preventing the normal passage of air. A hypoplastic trachea occurs when the windpipe doesn't develop to its full diameter, which in a normal pug would be about three-quarters of an inch. A pug with a hypoplastic trachea—one that's half to two-thirds of its normal diameter—must work harder to breathe through the windpipe.

Brachycephalic syndrome can affect pugs of any age, but it often doesn't become an issue until they get older. Over time, pugs with brachycephalic syndrome suffer an oxygen deficit. A pug that can't walk across the room without turning blue and gasping for air is definitely a candidate for reconstructive surgery. This involves relieving the airway obstruction by opening the nostrils and removing the excess soft palate and the everted sacules, a procedure that effectively doubles the diameter of the air passage. This common, straightforward surgery is ideally done using a laser instead of surgical instruments. With the use of a laser, there's no bleeding and no postoperative swelling, so recovery is easier on the dog. You'll be able to hear the difference in breathing immediately after surgery. Your pug will need a diet of soft food for about a week after surgery.

Cancer

The risk of cancer increases with age, and cancer is one of the most common problems in older dogs. The good news is that cancer, far from being a death sentence, is the single most treatable chronic disease that dogs face—when it's detected and treated early. There's no specific type of cancer that affects pugs, but common forms of cancer seen in dogs include mammary (breast) tumors, skin tumors, testicular tumors (in dogs that haven't been neutered), mouth cancer, and lymphoma.

Cancer occurs when cells grow uncontrollably on or inside the body, forming tumors. Tumors may stay in a single area of the body, or they may metastasize, meaning they spread to other parts of the body. Most types of cancer are diagnosed through a biopsy, which involves removing and studying a section of tissue. Blood tests, x-rays, and physical signs can also play a role in a diagnosis of cancer. The following physical signs can indicate cancer:

- Abnormal swellings or lumps that don't go away or that grow larger
- Sores that don't heal
- Unusual or excessive weight loss
- Lack of appetite for any length of time
- Bleeding or discharge from any body opening
- Unusual or bad-smelling odors
- Difficulty eating or swallowing
- Lack of energy
- Persistent lameness or stiffness
- Difficulty breathing, urinating, or defecating

Breast Cancer

Mammary tumors are the most common type of cancer in female dogs and make up 25 to 50 percent of all tumors seen in older, unspayed females. The highest incidence is in dogs older than six years. Half of all breast tumors in dogs are malignant. Breast cancer is treated surgically by removing the tumor. You can prevent or greatly reduce your female pug's risk of mammary cancer by spaying her before her first heat cycle (see Chapter 11).

Skin Tumors

Lots of older dogs develop lumps and bumps on or beneath their skin. These growths are usually harmless, but you should always have your veterinarian take a look just to be sure. Benign (harmless) tumors often seen on the surface of the skin include cysts, papillomas (warts), adenomas, and lipomas. Once your veterinarian has deemed these tumors harmless, you can just leave them alone or have them removed surgically if they affect your pug's mobility, are growing rapidly, or you just don't like the way they look.

 Fact

Dogs are fortunate in that they don't suffer the same side effects from chemotherapy as people. If your pug requires chemotherapy, he won't throw up or lose his hair. You may notice, however, that he's tired for a few days afterward.

Mast cell tumors are among the most commonly seen malignant (harmful) tumors in dogs and can occur anywhere on or in the body. They look like raised, nodular masses and can feel soft or solid when touched. Mast cell tumors can occur in dogs of any age, but they usually develop when a dog is eight to ten years old. When mast cell tumors are caught early, surgical removal is the treatment of choice. Depending on the stage of the disease, your veterinarian may recommend radiation therapy to ensure that any remaining tumor cells are destroyed. Chemotherapy can be helpful in advanced stages of the disease.

Testicular Tumors

Testicular tumors are common in dogs. The average age at which they develop is ten years, but they've been known to occur as early as three years and as late as nineteen years. They're often seen in dogs with retained testicles. This type of tumor can be removed surgically. Follow-up treatment with chemotherapy or radiation may be necessary if the tumor has spread. Testicular tumors are preventable entirely with neutering.

Oral Cancer

Canine malignant melanoma is the most common oral cancer in dogs and accounts for one out of twenty cancer diagnoses. This highly aggressive cancer can occur not only in the mouth but also in the nail bed and footpad.

One of the best reasons for brushing your pug's teeth on a frequent basis is so you can spot the signs of mouth cancer. Often, the signs are not recognized until the disease is advanced, making it difficult to provide effective treatment. Signs of mouth cancer include a mass on the gums, bleeding gums, bad breath, or difficulty eating. Oral cancers are diagnosed through biopsies and X-rays. Treatment requires surgery, sometimes followed by radiation therapy. Get in the habit of examining your pug's mouth, because this type of cancer requires early, aggressive treatment.

A new approach to treating canine malignant melanoma is the DNA-based vaccine studied at New York City's Animal Medical Center. The vaccine more than tripled the survival rate of the nine dogs in the study, from an expected 90 days to an average of 389 days. Four dogs survived for more than 400 days, and one was still alive after 615 days.

Lymphoma

Unusual swellings or enlargements in the lower neck area are often the first sign of lymphoma, a tumor of the blood-forming system. Further examination may show that all of the body's lymph nodes are enlarged. A biopsy can confirm the diagnosis, but further testing in the form of blood work, a bone marrow examination, and chest and abdominal images are necessary to determine the site and magnitude of the tumor. Lymphoma responds well to chemotherapy.

Cognitive Dysfunction Syndrome

Sometimes referred to as senility, cognitive dysfunction syndrome (or CDS) is defined as any age-related mental decline not caused by hearing or vision loss, organ failure, or a tumor. It doesn't appear to be common in pugs; they seem to be lucid late in life. If your pug does develop CDS, he may act disoriented or confused, wandering aimlessly, staring into space, or acting as if he's lost. Dogs with CDS interact less with family members or show changes in sleep and activity patterns. Sometimes they break housetraining. Signs of CDS can occur in dogs as young as eight years of age.

 Fact

Choline supplements sometimes help to increase mental alertness. Look for Cholodin Canine at holistic veterinary clinics, pet supply stores, online pet supply sources, or health food stores.

If your pug shows signs of CDS, take him to the veterinarian. A definite diagnosis is essential, because other health problems such as kidney, thyroid, or adrenal gland disease can resemble CDS. Once other health problems are ruled out, CDS can be managed with medication. Watch for side effects that can include vomiting, diarrhea, hyperactivity, or restlessness.

Congestive Heart Failure

Old, overweight pugs may be prone to congestive heart failure. This condition occurs when the heart is too weak to pump blood adequately, causing fluid to accumulate in the lungs. Suspect congestive heart failure if your pug coughs frequently, has trouble breathing, seems restless at night, or tires easily with only mild exercise. Congestive heart failure can't be cured, but diet, medication, and rest can ease the signs for a time. Also, weight loss can help.

Dental Disease

Dental disease is a serious problem in most older dogs, especially in toy breeds. Dental disease has even been described as the scourge of the old pug. Because pugs have underbites—the lower jaw is longer than the upper jaw—they often develop a heavy buildup of plaque and tartar.

 fact

When dental disease goes untreated, the mouth becomes a breeding ground for bacteria, which can enter the bloodstream and go on to infect organs such as the heart or kidneys. After a cleaning, your veterinarian may prescribe a course of antibiotics to help prevent bacterial infections.

Preventive dentistry throughout your pug's life is important. Keep his mouth healthy by brushing teeth regularly, encouraging play with chew toys, giving hard biscuits to help chip off tartar, and scheduling annual or as-needed veterinary cleanings. Signs of dental disease include bad breath, tartar buildup on teeth (that hard brown stuff you may see coating them), and inflammation of the gums. If your pug is picking at his food, his teeth may hurt. Take him in for a veterinary cleaning or, if that's not possible, moisten his dry food or switch to canned food.

Diabetes

Pugs are one of the breeds at high risk for developing diabetes mellitus, according to statistics from the School of Veterinary Medicine at the University of Pennsylvania. That's not surprising, considering their tendency toward obesity. It's just one more reason to keep your pug at a healthy weight.

Diabetes is a disorder of the pancreas gland and is a common problem in older dogs. It occurs when the pancreas doesn't produce enough insulin—a substance the body uses to drive glucose, or blood sugar, into the cells—or stops producing insulin altogether. The result is that glucose levels build up in the bloodstream, causing high blood sugar. Contributing factors include obesity and genetic predisposition.

Signs of diabetes include excessive thirst and urination, which often leads to accidents in the house, weight loss despite a ravenous appetite, and sudden blindness. If your pug shows any of these signs, take him to the veterinarian. Diabetes is diagnosed through blood work and urinalysis.

Diabetes can't be cured, but it can be managed successfully. Pugs with diabetes will require one or two daily insulin injections to keep the disease under control. Your veterinarian can show you how to give the shot. Most dogs don't seem to mind the injection, especially if they receive a treat or a meal immediately afterward. Weight loss through exercise and dietary control is another factor in successfully managing diabetes.

Hearing Loss

As dogs age, the eardrum stiffens and hearing becomes less acute. It's possible your pug is simply ignoring you when you call, but there's a good chance that he just can't hear you. Test his hearing by sneaking up behind him and making a noise by dropping your keys or clapping your hands. If he doesn't respond, he probably has suffered partial or total hearing loss. Take him to the veterinarian to confirm the diagnosis of deafness. You'll want to make sure that it's not related to a treatable condition such as an ear infection or to neurological disease.

If your pug is deaf, he can still get along just fine using his senses of sight and smell. Make a habit of announcing your presence to him by stomping your foot when you're behind him. He'll feel the vibrations and know where you are. You can also communicate with him by using hand signals instead of verbal commands. If you're reading this while your pug is still a pup, start teaching him hand signals now; you may need them later on his life.

Hypothyroidism

This decrease in thyroid function is the most common hormonal disorder seen in dogs, pugs included. Hypothyroidism occurs when the level of thyroid hormones falls below normal and usually affects middle-aged or older dogs. When dogs don't have enough thyroid hormone circulating in the body, it's evident in their physical condition. They often have rough, scaly skin or skin infections; symmetrical hair loss on the trunk and rear end; and unexplained weight gain. Dogs with hypothyroidism may also seem apathetic or mentally dull, becoming forgetful or having a shorter attention span. They lack energy and are unwilling to exercise.

Hypothyroidism is diagnosed with a blood test, which indicates the level of circulating thyroid hormones (T3 and T4). It's treatable with daily medication: synthetic thyroid hormone taken in the form of a chewable tablet. The amount your pug will need depends on his weight. Once the appropriate dose is determined, your pug will be back to his old self. Your veterinarian will recommend blood work every six months to ensure that the dose doesn't need to be changed.

Kidney Disease

When it comes to the health problems of old dogs, kidney disease is second only to cancer. The kidneys remove waste products from the body, so when they begin to deteriorate, toxic waste products build up in the body—often indicated by increased water consumption and urination. Fortunately, a relatively new early renal disease test allows veterinarians to identify kidney disease in the early stages, when it's manageable through diet and sometimes medication. In the past, kidney dysfunction wasn't detectable in blood work until 75 percent of the kidney's function was destroyed, so this test is a big step forward. When kidney disease is caught early, your veterinarian can prescribe a special low-protein diet that won't overwork the kidneys. This change in diet can greatly increase your pug's life span. Remember that a normal, healthy pug doesn't need a low-protein diet. Feeding reduced-protein dog food does nothing for preventing the development of kidney disease.

Vision Loss

As with hearing, vision too can decline with age. Nuclear sclerosis and cataracts are common vision problems in aging dogs. Vision loss can also cause pugs to run into objects such as furniture, injuring their protruding eyes. Signs of vision loss include hesitation at going down stairs, reluctance to move about in darkened rooms, or having problems navigating familiar areas, even in well-lit rooms.

 Essential

To help your vision-impaired pug get around, scent the furniture with perfume at your pug's nose level. He can use the smell as an olfactory "map" to find his way around. Vision-compromised dogs can also respond well to a sports whistle and can learn to associate various commands with different whistle sounds. A trainer can help you teach this form of communication.

Nuclear sclerosis is the hazing or graying of the nucleus, or center, of the eye's lens. This occurs when new fibers form at the edge of the lens and push inward toward the center and is a normal part of the eye's aging process. Nuclear sclerosis eventually occurs in all dogs. The good news is that it doesn't significantly affect vision, although some dogs may have difficulty with close-up focus on objects.

Cataracts, an opacity of the lens, begin to form at the center of the lens and spread outward. Eventually, the lens becomes entirely opaque and the dog can no longer see. While cataracts are common in old dogs, pugs don't have an increased frequency of cataracts compared to other breeds.

Cataracts can sometimes be removed surgically by a veterinary ophthalmologist, but that's not always feasible or cost-effective. Fortunately, your pug, like most dogs, can adapt to sightlessness quite well by using his senses of smell and hearing. As long as you don't move the furniture around, your pug with cataracts should do just fine. And with his small size, you won't have any difficulty carrying him down the stairs if he's fearful of navigating them on his own.

Keeping Your Old Pug Comfortable

As your pug ages, take steps to keep his life comfortable. No doubt you've always spoiled him, but there are plenty of special things you can do for him that will ease his aches and pains and help him continue to enjoy life as he always has. Here are some tips:

- Provide soft bedding or a heated bed.
- Lift him on and off furniture and in and out of the car, or purchase a ramp to make it easier for him to access those areas.
- Install a dog door so he can go outside to potty as needed, or provide a litter box indoors.
- Keep his blood moving with short walks in the cool of the day.
- Provide a sweater or jacket in winter months so he doesn't get a chill.
- Brush his teeth and schedule regular veterinary cleanings.
- Groom him weekly and keep the skin fold over the nose clean, as the skin of older dogs is less forgiving of neglect.

Aging dogs need to pee more often, so take your pug out more often or provide him with a way to get out on his own. Mental and physical stimulation in the form of mild exercise and play will improve his circulation, promote good digestion, and keep his weight under control. All of these factors will enhance your pug's golden years.

When to Say Goodbye

This is the most difficult decision a dog owner must make. When your pug is very old or sick and no longer enjoying life, you can decide to give him a peaceful release from pain. Because you know your pug best, only you can make this decision, although your veterinarian can certainly advise you. Factors to consider in determining your pug's quality of life include appetite, attitude, activity level, elimination habits, comfort, and interaction with family members. Questions to ask yourself are whether your pug has more good days than bad, whether he can still do his favorite things, and whether he acts as if he's in pain. When your pug is no longer interested in food, finds movement painful, loses bladder and bowel control, and seems indifferent to you, it's time to make that final call to the veterinarian to set up an appointment for euthanasia. A caring veterinarian will give you all the time you need to say your goodbyes. Stay with your pug as he goes to his final rest, giving him the comfort of your presence. Afterward, it's okay to cry; you've lost a very special friend. Remember the good times and cherish your pug forever in your heart and memories. And when you're ready, one of the best ways you can honor his memory is to welcome a new pug into your home.

Resources

Breed Clubs, Registries, and Organizations

American Kennel Club
5580 Centerview Dr.
Raleigh, NC 27606-3390
✐ www.akc.org

AKC Canine Health Foundation
251 W. Garfield Rd., Ste. 160
Aurora, OH 44202-8856
888-682-9696
✐ www.akcchf.org

ASPCA Animal Poison Control Center
1717 S. Philo, Ste. 36
Urbana, IL 61802
888-426-4435
✐ www.napcc.aspca.org

Association of Pet Dog Trainers
17000 Commerce Pkwy., Ste. C
Mt. Laurel, NJ 08054
800-738-3647
✐ www.apdt.com

Canine Epilepsy Research Consortium
✐ www.canine-epilepsy.net/cerc.html

Canine Eye Registry Foundation
Purdue University
CERF/Lynn Hall
625 Harrison St.
West Lafayette, IN 47907-2026
765-494-8179
✐ www.vet.purdue.edu/~yshen/
cerf.html

Love on a Leash (therapy dog organization)
P.O. Box 6308
Oceanside, CA 92058
✐ www.loveonaleash.org

Morris Animal Foundation
45 Inverness Dr. E.
Englewood, CO 80112-5480
800-243-2345
✐ www.morrisanimalfoundation.org

National Association of Dog Obedience Instructors
PMB #369
729 Grapevine Hwy.
Hurst, TX 76054-2085

National Association of Professional Pet Sitters
17000 Commerce Pkwy., Ste. C
Mt. Laurel, NJ 08054
800-296-7387
www.petsitters.org

National Dog Registry
Box 116
Woodstock, NY 12498
800-637-3647
www.natldogregistry.com

North American Dog Agility Council
11522 South Hwy. 3
Cataldo, ID 83810
www.nadac.com

Orthopedic Foundation for Animals
2300 E. Nifong Blvd.
Columbia, MO 65201
www.offa.org

Pet Sitters International
201 E. King St.
King, NC 27021-9161
336-983-9222
www.petsit.com

Pug Dog Club of America (PDCA)
Polly Lamarine, Secretary
61 Fairfax Ave.
Meriden, CT 06450-2725
lamarine@sbcglobal.net
www.pugs.org

Therapy Dogs Inc.
P.O. Box 5868
Cheyenne, WY 82003
877-843-7364
www.therapydogs.com

Therapy Dogs International
88 Bartley Rd.
Flanders, NJ 07836
973-252-9800
www.tdi-dog.org

United Kennel Club
100 East Kilgore Rd.
Kalamazoo, MI 49002-5584
www.ukcdogs.com

United States Dog Agility Association
P.O. Box 850955
Richardson, TX 75085-0955
888-244-5489
www.usdaa.com

World Canine Freestyle Organization
P.O. Box 350122
Brooklyn, NY 11235-2525
718-332-8336
www.worldcaninefreestyle.org

Books, Magazines, and Web Sites

Books

Activities

Introduction to Dog Agility, by Margaret H. Bonham (Hauppauge, NY: Barron's Educational Series, Incorporated, 2000).

Show Me! A Dog-Showing Primer, by D. Caroline Coile (Hauppauge, NY: Barron's Educational Series, Incorporated, 1997).

The Simple Guide to Getting Active with Your Dog, by Margaret H. Bonham (Neptune City, NJ: TFH Publications, 2002).

Volunteering with Your Pet: How to Get Involved in Animal-Assisted Therapy with Any Kind of Pet, by Mary R. Burch and Aaron Honori Katcher (Hungry Minds, 1996).

Adoption and Rescue

The Adoption Option, by Eliza Rubenstein and Shari Kalina (Howell Book House, 1996).

Save That Dog! by Liz Palika (Howell Book House, 1997).

Behavior, Intelligence, and Training

All Dogs Need Some Training, by Liz Palika (Howell Book House, 1997).

Dog Behavior: A Guide to a Happy, Healthy Pet, by Ian Dunbar (Howell Book House, 1998).

The Everything® Dog Training and Tricks Book, by Gerilyn J. Bielakiewicz (Adams Media, 2003).

Getting Started: Clicker Training for Dogs, by Karen Pryor (Sunshine Books, 2002).

How to Teach a New Dog Old Tricks, 3rd ed., by Ian Dunbar (James & Kenneth Publishers, 1998).

The Intelligence of Dogs: A Guide to the Thoughts, Emotions, and Inner Lives of Our Canine Companions, by Stanley Coren (Bantam Books, 1995).

The Only Dog Training Book You'll Ever Need, by Gerilyn J. Bielakiewicz (Adams Media, 2004).

The Trick Is in the Training: 25 Fun Tricks to Teach Your Dog, by Stephanie Taunton and Cheryl S. Smith (Barron's Educational Series, Incorporated, 1998).

Health and Nutrition

Dr. Pitcairn's Complete Guide to Natural Health for Dogs and Cats, by Richard Pitcairn, D.V.M., Ph.D., and Susan Hubble Pitcairn (Rodale Books, 1995).

The Dog Owner's Home Veterinary Handbook, by James M. Giffin, M.D., and Liisa D. Carlson, D.V.M. (Howell Book House, 1999).

Hands-On Dog Care, by Sue M. Copeland and John M. Hamil, D.V.M. (Doral Publishing, 2000).

Home-Prepared Dog and Cat Diets: The Healthful Alternative, by Donald R. Strombeck, D.V.M., Ph.D. (Iowa State University Press, 1999).

Pills for Pets: The A to Z Guide to Drugs and Medications for Your Animal Companion, by Debra Eldredge, D.V.M. (Citadel Press, 2003).

UC Davis Book of Dogs: The Complete Medical Reference Guide for Dogs and Puppies, edited by Mordecai Siegal (Harper Resource, 1995).

Travel

The Dog Lover's Companion, series (Avalon Travel Publishing). City and state guides on traveling with dogs.

Take Your Pet USA, by Arthur Frank (Artco Publishing).

Traveling with Your Pet, The AAA Petbook, edited by Greg Weeks (American Automobile Association). Guide to pet-friendly lodging in the United States and Canada.

Magazines

AKC Family Dog
American Kennel Club
260 Madison Ave.
New York, NY 10016

AKC Gazette
American Kennel Club
260 Madison Ave.
New York, NY 10016

Dog Fancy
Fancy Publications
P.O. Box 6050
Mission Viejo, CA 92690

Dogs USA
Fancy Publications
P.O. Box 6050
Mission Viejo, CA 92690

Dog World
Fancy Publications
P.O. Box 6050
Mission Viejo, CA 92690

Popular Dogs: Pugs
Fancy Publications
P.O. Box 6050
Mission Viejo, CA 92690

Pug Talk
5031 Plover Rd.
Wisconsin Rapids, WI 54494-9705
www.pugtalk.com

Web Sites

www.dogfriendly.com
www.dogslife.com
www.findapet.com/petnames.htm
www.nopuppymills.com
www.nps.gov
  (National Park Service)
www.petfinder.com
www.petrix.com/dognames
www.petswelcome.com
www.pettrax.com

Index

Trade paperback, $14.95
1-55850-710-8, 320 pages

Have you ever wondered how to tempt your finicky cat to eat, or how to put that fat cat on a diet? What is the best way to keep your cat from eating your house plants? You'll find the answers to these and many other questions in *The Everything® Cat Book*. From choosing a veterinarian and basic first-aid to fascinating cat lore and trivia, this title offers everything you need to know about living with your favorite feline friend.

Whether you're the proud owner of a registered pure-bred Jack Russell Terrier or a happy-go-lucky mutt from the pound, it's the one book you'll turn to again and again. Packed with illustrations, instructions, historical information, and useful tips, *The Everything® Dog Book* covers everything from training to breed behavior, from grooming to exercise, from traveling with your pooch to keeping him from destroying your slippers.

Trade paperback, $14.95
1-58062-144-9, 304 pages

Trade paperback, $14.95
1-58062-666-1, 304
pages

As every dog owner knows, it takes a lot of time and patience to train a dog—and even more to get him to do tricks and show off in front of friends. In *The Everything®Dog Training and Tricks Book*, Canine University® cofounder Gerilyn Bielakiewicz explains how to solve virtually every behavioral issue—from aggressiveness to digging—and guides you through teaching all kinds of feats, whether your dog is in "kindergarten" or has graduated to "circus dog."

This exciting book is perfect for horse lovers of all ages and skill levels. You'll learn what breed is best suited to a rider's needs and skills, as well as how to buy a horse, how to choose a reliable vet, and how to detect early symptoms of various health issues. Packed with professional suggestions, horse trivia, and definitions of equine jargon, *The Everything® Horse Book* would make an ideal gift for anyone who has ever been interested in our equestrian friends.

Trade paperback, $14.95
1-58062-564-9, 304 pages

Trade paperback, $14.95
1-58062-576-2, 320 pages

Nothing is more adorable than a new puppy! But no matter how cute, puppies take a lot of hard work and loving care. *The Everything® Puppy Book* teaches you absolutely everything you need to raise your precious pet through the most critical stages of his or her life. Including photographs of your favorite breeds and a color insert, this book covers everything from grooming to exercise, and training to breed behavior.

Whether you are interested in fresh water or salt water tropical fish, *The Everything® Tropical Fish Book* is a complete resource for creating environments for fish to thrive. In this book, readers will find complete descriptions of various species, from freshwater goldfish and koi to rare tropical breeds. There are hundreds of tips on how to choose the right fish for every aquarium, and subsequently feed, breed, and maintain them.

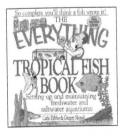

Trade paperback, $14.95
1-58062-343-3, 320 pages
plus 8-page color insert

EVERYTHING
DOG BREED GUIDES ®